BARRON'S

HOW TO PREPARE FOR THE

TOEFL®
ESSAY

TEST OF ENGLISH
AS A FOREIGN LANGUAGE

2ND EDITION

Lin Lougheed, Ed.D.

President, Instructional Design International, Inc.

Former TESOL Executive Board Member

BARRON'S

Published in 2004, 2000 by Barron's Educational Series, Inc.

Text © copyright 2004, 2000 by Lin Lougheed

Text design and cover © copyright 2004, 2000
by Barron's Educational Series, Inc.

All inquiries should be addressed to:
Barron's Educational Series, Inc.
250 Wireless Boulevard
Hauppauge, New York 11788
http://www.barronseduc.com

ISBN-13: 978-0-7641-2313-9
ISBN-10: 0-7641-2313-0
Library of Congress Catalog Card No.: 2003052090

Library of Congress Cataloging-in-Publication Data

Lougheed, Lin, 1946–
    How to prepare for the TOEFL essay : test of English as a foreign language /
by Lin Lougheed.—2nd ed.
        p.   cm.
    At head of title: Barron's
    ISBN 0-7641-2313-0
    1. English language—Textbooks for foreign speakers.   2. Test of English as a
foreign language—Study guides.   3. English language—Examinations—Study
guides.   I. Title: Barron's how to prepare for the TOEFL essay.   II. Lougheed,
Lin, 1946–Barron's how to prepare for the computer-based TOEFL essay.   III. Title.

PE1128.L6438 2004
428^1.0076—dc21

                                                                        2003052090

Printed in the United States of America

9 8 7

Contents

Introduction

1. Essay Writing in Twelve Steps

2. Planning the Essay

3. Writing the Essay

4. Revising the Essay

Appendix

Introduction

HOW TO USE THIS BOOK

There are three stages in creating an essay: planning, writing, and revising. When you write the TOEFL essay, you will have only thirty minutes to do all of this. In that short, thirty minutes, your writing must make an impression. Your writing must be clear, coherent, and correct. This book will help you do that.

How to Prepare for the TOEFL Essay, 2nd Edition provides a step-by-step guide for planning, writing, and revising your essay.

PLAN

This book will help you plan your essay. You will learn how to

understand the essay topic,
write a thesis statement, and
organize your thoughts with concept maps.

You also must have a plan for studying. Start with the first chapter of this book. Do every activity on every page until you reach the end. Follow the sequence of the book. When you write an essay, you start with the first word of the first sentence and end with the last word of the conclusion. Study this book the same way. Begin at the beginning and work your way through the book.

You will need to measure your success. The answer key in the back of the book will tell you how well you are doing. At the end of each chapter, there are Free Practice activities that ask you to write something on your own. There is, of course, no answer key for these activities. Share your writing with friends or teachers. They will tell you how well you are doing. You can find additional essays and topics, including any new topics from ETS, on Dr. Lougheed's Web site: *www.lougheed.com*.

WRITE

This book will help you write your essay. You will learn how to

state opinions,
write topic statements,
write supporting details,
write a conclusion, and
use syntactic and semantic variety in your essay.

The best way to learn to write is by writing. You will do a great deal of writing while you study this book. You will want to have a measure of how well you have progressed. Therefore, you will end each section with a self-test. You will be responsible for measuring your achievements.

The first self-test is at the end of the Introduction. You will be instructed to select an essay topic from the list in the Appendix and write on that topic. Pretend you are taking the TOEFL; write the essay in thirty minutes. When you are finished, don't show the essay to anyone. You will return to this first essay later.

At the end of the Planning section, you will take another self-test. Write a second essay on the same topic as your first essay. Write this essay in thirty minutes, too. Compare this second essay with the first one that you wrote on the same topic. Do you feel that you improved?

At the end of the Writing section and at the end of the Revision section, you will again write essays on the same topic. By the end of the book, you will have written four essays on the same topic. Compare all four essays. Compare your thesis statements, topic sentences, supporting details, and conclusions. Can you see your progress? Show your essay to someone else. What do they think?

REVISE

This book will help you revise your essay. You will learn how to

correct sentence fragments,

correct run-on sentences,

combine clauses and modifiers, and

use correct punctuation.

Writing is a solitary activity, but rewriting doesn't have to be. Get some help. Show your work to anyone who is willing to help you. Give them the Proofing Checklist on page 28 and have them rate the essays you write.

When you are learning how to write, you must, at the same time, learn to rewrite. You must make it a habit to rewrite the essays you write in this book. Try to incorporate your friends' suggestions into your revised essay. The more you write, the better you will write.

A good essay takes time: time to plan; time to write, and time to revise. On the TOEFL Essay you only have thirty minutes. If you take time now to learn how to write, you'll easily be able to write your essay in thirty minutes.

WARNING Study the model essays carefully. Analyze them completely. **Do NOT memorize them.** Your essay will not be scored if it matches an essay in this book. Your essay on the TOEFL must be your OWN original essay.

TO THE TEACHER

This book is perfectly suited for use in the classroom. The activities are carefully structured and can easily be completed in class. The activities can also be done as homework and corrected in class.

This book contains two types of activities: structured and free. The structured activities present models and controlled writing activities for the students. The free activities encourage them to write on their own using the controlled, structured activities as models.

EXPANDING THE ACTIVITIES

This book is a gold mine. Each chapter has examples and structured activities showing how a particular part of an essay is developed. In addition, the model essays in the Appendix provide further examples of essay development. Use these essays to expand the activities in the book. For example, in Chapter 3 the students are asked to identify the topic sentence and supporting details in an introductory paragraph. There are five examples in the exercise in that chapter, but more than one hundred introductory paragraphs in the model essays in the Appendix, which can be used to continue the exercise. You can have the students use the model essays to look for examples of transition words, cohesion, conclusions, or any other aspect of essay writing that you want to illustrate. All of the essays in this book, both those used in the text and those in the Appendix, follow a model of essay organization. This model is presented at the end of Chapter 1 and is repeated next to every essay in the book to show how each essay is organized. You can have the students use this model to analyze the essays in the book. Ask them to find where the theme is stated in an essay, where each point is mentioned, and where the examples are explained. Your students need to follow this model in their own writing.

You might advise your students that the model essays show a great diversity of writing. Everyone has a different writing style and the essays reflect this difference. This book is prescriptive in its approach to essay writing, but one can present one's ideas in many ways. By analyzing the style of a model essay (how the writer developed an idea and how the writer introduced and concluded the essay), your students will gain a broader understanding of essay writing.

GETTING STUDENTS TO DO MORE

Writing is a very personal activity, and students must be encouraged to write on their own. The Strategies and Tips section contains activities that the student can do to improve general writing ability (*General Writing Improvement Strategies*).

Students, of course, don't want to waste their time learning "general" writing, even though it will improve their essay writing. They want their preparation to be TOEFL-specific. To this end, there are more than 133 topics in the Appendix that have appeared or could appear on the actual TOEFL test. Assign essay topics from this list frequently. Have the students do one a night or one a week. Use these essays for practice in class as the students work through the stages of planning, writing, and revising the essay.

PLAN

Have the students work together as they learn to plan, write, and revise their essays. In order to be able to address the writing topics, students need to begin to form opinions on these topics. They must get used to thinking about why a school needs more teachers, or why a landscaper is needed by our community. In small groups they can brainstorm and discuss their ideas on the various writing topics presented throughout the book and in the Appendix. Following these discussions, they can practice writing thesis statements and developing concept maps on the same topics. They can do this in groups, or they can do it alone and bring their work to the group for critique.

WRITE

When the class is working through Chapter 3, have the students check each other's essays to make sure there is a topic sentence in each paragraph. Have them check the introduction to make sure the theme and its supporting points are all mentioned. After they have done the exercises on conclusions, have them look at the conclusions of their own work to see if they summarize the theme that was presented in the introduction. They can also look at the use of transition words in their own or their classmate's essays; they can look for passive and active voice, and the other items that are covered in the chapter.

REVISE

After the students have worked on the exercises about run-on sentences and sentence fragments in Chapter 4, have them check each other's work for these problems. Have them correct the spelling and punctuation. This chapter provides several model essays for revision practice. They can continue this practice by revising each other's essays in groups. They should also get used to using the Proofing Checklist on page 28 to revise their own and their classmates' work.

Whatever your students write, they will profit from doing it again. Even though they can't revise extensively on the TOEFL Essay, learning to rethink and redo will help them develop sound writing habits.

A word of caution. Please remind the students not to memorize the essays in this book. An essay will not be rated if the reader suspects it was taken from the model essays.

QUESTIONS AND ANSWERS ABOUT THE TOEFL ESSAY

1. How long do I have to write the essay?
Thirty minutes.

2. Do I have to use the computer?
No, you can write your essay by hand. You can decide on test day. (See the section *To Type or Not to Type*.)

3. Do I have a choice of topics?
No, you will only be given one topic.

4. Will all test-takers have the same topic?
No. Not every test-taker will have the same topic.

5. What will happen if I don't understand the question?
If you study this book, that won't be a problem. You will understand all the possible topics. On the day of the test, you will not receive any help with the topic.

6. What will happen if I don't understand how to work the computer?
There will be test administrators in the room who can answer your questions about using the computer. They will not answer any question about the use of English.

7. What kind of pencils should I bring?
None. Everything you need to write your essay will be given to you at the testing center. If you need extra pencils or paper, ask your test administrator.

8. Can I bring a clock with me?
No. Nothing can be brought into the test room. You can wear your watch or look at the clock on the computer screen. There will be a clock in the upper left corner that counts down the time remaining.

9. Can I bring a dictionary with me?
No. Nothing can be brought into the test room.

10. Can I bring paper with me?
No. Nothing can be brought into the test room. Scratch paper and paper on which to write your essay will be supplied.

11. What happens to the notes I take?
You can write your notes in English or your first language. They will be collected and discarded. They will not be seen by the raters.

12. Is there a spell checker or a grammar checker on the computer?
No. You will have to do your own proofreading. (See the section, *To Type or Not to Type*.) Don't worry about a few spelling errors or a few mistakes with punctuation or grammar. A few small errors will not count against your score. Hint: If you are unsure how to spell a word, use a word you do know how to spell.

13. How long should the essay be?
It should be around 300 words. You should be able to address your topic completely in three to five short paragraphs.

14. What's more important in the essay: organization or grammar.
Both are important. A reader judges an essay on its organization, your use of details to support your opinions, and your facility with English. (See the section, *Scoring the Essay*.)

15. Do I need a title?
No. However, a title helps the readers focus attention on your thesis. It helps them understand your point of view.

16. Do I need an introduction?
You need something to introduce your readers to your topic. This will help them understand what you are going to say and how you plan to develop your ideas.

17. **How many paragraphs do I need?**

    You need enough to cover your topic and show that you are proficient in English. A general rule is that you should have five paragraphs: the first paragraph is the introduction, the next three paragraphs are the body, and the fifth paragraph is the conclusion. In the three paragraphs of the body, you should have one paragraph for each topic sentence.

    You will not be scored on how many paragraphs you write. You will be scored on how well you address your topic.

18. **What happens if I don't finish?**

    You do not need to have an elegantly stated conclusion. What you do write should demonstrate your facility with English. Do not end with an apology. DO not apologize to the reader for what you did not do or for what you think should have been better.

19. **Is there an extra fee for the essay?**

    No. The test fee covers all parts of the TOEFL.

20. **Is the essay required?**

    Yes. All test takers who take the TOEFL must write an essay.

21. **How is my essay scored?**

    Your essay will be read by two readers. Neither reader will know the score the other reader gives your essay. If the scores are more than one point apart (one reader gives your essay a 6 and another reader gives it a 4), your essay will be read by a third person. If that reader gives your essay a 4.5, your score will be the approximate average of the three scores, 5.

22. **Will I see my essay score immediately?**

    No. If you type your essay on the computer, your score will be mailed to you approximately 2 weeks after the test date. If you write your essay by hand, your score will be sent to you in 5 weeks. If you change your address, let the Educational Testing Service (ETS) know your new address.

23. **Can I get my score by phone?**

    Yes. You can get your score report by phone on the day that the scores are mailed. See the latest edition of ETS' *Information Bulletin for the TOEFL* for precise instructions.

24. **What if I don't like my rating?**

    Take the test again.

25. **Can I cancel my essay score?**

    Yes. At the end of the CBT test, you have the option to cancel your scores BEFORE you see them. If you choose this option, all of your scores, including your essay score, will be cancelled.

TOEFL ESSAY BASICS

TO TYPE OR NOT TO TYPE

When you sit down in front of the computer on test day, you will have to decide whether you will type your essay on the computer or whether you will write it out longhand. The following chart gives you some pros (+) and cons (−) for writing by computer or by hand.

	By Computer	By Hand
Input	+ Your essay will be legible, clear. − Readers may unconsciously expect more from a clean-looking essay.	+ Your essay will be as clear as your handwriting. − If your handwriting is illegible, your essay will be impossible to score. − Revisions/changes could make the essay look disorganized.
Speed	+ Faster if you are familiar with a computer or a keyboard. + If you are familiar with Windows, you will understand the functions. − Slow if you do not know how to type. − Potentially slow if you are used to standard word processing functions like tabs that are disabled on the Computer-Based TOEFL. You may waste time hitting these buttons by accident.	+ If you aren't familiar with a keyboard, you probably can write faster than you type. − If you have difficulty forming the letters, your brain will race ahead of you, causing you to skip letters and words. When you go back and revise, your essay may look messy.
Proofreading	− You have to scroll up and down to reread your essay.	+ You can see your entire essay at a glance.
Revising	+ You can easily cut/paste/delete words or sentences, and the essay will look clean. − No spell checker or grammar checker. It's all up to you.	+ You might be more careful when you write so that you won't need to revise so much. − Revisions/changes could make the essay look messy. − No spell checker or grammar checker. It's all up to you.

As part of your preparation, you should practice both ways. First write some practice essays out by hand. Then, if you have access to a computer, type the same essays without looking at the handwritten versions. Then switch the order. First type some essays and then write them out by hand without looking at the handwritten versions.

Ask yourself which was easier, which was more comfortable. Choose the option that was easier and more comfortable.

Get some other opinions. You might ask your teacher or a friend with good English skills to read your essays, both handwritten and typed. Which do they think are better essays? If your informal judges thought that the handwritten essays were better, you might want to consider writing your essay by hand.

A word of caution: opinions are subjective. When some readers read a perfectly typed essay, they have the expectation that the English will be perfect, too. Their expectations are high. The essay looks like a finished, proofed piece of writing. If there are mistakes in the essay, they are more evident. They stand out. A handwritten essay looks more like a draft and consequently the reader may not judge it so harshly.

TEST DAY

On the day of the test, you will have to make the decision: by computer or by hand. Even though you don't have to decide until test day, make your decision in advance. Don't waste time on test day making a decision. Spend that extra time on your essay.

You will be given paper and pencils to write your essay. If you type your essay, you can use the paper to make notes and to draw your concept maps. If you write your essay by hand, you will need to keep a few sheets clean for your essay; use the rest to make notes and draw your concept maps. You will have to turn in all paper at the end of the essay section.

If you write your essay by hand, write on the white areas only. Do not write on the shaded margins. Your handwritten essay will be scanned and sent over the Internet to the readers who score the essays. Words written in the gray, shaded margins will not appear.

THE TOPIC

The topic will be shown on the computer even though you choose to write by hand. The screen will look similar to this:

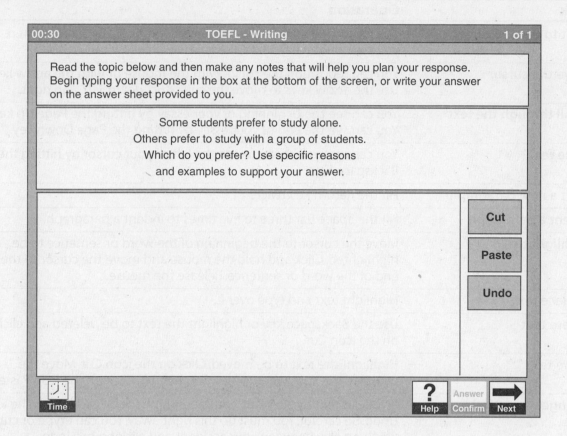

Notice the clock in the upper left corner. Use that to help you plan your essay. You can end the essay section at any time by clicking on Next and Confirm. Do NOT click on Next and Confirm until you have finished your essay. After you click on Next and Confirm, you will not be allowed to write or revise your essay.

At the end of thirty minutes, the computer will automatically end the essay section.

TIME SCHEDULE

You only have thirty minutes to write your essay. Here is a plan to use that thirty minutes efficiently.

Time		Activity
30:00 – 25:00	PLAN	Read the topic and write your thesis statement. Create your concept map with supporting details.
25:00 – 05:00	WRITE	Write draft topic sentences for each of the supporting details on your scratch paper. Write your essay using your concept map as a guide.
05:00 – 00:00	REVISE	Reread and revise your essay.

COMPUTER TUTORIAL

The keyboard functions for the Computer-Based TOEFL are similar to that of any other word processing program. To perform standard tasks, follow the directions below.

Task	Operation
Start to type	The cursor will blink on the upper left corner of the screen. When you type on the keyboard, the letters will follow this cursor.
Move the cursor	You can reposition the cursor with the mouse or with the arrow keys. Use the arrow keys to move the cursor up, down, left, and right.
Scroll through the text	You can see the beginning of your essay by hitting the Page Up key. You can see the end of your essay by hitting the Page Down key.
Erase text	You can erase all characters to the left of your cursor by hitting the Backspace key.
Start a new paragraph	Hit the Return key twice.
Indent a paragraph	Hit the Space Bar three to five times to indent a paragraph.
Highlight text	Move the cursor to the beginning of the word or sentence to be highlighted. Click and hold the mouse and move the cursor to the end of the word or sentence. Release the mouse.
Replace text	Highlight text and type over it.
Delete text	Use the Backspace key or highlight the text to be deleted and click on the icon Cut.
Move text	Highlight the text to be moved. Click on the icon Cut. Move the cursor to the spot where you want the text. Click on the icon Paste.
Change your mind	If you cut text by accident, you can put it back by clicking on the icon Undo. Be careful. You must do this right away. You can't type or cut anything else between your accident and clicking on Undo.

KEYBOARD FOR THE ESSAY

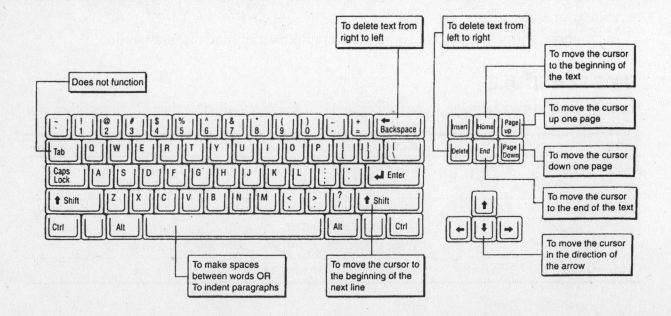

COMPUTER SCREEN FOR THE ESSAY

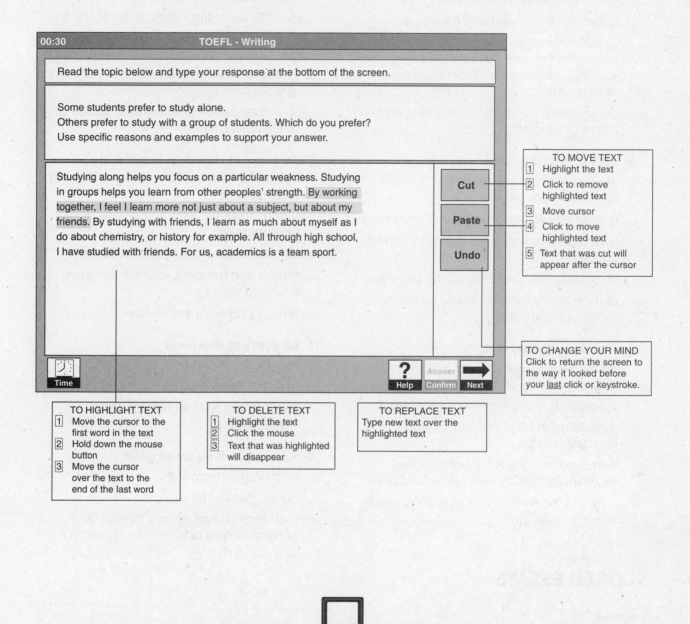

00:30	TOEFL - Writing

Read the topic below and type your response at the bottom of the screen.

Some students prefer to study alone.
Others prefer to study with a group of students. Which do you prefer?
Use specific reasons and examples to support your answer.

Studying along helps you focus on a particular weakness. Studying in groups helps you learn from other peoples' strength. By working together, I feel I learn more not just about a subject, but about my friends. By studying with friends, I learn as much about myself as I do about chemistry, or history for example. All through high school, I have studied with friends. For us, academics is a team sport.

Cut

Paste

Undo

Time

? Help   Answer Confirm   **→** Next

TO MOVE TEXT
1. Highlight the text
2. Click to remove highlighted text
3. Move cursor
4. Click to move highlighted text
5. Text that was cut will appear after the cursor

TO CHANGE YOUR MIND
Click to return the screen to the way it looked before your last click or keystroke.

TO HIGHLIGHT TEXT
1. Move the cursor to the first word in the text
2. Hold down the mouse button
3. Move the cursor over the text to the end of the last word

TO DELETE TEXT
1. Highlight the text
2. Click the mouse
3. Text that was highlighted will disappear

TO REPLACE TEXT
Type new text over the highlighted text

SCORING THE ESSAY

The score for your essay will count for almost 50 percent of your Structure score. Two people will read your essay. These readers will judge your essay according to the rating criteria on the following pages. The scores they give your essay will be averaged. If one rater gives your essay a 5 and the second rater gives your essay a 4, your score will be 4.5.

The raters' scores must be within one point of each other. If one of the raters gives your essay a 5 and the second rater gives your essay a 3, a third rater will read your essay. Your final score will be the average of the three readers' ratings.

RATING SCALE

6 An essay at this level

_____effectively addresses the writing task

_____is well organized and well developed

_____uses clearly appropriate details to support a thesis or illustrate ideas

_____displays consistent facility in the use of language

_____demonstrates syntactic variety and appropriate word choice

5 An essay at this level

_____may address some parts of the task more effectively than others

_____is generally well-organized and developed

_____uses details to support a thesis or illustrate an idea

_____displays facility in the use of the language

_____demonstrates some syntactic variety and range of vocabulary

4 An essay at this level

_____addresses the writing topic adequately but may slight parts of the task

_____is adequately organized and developed

_____uses some details to support a thesis or illustrate an idea

_____demonstrates adequate but possibly inconsistent facility with syntax and usage

_____may contain some errors that occasionally obscure meaning

3 An essay at this level may reveal one or more of the following weaknesses:

_____inadequate organization or development

_____inappropriate or insufficient details to support or illustrate generalizations

_____a noticeably inappropriate choice of words or word forms

_____an accumulation of errors in sentence structure and/or usage

2 An essay at this level is seriously flawed by one or more of the following weaknesses:

_____serious disorganization or under-development

_____little or no detail, or irrelevant specifics

_____serious and frequent errors in sentence structure or usage

_____serious problems with focus

1 An essay at this level

_____may be incoherent

_____may be undeveloped

_____may contain severe and persistent writing errors

0 An essay will be rated 0 if it

_____contains no response

_____merely copies the topic

_____is off-topic, is written in a foreign language, or consists only of keystroke characters

SCORED ESSAYS

Score 6

Topic 13

Some people prefer to eat at food stands or restaurants. Other people prefer to prepare and eat food at home. Which do you prefer? Use specific reasons and examples to support your answer.

Eating Out

Although many people prefer to cook at home, I prefer to eat out. The main reason is that I am not a very good cook. In addition, eating out allows me to spend more time studying and less time in the kitchen. And, believe it or not, eating out can be cheaper than cooking at home.

To begin with, I don't know how to cook. When you don't know how to cook, there is a good chance that what you cook will not be worth of eating. This results in a waste of food, as well as a waste of money and effort.

Also, cooking takes a lot of time. While the food might not actually be on the stove for very long, you also have to consider the time that is spent shopping for the food, cleaning and chopping it, and cleaning up the kitchen after it is cooked.

Finally, eating out is surprisingly economical. Of course going to elegant restaurants is expensive, but there are other ways to eat out. Food stands and some small, casual restaurants provides plenty of good food for very little cost. Many places of this type are located near the university and are very convenient for students.

As my life changes, my preferences about where to eat may change, too. For the life of a student, eating out is the only practical choice.

Proofing Checklist

✓	**CONTENT**
	This essay has a clear thesis in the beginning and is also very well organized. The first two of the three body paragraphs give reasons why the writer does not want to cook at home, while the third gives reasons why eating out is better. Although there is not a great deal of development, there are sufficient details to support the topic sentence in each paragraph. The conclusion paraphrases the main idea rather than simply repeating it.
✓	**CLARITY**
	There is good use of cohesive devices like repeating verbs, parallel structures, and rephrasing. This essay shows syntactic and semantic variety.
	There are very few grammar errors, and they do not interfere with comprehension. . . . there is a good chance that what you cook will not be <u>worth of </u>eating. . . . there is a good chance that what you cook will not be worth eating / worthy of eating. Food stands and some small, casual restaurants <u>provides</u> plenty of good food . . . Food stands and some small, casual restaurants <u>provide</u> plenty of good food . . .
✓	**PUNCTUATION**
	There are no punctuation errors.
✓	**SPELLING**
	There are no spelling errors.

Score 5

Topic 114

Some people think that the family is the most important influence on young adults. Other people think that friends are the most important influence on young adults. Which view do you agree with? Use examples to support your position.

The Important Influence

We are all influence by whomever we meet. We all stand as models to everyone in this world. However, our choice of a model is important especially when choosing a career. I believe that in the case concerning our future and our career, families have more influence on us than friends.

Friends are the ones we spend time having fun, enjoying, playing and so forth. Friends also teach good things and help us. Friends advice good things about life, but not like family. Family always thinks that their children will become superior ones in the future. They want their children be smarter than anyone else. However, friends are not such an influential adviser like family. Family feels that time is waste when their adult children have too much fun. However, friends influence us more to play or have fun rather than advising us about our career. Therefore, family puts their substantial impact on heir children in order to shape up their future career.

In the US, most young adults are usually influence by their friends rather than their parents. It depends upon what type of influence it is. Usually, people are busier in the US. They don't have time to give important influence to their children. Therefore, the children choose their own way to catch up their careers. Whatever they see around impacts these adult children, and they are influence by that. However, this impact might not better them for their future career.

Therefore, I'd say family influences their adult children more and better than friends and relatives.

Proofing Checklist

✓	**CONTENT**
	The thesis of this essay is very clear and easy to locate at the end of the introduction. This essay is generally well organized. The writer carefully compares and contrasts the level of influence one receives from one's parents with the influence one receives from one's friends. The writer is able to develop his/her thesis. There is a conclusion that restates the thesis.
✓	**CLARITY**
	The author displays facility in the use of language, but there are some repeated errors in usage and grammar that slow the reader down. S/he seems to be comfortable with expressing ideas in English. Word choice is not always ideal, but ideas are understandable.
	Friends <u>advice</u> good things about life, but not like family. Friends advise good things about life, but not like family. Therefore, <u>family puts their substantial impact on heir children</u> … Therefore, families have a substantial impact on their children… In the US, most young adults <u>are usually influence by</u> their friends… In the US, most young adults are usually influenced by their friends…
✓	**PUNCTUATION**
	There are no punctuation errors.
✓	**SPELLING**
	There is only one spelling error.
	Therefore, family puts their substantial impact on <u>heir</u> children… Therefore, family puts their substantial impact on their children…

Score 4

Topic 136

Do you agree or disagree with the following statement? Playing a game is fun only when you win. Use specific reasons and examples to support your answer.

Playing Is Fun if We Win

Some would like to play the game such as, basketball, tennis, swimming, and riding bike for exercises and fun. But some, they play for their acheivement. I agree that playing game is fun when we win.

As a matter of fact, when I was in High school, I like to play basketball as my hobby. I was very excited when I won the game. All high schools in Cambodia, they required students to choose one kind of game such as, volleyball, soccer, basketball, tennis and swimming. By that time, I took basketball as my favorite hobby. My school gave me the best basketball coach. He had lot of experience of training basketball players. My teams and I were trained by him everyday for two months. After two monthes of training, My coach wanted us to compete with the other schools.

When the competition day came, our emotion was combined with happy and scare of losing the game. But our coach encourage us. He told us that "don't be afraid of your competitors, they are as same as you, so you have to have a confident in yourself." When time of competition of game started, our coach led us to basketball course to get to know our competitors. The result of competition was my team completely won. My coach and our team were very happy to win that game.

I believe that playing game is very difficult if we don't know a weakness of our competitors. We have to have a confident in ourselves. I agree that playing game is very fun when we win.

Proofing Checklist

✓	CONTENT
	This essay is adequately organized and developed. It shows development of ideas and some facility with English. In the first paragraph and in the conclusion, the writer states his/her opinion that playing a game is fun when one wins. He/She does not directly address the topic, which is more black and white: playing a game is fun ONLY when one wins. It is likely that the writer did not understand the question clearly.
	The writer uses a personal story to illustrate his/her thesis. This story seems to indicate that the writer also had a good time just playing basketball even when he/she didn't win.
✓	**CLARITY**
	Syntax and usage are inconsistent and distract the reader from the meaning.
	Everyone who is born into this world, <u>they have different idea of playing game</u>. Everyone who is born into this world has a different idea about playing games.
	… our emotion was <u>combined with happy and scare</u> of losing the game. … our emotion was a combination of happiness and fear of losing the game.
	We have to have <u>a confident </u>in ourselves. We have to have confidence in ourselves.
✓	**PUNCTUATION**
	There are some punctuation errors.
	After two month of training, <u>My</u> coach wanted us to compete … After two month of training, my coach wanted us to compete …
	He told us that "<u>d</u>on't be afraid of your competitors … He told us, "Don't be afraid of your competitors …
✓	**SPELLING**
	There are a couple of spelling errors.
	But some, they play for their <u>acheivement</u>. But some, they play for their achievement.
	After two <u>monthes</u> of training … After two months of training …

Score 3

Topic 111

Some people prefer to spend time with one or two close friends. Others choose to spend time with a large number of friends. Compare the advantages of each choice. Which of these two ways of spending time do you prefer? Use specific reasons to support your answer.

Friends

People need friends they include in a society. Some people try to find good people but some people just take any person who is around them. Which means first one is very serious to find friends and second people are not too serious to have friends. However, there are two types of character to make friends. Some people prefer to spend time with one or two friends. Others choose to spend time with a large number of friends.

First of all, some people want to spend time with one or two friends. Those people always take care of their friends very well. For example, when they have a party they can invite everyone their home even though her/his home is small. Also he/she can talk with each friend before party is over. Because he/she does not have many friends so he/she can be able to talk everyone. Therefore, his/her friends returns home very happy after party.

Secondly, some people want to spend time with a large number of friends. Those people love people also they can get a good advice from friends. For example, when they have a problem they can ask their many friends and then they can collect every answer. Therefore, they are figure it out to fix their problem easily.

Proofing Checklist

✓	**CONTENT**
	The organization and development of the topic is not fully adequate. The writer talks about each choice, but never accomplishes the task: to express a preference. There is no conclusion to this essay. There is a good attempt at addressing the task, discussing the topic in English, and demonstrating a basic level of competence as a writer in English. The writing is lively and earnest.
✓	**CLARITY**
	The writing is understandable, but syntax and usage are very inconsistent. <u>Which means first one is very serious to find friends</u> … This means the first one is very serious about finding friends … Because he/she does not have many friends <u>so he/she can be able to talk everyone</u>. Because he/she does not have many friends, he/she can talk to everyone / is able to talk to everyone. Those people love <u>people also they</u> can get <u>a</u> good advice from friends. Those people love people; also, they can get good advice from friends.
✓	**PUNCTUATION**
	There are a few punctuation errors. For example, when they have a <u>problem they</u> can ask their many friends… For example, when they have a problem, they can ask their many friends…
✓	**SPELLING**
	There are no spelling errors.

Score 2

Topic 128

Some people say that physical exercise should be a required part of every school day. Other people believe that students should spend the whole school day on academic studies. Which opinion do you agree with? Use specific reasons and details to support your answer.

Staying in School

I agree an opinion that students should spend the whole day on academic studies. Because there are have many opportunites for students to be a very good student, like, they have a lot time to spend studies, also, they will be effected by school when they are staying in school. Because of many people staying in library to spend their study, I think that, It will advise me to follow to them. Moreover, staying in school is good for students to enrolling to university. Because they don't have to think something of outside so they really have to think of their learning, this is a good idea for students to stay. Besides that, if they go home to study, it is ok. But when you are studying in your home, suddenly your father or someone call you at that time, I think, you are confusing about your study. Anyway, I still like to spend the whole school day on academic studies, Because there are have enough books and have many things to use in my knowledge. So I love staying in school day to increase my knowledge.

Proofing Checklist

✓	**CONTENT**
	This essay demonstrates "developing competence," but is flawed on several levels. It is possible that the writer does not fully understand the prompt. The writer seems to think the choice is between staying home or staying in school. S/he doesn't say why one should spend the day on academics and does not address why some physical education would be bad. The information is not organized into an essay, but is all one paragraph. There are insufficient details to support the author's opinions.
✓	**CLARITY**
	There is an accumulation of errors in sentence structure; in fact, there are errors in nearly every sentence.
	I agree <u>an opinion</u> that students should spend the whole day on academic studies.
	I agree that students should spend the whole day on academic studies.
	Because <u>there are have</u> many opportunites for <u>students to be a very good student</u>,
	Because there are many opportunities for them to be very good students,
	…they have <u>a lot time</u> to spend <u>studies</u>…
	…they have a lot of time to spend on their studies…
✓	**PUNCTUATION**
	There are a number of punctuation errors, mixed in with other errors.
	I think <u>that, It</u> will advise me to follow to them.
	I think that it will be advisable for me to follow to them.
✓	**SPELLING**
	There are a few spelling errors.
	…they will be <u>effected</u> by school…
	…they will be affected by school…
	Because there are have many <u>opportunites</u> for students to be a very good student,…
	Because there are have many opportunities for students to be a very good student,…

Score 1

Topic 145

Some people say that advertising encourages us to buy things we really do not need. Others say that advertisements tell us about new products that may improve our lives. Which viewpoint do you agree with? Use specific reasons and examples to support your answer.

Ads

Some people say that advertising encourages us to buy things we really do not need. Others say that advertisements tell us about new products that may improve our lives. Yes. It is. I buyed much, because TV ads.

Proofing Checklist

✓	**CONTENT**
	The student here simply rewrote the topic and added a few words. The essay is on topic, but there is no development of the topic. The author implies, but does not directly state, that s/he agrees with people who say that advertising encourages us to buy things we really do not need.
✓	**CLARITY**
	The few sentences or sentence fragments contain severe errors. The past tense of *buy* is *bought*. *Much* is not an appropriate word choice; *a lot* or *many things* would be better. *Because* should be *because of* or the phrase can be made into a sentence. *Because TV ads make me want to have everything.*

Essay Score 0

If the essay writer simply rewrites the topic question and doesn't add any additional words, the score will be 0.

If the essay writer creates a perfect essay or any essay on a topic that does not match the given topic, the score will be 0.

STRATEGIES AND TIPS

SPECIFIC TOEFL WRITING IMPROVEMENT STRATEGIES

1. Every day choose one TOEFL essay topic, study the concept map, and read the model essay.

2. Think about the essay topics you read. You may have never thought about a particular subject. After you read an essay topic, form an opinion about that subject. You need an opinion before you can write about one.

The general writing improvement strategies below will help you learn to think about a topic.

3. Once you have thought about a topic, write an essay on that topic. Follow the proposed time schedule to finish your essay in thirty minutes.

Time		Activity
30:00 – 25:00	PLAN	Read the topic and write your thesis statement. Create your concept map with supporting details.
25:00 – 05:00	WRITE	Write draft topic sentences for each of the supporting details on your scratch paper. Write your essay using your concept map as a guide.
05:00 – 00:00	REVISE	Reread and revise your essay.

GENERAL WRITING IMPROVEMENT STRATEGIES

Writing is a skill like playing tennis. You have to practice. There is a lot of extra work you can do on your own to help you become a better writer. Doing these activities, you'll practice your writing, practice your penmanship, and practice forming opinions.

1. To improve your writing, pay attention when you read. Notice how the author of your book organizes thoughts and expresses ideas. *Gone with the Wind* is a famous American novel by Margaret Mitchell. Many years after she died, a sequel was published. The author of that sequel wrote out, by hand, the entire 1037 pages of *Gone with the Wind* three times! She wanted to mimic the style of Margaret Mitchell. She wanted to get a feel for the way Mitchell put sentences together.

   You can do the same thing. Take the model essays in this book and write them out by hand. Write them several times until you get a feel for the use of transition phrases and other cohesive devices. Try to understand how the details support the topic sentences. Pay attention to the introductions and conclusions.

   Once you have copied the model essay several times, think about whether you agree or disagree with the opinion of the author. Then create your own essay on the same topic. Compare your essay with the model essay. Show your essay to a friend or teacher.

2. Read more. A lot of research has shown that reading improves your writing. Reading will build your vocabulary and your understanding of the way ideas are expressed. Read every chance you get.

3. An essay is made up of sentences. If you have some extra time, for example, while waiting for someone, don't just stare at the wall. Write!

   You don't have to write an essay; write just a sentence or two. Look around you. What do you see? Write what you see: *The wall is painted a light yellow*. Write what you think about it: *Yellow is too colorful for me; I'd prefer gray*. Write why you think so: *Yellow is too bright a color; it's hard to relax in a yellow room*.

4. Buy a notebook to record your thoughts and your writing. Don't use this notebook for anything but writing practice. This notebook will be your private classroom.

5. Keep a journal. Record the events of the day. Tell what happened and what you felt about the event. Record what you thought about the events and what conclusions you reached. This will give you practice in writing about your opinions. Review these notes periodically to see if any of these opinions can be used in your essays.

   Date every entry. Put the time of day you are writing. Dates will help you remember the event more clearly later on. A date is a detail, and details are important to good writing.

   Keep every other page blank. If you want to rewrite an entry or to expand on one, you will have the space. This will give you practice in revision.

   The journal does not have to be serious. It can be anything from words, to poems, to jokes, to a complete essay. It can be about your school, your family, or you. The important thing is to write.

6. When events happen, take notes. Later in the day reread your notes and turn them into sentences. Turn the sentences into paragraphs.

7. Write every day. Give yourself a gift of time. Spend five minutes a day writing, and do it faithfully everyday. Once a week, assign yourself a topic and write an essay in thirty minutes.

8. Go back over your writing frequently. The more you write, the better writer you will become. You may think of a better, or a different, way of expressing a thought. Use the blank page to experiment with different ways of expressing the same idea.

9. When you rewrite, imagine you are writing for a different audience. The first time you wrote for yourself. How would you change your writing if your friends were to read it? Your teacher? Your mother? A stranger?

TIPS ON TEST DAY

1. Decide before the test whether you will use the computer or whether you will write the essay by hand. (See section *To Type or Not to Type*.)

2. If you write by hand, your penmanship must be legible.

3. Take full advantage of the paper you are provided. Use it to draw your concept maps. Use it to plan your essay. Write in your first language if you want.

4. Don't be afraid to exaggerate. This essay does not have to be the truth. You do not have to give your real feelings. You can write whatever you want as long as it is on the topic and is grammatically and syntactically correct.

5. You may revise your essay. However, do not completely rewrite it. Think before you write. Try the sentence in your head before you put it on paper.

6. Try to save a few minutes to look over your essay. Look for errors and correct them. Do not do major rewrites here; correct only sentences that would make your essay difficult to understand.

Don't be tempted to memorize the essays in this book. The readers will be familiar with these essays. Use these essays as springboards for your own ideas. Develop your own concept maps and essays from the topics.

SELF-TEST ESSAY #1

Select a topic from the list in the *Appendix, Essay Topic Index*. Plan, write, and revise an essay on that topic within thirty minutes. Use the space on the pages following. Do NOT write in the shaded areas.

Divide your time like this.

PLAN	5 minutes	30:00 – 25:00
WRITE	20 minutes	25:00 – 05:00
REVISE	5 minutes	05:00 – 00:00

Topic Number: _____

PLAN

Concept Map

Thesis Statement

General Ideas

Supporting Details

WRITE

REVISE

Proofing Checklist

Reread your essay. Use this checklist as a guide.

You will not be familiar with many of these items now. You will learn about them all as you study this book.

✓	CONTENT
	Is there a thesis statement or introduction?
	Is there a topic sentence for each paragraph?
	Are there supporting details for each topic statement?
	Is there a conclusion?
✓	CLARITY
	Are there run-on sentences or sentence fragments?
	Are there misplaced modifiers or dangling modifiers?
	Are the structures parallel?
	Are there transition words?
	Are the sentences and paragraphs cohesive?
✓	PUNCTUATION AND SPELLING
	Are the paragraphs indented?
	Are there punctuation marks such as periods at the end of each sentence?
	Do all sentences begin with capital letters?
	Are all the words spelled correctly?

Essay Writing in Twelve Steps

In this chapter you will learn a twelve-step program for writing an essay. You can follow these steps when writing any essay for any purpose. The only difference between writing the TOEFL Essay and writing other essays is the time. You only have thirty minutes to write an essay. If you follow these twelve steps, you will be able to write a good essay for any purpose. You can find additional essays and topics, including new topics from ETS, on Dr. Lougheed's Web site: *www.lougheed.com.*

PLANNING THE ESSAY

There are two important parts to planning an essay:

addressing the writing task and

organizing the topic.

Here is an overview of the step-by-step process you will use to address the task and organize the topic.

Step 1	Read the essay topic.
Step 2	Identify the task.
Step 3	Write your thesis statement.
Step 4	Make notes about your general ideas.
Step 5	Expand your notes to include specific details.

The example that follows is a short introduction to the steps of planning an essay. Planning an essay will be discussed thoroughly in the chapter by the same name beginning on page 39. You will learn different ways to address a topic and different ways to organize a topic. You will learn different ways to plan your essay, but the steps remain the same. You must always follow these steps.

STEP 1: READ THE ESSAY TOPIC

(Topic 157) In the future, students may have the choice of studying at home by using technology such as computers or television or of studying at traditional schools. Which would you prefer? Use reasons and specific details to explain your choice.

STEP 2: IDENTIFY THE TASK

The topic wants you to state a preference. *Do you prefer to study at home using computers or study at school?* The instructions suggest you give reasons and specific details to support your answer.

STEP 3: WRITE YOUR THESIS STATEMENT

Thesis statement: *Studying at school is best for me*.

The thesis statement is a one-sentence summary of your ideas about the topic. In this case, it states your preference.

STEP 4: MAKE NOTES ABOUT YOUR GENERAL IDEAS

These notes are the start of your concept map. The concept map, like a road map, will guide you as you write your essay.

As the writer, I need to plan the organization of the topic. I make two columns so that I can compare the quality of education at home with the quality of education at school.

home		school
	~~activities~~ ~~people~~ ~~day-to-day~~ interaction	
	subjects	
	~~future~~ technology	
	motivation	

I then make a list of all the general ideas that affect education at home and at school. As I write, I may change my mind and cross out a few ideas. I may not like them, or I may not think I could give any examples about them. If I can't give any examples, I shouldn't mention them. I must give reasons and specific details to support my ideas.

STEP 5: EXPAND YOUR NOTES TO INCLUDE SPECIFIC DETAILS

You started your concept map with general notes. Now expand your concept map with specific details.

home		school
alone	~~activities~~ ~~people~~	talk to others
nobody to talk to	~~day-to-day~~ interaction	learn from others
technology only	technology plus teachers ~~subjects~~ information	and classmates
limited	~~future~~ ~~technology~~	~~more au~~
nobody sees my work	motivation	competition with classmates

In my first general idea, *interaction*, I added the specific details of *alone* and *nobody to talk to* at home. I would find studying at home all by myself lonely. At school, I would be able to talk to other students and learn from them as well. Therefore, I put the specific details *talk to others* and *learn from others* under school.

I crossed out *activities* and *day-to-day* because they weren't exactly the words I was looking for. Similarly *people* wasn't as precise a term as *interaction*.

In the third row for general ideas I thought more about what I wanted to say. I decided I had already talked about *technology* under *subjects* so I crossed it out.

In the second row for general ideas, the word *subjects* was not parallel with the other nouns. I needed a word that ended with *-tion*. I chose *information*.

WRITING THE ESSAY

There are two important parts to writing an essay:

developing the topic and

demonstrating facility with English.

We learned the five steps in planning the essay in the preceding section. Here is an overview of the step-by-step process that you will use to develop the topic and demonstrate your facility with English.

Step 6	Write the topic sentence for each paragraph.
Step 7	Write the introduction.
Step 8	Write the body of the essay.
Step 9	Write the conclusion.

The example that follows is a short introduction to the steps of writing an essay. Writing an essay will be discussed thoroughly in the chapter by the same name. You will learn different ways to develop a topic and demonstrate your facility with English. You will learn different ways to write your essay, but the steps remain the same. You must always follow these steps.

In Steps 1–5 we planned the essay. Now let's write it.

STEP 6: WRITE THE TOPIC SENTENCE FOR EACH PARAGRAPH

Each of the rows in the concept map could be a paragraph: one paragraph could be about interaction; one paragraph could be about course subjects; one paragraph could be about motivation.

Topic sentence for general idea: information

> *Information comes from technology, but it also comes from people.*

Topic sentence for general idea: interaction

> *Interaction with other people increases my knowledge.*

Topic sentence for general idea: motivation

> *Competition motivates me.*

Once I have the topic sentences for my paragraphs, I can begin to write the essay.

STEP 7: WRITE THE INTRODUCTION

The introduction lets the reader know what my point of view is and how I plan to develop the essay.

> *I believe that it is better to study at school than at home. I can learn a lot if I study alone at home, but I can learn more if I study at school with other people. I can gain a lot of information from other people. I also learn a lot by interacting with them. I am motivated to study more if I don't work alone. Therefore, I believe I can learn a lot more at school.*

In this introduction, I have stated my opinion, *Studying at school is best for me*. I have indicated that I will develop my topic by discussing *information*, *interaction*, and *motivation*.

STEP 8: WRITE THE BODY OF THE ESSAY

Paragraph 2

> *Information comes from technology, but it also comes from people. If I study at home, I can get a lot of information from my computer, DVD player, and television. If I study at school, I can get all this information, and I can also get information from my teachers and classmates. So, I learn more at school.*

In this paragraph, I chose one of my topic sentences and developed it using the specific details in my concept map. I could pick any topic sentence I wanted. I did not have to follow any particular order.

Paragraph 3

Interaction with other people increases my knowledge. At home I have nobody to talk to. Nobody can hear my ideas. At school I have the opportunity to interact with other people. We can explain our ideas to each other. We can agree and disagree. Together we can develop our ideas and learn to understand new things.

In this paragraph, I chose another topic sentence and developed it using the specific details in my concept map.

Paragraph 4

Competition motivates me. When I am at home, nobody can see my work. Nobody can tell me that I did a good job or a bad job. When I am at school, my teacher and my classmates see my work, and I can see my classmates' work. I want to do a good job like my classmates, or even a better job. So, I want to study harder.

In this paragraph, I chose another topic sentence and developed it using the specific details in my concept map. I don't have to have a specific number of paragraphs. I can have three or I can have ten. I need enough paragraphs to develop my essay thoroughly.

STEP 9: WRITE THE CONCLUSION

Some people can study very well when they are alone at home, but I can't. I need to have other people near me. When I am with other people, I have the possibility to learn more information. I have the opportunity to develop my ideas more completely. I have the motivation to do a better job. Therefore, school is the best place for me.

In this paragraph, I summarized why I preferred studying in school. I rephrased my ideas. I did not simply repeat them.

REVISING THE ESSAY

There are two important parts to revising an essay:

checking the content and clarity and

checking the punctuation and spelling.

Here is an overview of the step-by-step process that you will use to check the clarity and proof the essay. These steps parallel the Proofing Checklist (see page 28). Follow this checklist to help you proof all of your essays.

Step 10	Check the content.
Step 11	Check the clarity.
Step 12	Check the punctuation and spelling.

For this overview, we will proof the essay written on Topic 157. Since this is a model essay, there will be no major problems. Observe how the proofing checklist can help you review your own work.

Here is the essay on Topic 157 that we wrote following Steps 1 to 9.

In the future, students may have the choice of studying at home by using technology such as computers or television or of studying at traditional schools. Which would you prefer? Use reasons and specific details to explain your choice.

I believe that it is better to study at school than at home. I can learn a lot if I study alone at home, but I can learn more if I study at school with other people. I can gain a lot of information from other people. I also learn a lot by interacting with them. I am motivated to study more if I don't work alone. Therefore, I believe I can learn a lot more at school.

Information comes from technology, but it also comes from people. If I study at home, I can get a lot of information from my computer, DVD player, and television. If I study at school, I can get all this information, and I can also get information from my teachers and classmates. So, I learn more.

Interaction with other people increases my knowledge. At home I have nobody to talk to. Nobody can hear my ideas. At school I have the opportunity to interact with other people. We can explain our ideas to each other. We can agree and disagree. Together we can develop our ideas and learn to understand new things.

Competition motivates me. When I am at home, nobody can see my work. Nobody can tell me that I did a good job or a bad job. When I am at school, my teacher and my classmates see my work, and I can see my classmates' work. I want to do a good job like my classmates, or even a better job. So, I want to study harder.

Some people can study very well when they are alone at home, but I can't. I need to have other people near me. When I am with other people, I have the possibility to learn more information. I have the opportunity to develop my ideas more completely. I have the motivation to do a better job. Therefore, school is the best place for me.

Let's proof this essay following Steps 10, 11, and 12.

STEP 10: CHECK THE CONTENT

Is there a thesis statement?	✔ Yes	I believe that it is better to study at school than at home.
Is there a topic sentence for each paragraph?	✔ Yes	**Paragraph 2** Information comes from technology, but it also comes from people. **Paragraph 3** Interaction with other people increases my knowledge. **Paragraph 4** Competition motivates me.
Are there supporting details for each paragraph?	✔ Yes	**Paragraph 2** If I study at home, I can get a lot of information from my computer, DVD player, and television. If I study at school, I can get all this information, and I can also get information from my teachers and classmates. **Paragraph 3** At home I have nobody to talk to. Nobody can hear my ideas. At school I have the opportunity to interact with other people. We can explain our ideas to each other. We can agree and disagree. Together we can develop our ideas and learn to understand new things. **Paragraph 4** When I am at home, nobody can see my work. Nobody can tell me that I did a good job or a bad job. When I am at school, my teacher and my classmates see my work, and I can see my classmates' work. I want to do a good job like my classmates, or even a better job. So, I want to study harder.
Is there a conclusion?	✔ Yes	Some people can study very well when they are alone at home, but I can't. I need to have other people near me. When I am with other people, I have the possibility to learn more information. I have the opportunity to develop my ideas more completely. I have the motivation to do a better job. Therefore, school is the best place for me.

STEP 11: CHECK THE CLARITY

Are there run-on sentences or sentence fragments?	✓ No	
Are there misplaced modifiers or dangling modifiers?	✓ No	
Are the structures parallel?	✓ Yes	**Introduction** *I can learn* a lot *if I study* alone at home, but *I can learn* more *if I study* at school
		Paragraph 2 *If I study at home, I can get* a lot of information from my computer, DVD player, and television. *If I study at school, I can get* all this information...
		Paragraph 3 *At home I have no*body to talk to.... *At school I have* the opportunity to....
		Conclusion *I have the possibility* to learn more information. *I have the opportunity* to develop my ideas more completely. *I have the motivation* to do a better job.
Are there transition words?	✓ Yes	**Introduction** *But* used for contrast *Therefore,* I believe I can learn...
		Paragraph 2 *But* used for contrast *So,* I learn more.
		Paragraph 4 *But* used for contrast *So,* I want to study harder.
		Conclusion *But* used for contrast *Therefore,* school is the best place for me.
Are the sentences and paragraphs cohesive?	✓ Yes	Repetition of *at home, at school* in every paragraph

STEP 12: CHECK THE PUNCTUATION AND SPELLING

Are paragraphs indented?	✓ Yes
Are there punctuation marks such as periods at the end of each sentence?	✓ Yes
Do all sentences begin with capital letters?	✓ Yes
Are the words spelled correctly?	✓ Yes

Planning the Essay

ADDRESSING THE WRITING TASK

STEP 1: READ THE ESSAY TOPIC

The first thing to do is read the essay topic carefully. It will be given to you on the computer monitor.

To write a good essay, you must know what the topic asks you to do. You should know how to address the writing task. You must write on the topic. If you write on another subject, you will receive a 0. Pay attention to the task.

STEP 2: IDENTIFY THE TASK

There are four essay types on the TOEFL. The most common essay types are *agreeing or disagreeing* and *stating a preference*. It is more likely that you will get one of these essay topics to write, but you could also be given one of the others. You must know how to recognize the tasks in all four types. The tasks in *making an argument* and *giving an explanation* are similar. Your approach will be similar.

Topic Type	Percentage of Topics
Making an argument	34%
Agreeing or disagreeing	29%
Stating a preference	21%
Giving an explanation	16%

Making an argument

In this essay, you will be presented with a hypothetical situation. You will have to determine what needs to be done, make a choice, and support your hypothesis. In these essays, the topic is usually written in the future or conditional tense.

KEY WORDS OR PHRASES
If…
How…
In your opinion…
If you could change (something), what would you change?
What is the best way to (do something)?
What should be the main focus?
Which of the following should you do?
Which of the following is most important to you?
What would you give to help someone?
How would you do something?
How would you do something/choose between two things?
How will (something) affect (something else)?

Examples

(**Topic 141**) If you could make one important change in a school that you attended, what change would you make? Use reasons and specific examples to support your answer.

(**Topic 172**) When students move to a new school, they sometimes face problems. How can schools help these students with their problems? Use specific reasons and examples to explain your answer.

Agreeing or disagreeing

In this essay, you must state an opinion and defend your point of view. You must give reasons for your thinking. You usually discuss only one side of the issue.

KEY WORDS OR PHRASES
Do you agree or disagree …?
Do you support or oppose …?
In your opinion, which is most effective?
Why or why not?

NOTE: Your opinion is an important part of every essay. You will see many different topics asking for your opinion. In determining the writing task, you must look at what the topic is asking you to do.

Examples

(**Topic 148**) Do you agree or disagree with the following statement? Playing games teaches us about life. Use specific reasons and examples to support your answer.

(**Topic 131**) Do you agree or disagree with the following statement: **Only** people who earn a lot of money are successful. Use specific reasons and examples to support your answer.

Stating a preference

In this essay, you must discuss both sides of an issue. You will be asked to compare and contrast both sides. You may be asked to give the pros and cons, the advantages and disadvantages of something. You must also state your own personal preference and give reasons to support your choice. You may be asked to state what you think someone else's preference is.

KEY WORDS OR PHRASES
Some do this; others do that.
Some say this; others say that.
Which opinion do you agree with?
In your opinion, which is better?
Which would you prefer?
Would you prefer to …?
Compare the advantages and disadvantages.
Compare these views.
Which viewpoint do you agree with?
Discuss the advantages and disadvantages.
Which is best for you?
Compare these attitudes.
How is (something) different from (another thing)?

Examples

(**Topic 177**) A friend of yours has received some money and plans to use all of it either

• to go on a vacation

• to buy a car.

Your friend has asked you for advice. Compare your friend's two choices and explain which one you think your friend should choose. Use specific reasons and details to support your choice.

(**Topic 4**) It has been said, "Not everything that is learned is contained in books." Compare and contrast knowledge gained from experience with knowledge gained from books. In your opinion, which source is more important. Why?

Giving an explanation

In this essay, you must describe what something is, how it happened, why it occurs, or how it is different. You may have to tell why something is good or bad. You will have to establish criteria and use those criteria to make a judgement.

KEY WORDS OR PHRASES
Describe . . .
Explain . . .
What do you consider most important: (list)?
What have you learned by (doing something)?
Why do you think (something happens)?
What are the qualities of (something)?
Choose an event and tell why you enjoyed it.
How has (something) changed?
Why is (something) important?
How does (something) affect (something else)?
How is (something) different?

Examples

(**Topic 152**) Many parts of the world are losing important natural resources, such as forests, animals, or clean water. Choose **one** resource that is disappearing and explain why it needs to be saved. Use specific reasons and examples to support your opinion.

(**Topic 1**) People attend college or university for many different reasons (for example, new experiences, career preparation, increased knowledge). Why do **you** think people attend college or university? Use specific reasons and examples to support your answer.

Practice 1

Read the following essay topics. Choose which task you are to do.

1. If you could change one important thing about your hometown, what would you change? Use reasons and specific examples to support your answer.

   (A) Make an argument   (B) Give an explanation

2. Some people say that physical exercise should be a required part of every school day. Other people believe that students should spend the whole school day on academic studies. Which opinion do you agree with? Give reasons to support your answer.

   (A) Make an argument   (B) State a preference

3. Do you agree or disagree with the following statement? Playing a game is fun only when you win. Use specific reasons and examples to support your answer.

   (A) Agree or disagree   (B) State a preference

4. Think of the most important class you have ever taken. Why did you enjoy this class so much? Use specific reasons and details to explain your answer.

   (A) Make an argument   (B) Give an explanation

5. Do you agree or disagree with the following statement? Books are not needed any more because people can read information on computers. Use specific reasons and details to explain your answer.

   (A) Make an argument   (B) Agree or disagree

6. In the twentieth century, food has become easier to prepare. Has this change improved the way people live? Use specific reasons and examples to support your answer.

   (A) State a preference   (B) Give an explanation

7. Some items (such as clothes or furniture) can be made by hand or by machine. Which do you prefer—items made by hand or items made by machine? Use reasons and specific examples to explain your choice.

   (A) State a preference   (B) Make an argument

8. A gift (such as a soccer ball, a camera, or an animal) can contribute to a child's development. What gift would you give to help a child develop? Why? Use reasons and specific examples to support your choice.

   (A) Give an explanation   (B) Agree or disagree

9. Do you agree or disagree with the following statement? Universities should give the same amount of money to their students' sports activities as they give to their university libraries. Use specific reasons and examples to support your opinion.

   (A) Agree or disagree   (B) Make an argument

10. Some people prefer to spend most of their time alone. Others like to be with friends most of the time. Do you prefer to spend your time alone or with friends? Give reasons to support your answer.

    (A) State a preference   (B) Make an argument

STEP 3: WRITE YOUR THESIS STATEMENT

In order to write a good essay, you must clearly state your thesis. Every essay must have a thesis. The thesis is the main idea of your essay. A thesis statement focuses the direction of the topic and helps the reader understand what you want to say. It tells the reader what your topic is.

Look at these example topics to see how different thesis statements can come from the same topic.

Topic 99

You have been told that dormitory rooms at your university must be shared by two students. Would you rather have the university assign a student to share a room with you, or would you rather choose your own roommate? Use specific reasons and details to explain your answer.

Thesis statement A

>Since I do not get along well with many people, I prefer to choose my own roommate.

From this statement, we can presume that the writer will discuss why s/he has difficulty having friendly relationships with people.

Thesis statement B

>The opportunity to meet new people is an important benefit of a university education, so I believe it is better to let the university choose my roommate for me.

From this statement, we can presume the writer will discuss the benefits of meeting new people at a university.

A thesis statement must be on the topic. Pay close attention to what the topic asks you to do.

Topic 95

Some people think governments should spend as much money as possible exploring outer space (for example, traveling to the moon and to other planets). Other people disagree and think governments should spend this money for our basic needs on Earth. Which of these two opinions do you agree with? Use specific reasons and details to support your answer.

Thesis statement A

>The moon is a better place to explore because it is nearer than the planets.

This thesis statement is NOT a good thesis statement for this topic. It takes two of the words from the topic and writes about exploration possibilities. The topic, though, is how best to spend limited resources: on space exploration or on needs on Earth. This thesis statement is off topic.

Thesis statement B

>While there is still hunger, poverty, and illiteracy on Earth, our resources should be focused here and not in outer space.

From this statement, we can presume the writer will discuss why hunger, poverty, and illiteracy on earth are more worthy of attention than space exploration.

Thesis statement C

>Gaining psychological and scientific knowledge through space exploration will benefit us more than trying to solve problems here on Earth.

From this statement, we can presume the writer will discuss in detail the psychological and scientific benefits that we receive from space exploration.

Practice 2

Choose the thesis statements that are appropriate to the topic. There can be more than one possible answer.

1. What is one of the most important decisions you have made? Why was this decision important? Use specific reasons and details to explain your answer.

    (A) Decisions are important because without them nothing would get done.

    (B) Deciding to leave home to attend school in the US has been so far the most important decision I've made.

    (C) Although my parents wanted me to study medicine, I knew that I should follow my heart and get a degree in nuclear physics.

2. Someone who was considered an educated person in the past (for example, in your parents' or grandparents' generation) would not be considered an educated person today. Do you agree or disagree? Use specific reasons and examples to support your answer.

    (A) If you define education as earning degrees, than I would have to agree that today people are more educated than they were in the past.

    (B) It was more difficult to get an education in the past since there weren't as many schools.

    (C) Both my grandfather and my grandmother attended university which is where they met.

3. Many people visit museums when they travel to new places. Why do you think people visit museums? Use specific reasons and examples to support your answer.

    (A) New museums are opening in almost every city in the world.

    (B) Museums hold the historic and artistic record of a region, so visiting museums is the best way to understand a new place.

    (C) Travelers want to see in person famous works of art that they have only seen in books so they head to museums when in new cities.

4. In the future, students may have the choice of studying at home by using technology such as computers or television or of studying at traditional schools. Which would you prefer? Use reasons and specific details to explain your choice.

    (A) Interaction with my fellow students is important to me so I would prefer to study in a more traditional setting.

    (B) Computers and television are two examples of technology that will change a lot in the future.

    (C) The advantages of studying what you want, when you want, and where you want do not, for me, outweigh the disadvantages of using technology for home education.

5. In general, people are living longer now. How will this change affect society? Use specific details and examples to develop your essay.

    (A) People are living longer now because of improvements in medical care.

    (B) As the majority of our population becomes older, our communities will have to shift their focus from providing services to the young, like schools, to services to aging adults, like medical care.

    (C) Society has been around a long time and it is always changing.

Free Practice

Do any or all of the following activities on your own or in a group. There are no answers provided.

1. Write your own thesis statement for the five topics above.

2. Look at the Model Essays in the Appendix. Note whether each topic is Agreeing or Disagreeing (AD), Stating a Preference (PR), Giving an Explanation (EX), or Making an Argument (MA).

3. Write essays on the above topics.

ORGANIZING THE ESSAY

STEP 4: MAKE NOTES ABOUT YOUR GENERAL IDEA

To write a good essay, you must organize your thoughts before you write. First, of course, you must have some thoughts. You must have an opinion about a subject. Your opinion about a subject is the thesis of your essay.

Concept maps will help you organize the topic. Use a concept map to make notes. There are many different types of concept maps. We will discuss five in this chapter. Some of them are more appropriate for certain topics. Some are appropriate for all topics. Use the one that works best for you.

Concept Map	Topic
Web	All topics
Fish bone	All topics
Venn Diagram	Stating a preference
Matrix	All topics
NPR	Making an argument

STEP 5: EXPAND YOUR NOTES TO INCLUDE SPECIFIC DETAILS

Regardless of its shape, each concept map has three components: the thesis statement, some general ideas, and some supporting details. As a rule, you should try to have three general ideas per essay and at least two supporting details per general idea. This will vary according to your topic and the way you choose to organize your topic.

Web

The web concept map is like a spider web. Many ideas are linked by a common thread.

1. Read the topic. (**Topic 159**) The twentieth century saw great change. In your opinion, what is **one** change that should be remembered about the twentieth century? Use specific reasons and details to explain your choice.

2. Identify the task. Explanation

3. Write a thesis. Medical advances are the most important change.

4. Add general ideas.

5. Add supporting details.

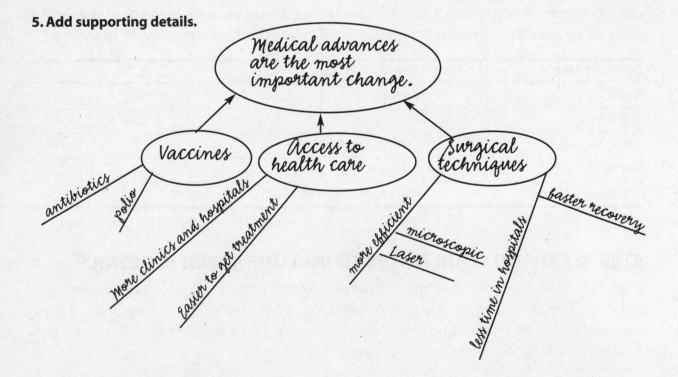

Essay Topic 159

Compare the web concept map with this essay.

Medical Advances: An Important Change
of the Twentieth Century

There were many important changes, both technological and cultural, during the twentieth century. In my opinion, the most important of these is the advances that were made in medical science. The development of vaccines and antibiotics, increased access to health care, and improvements in surgical techniques are all things that improved, and saved, the lives of people all around the world.

Vaccines and antibiotics have saved the lives of many people. Fifty years ago, many people became crippled or died from polio. Now the polio vaccine is available everywhere. In the past, people could die from even simple infections. Now penicillin and other antibiotics make it easy to cure infections.

Increased access to health care has also improved the lives of millions of people. In the past, many people lived far from hospitals or clinics. Now hospitals, clinics, and health centers have been built in many parts of the world. More people have the opportunity to visit a doctor or nurse before they become very sick. They can be treated more easily. They are sick less and this leads to a better quality of life.

Improved surgical techniques make it easier to treat many medical problems. Microscopic and laser surgery techniques are more efficient than older methods. It is easier for the doctor to perform them, and easier for the patient to recover. Surgery patients can return to their normal life more quickly now than they could in the past.

Everybody needs good health in order to have a good quality of life. Advances in medical science have improved the lives of people all around the world. They are improvements that are important to everyone.

Essay Organization

Theme:	Medical advances are the most important change of the twentieth century.
Point 1: **Examples:**	Development of vaccines and antibiotics Polio vaccine saves lives Penicillin and other antibiotics save lives
Point 2: **Examples:**	Increased access to health care Hospitals, clinics, health centers were built People are sick less because it's easier to get treatment
Point 3: **Examples:**	Improvements in surgical techniques Microscopic and laser surgery are easier to perform Patients recover faster

Fish bone

The fish bone concept map looks like a fish skeleton. The supporting reasons and specific examples point to the main idea.

1. Read the topic.   Think of the most important class you have ever taken. Why did you enjoy this class so much? Use specific reasons and details to explain your answer.

2. Identify the task.   Explanation

3. Write a thesis.   I learned a lot in Art History, and it was inspiring.

4. Add general ideas.

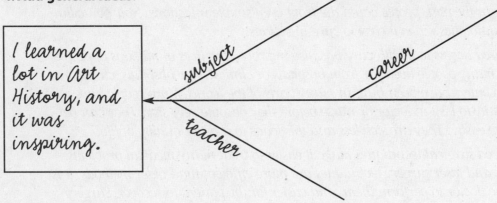

5. Add supporting details.

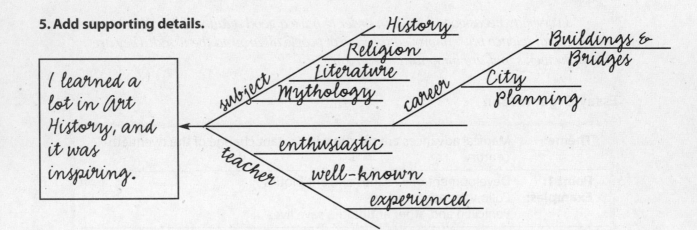

Essay

Compare the fish bone concept map with this essay.

Art History

Even though I am an engineer, I have to say that Introduction to Art History *is the most important class I have ever taken. In this class I had the opportunity to learn new things, not only about art, but about other areas as well. I had a teacher who inspired me. And, believe it or not, it was important to my career as an engineer.*

Art history should be a required course for everyone because it teaches you about so many things. I learned not only about art, but also about history, religion, literature, and mythology. These are subjects I didn't learn about in my engineering classes, so it was a wonderful opportunity for me.

Of course, the most important part of any class is the teacher, and I was lucky to have a very good teacher in this class. She was very experienced and well known in her field. She was enthusiastic about art, and she was able to make her students enthusiastic about it too. She inspired me to learn more.

Studying art history taught me some things about the history of engineering. In old paintings, I saw how buildings and bridges were built in the past. I saw how cities were planned. I realized that I could learn about my own field in different ways.

I learned a lot of things in my art history class. I learned about art, about engineering, and about other things I hadn't imagined. Both the subject and the teacher inspired me to expand my mind. I am very glad that I took this class.

Essay Organization

Theme:	I learned a lot in Art History, and it was inspiring.
Point 1: **Examples:**	I learned many things in this class. Art History, religion, literature, and mythology
Point 2: **Examples:**	I had a very good teacher. Experienced and well known Enthusiastic Inspiring
Point 3: **Examples:**	It was important to my career as an engineer. I learned how bridges and buildings were built in the past. I learned how cities were planned in the past.

Venn Diagram

The Venn Diagram is most appropriate for comparing and contrasting two issues. The circles represent the qualities of each issue. Where they overlap in the center represents where they are similar. Usually, the center contains the general ideas and the outside sections contain the specific differences. A Venn Diagram is often not as complete as a web. The topics are not as fully developed.

1. Read the topic.   (Topic 112) Some people think that children should begin their formal educa-
tion at a very early age and should spend most of their time on school studies.
Others believe that young children should spend most of their time playing.
Compare these two views. Which view do you agree with? Why?

2. Identify the task.   Stating a preference

3. Write a thesis.   Children can learn at school and at play.

4. Add general ideas.   Socialize and competition

**5. Add supporting
details.**

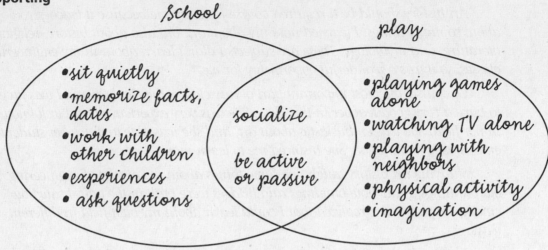

Essay Topic 112

Compare the Venn Diagram with this essay.

Educating Children

*Should a child spend more time on school studies or more time on play? The
answer to this question depends on the quality of the school and the quality of the
play. Wherever children spend their time, they should be active participants, not passive observers.*

*Not all schools are the same. In some schools, children must sit quietly all day
and memorize dates and facts. In other schools, children are encouraged to participate in different kinds of activities. They are encouraged to ask questions, to interact
with other children, and to experience things.*

*Not all children play the same way. Some children prefer to watch TV or video
games. Other children enjoy games that involve physical activity, using their imagination, or playing with other children.*

*Not all children are the same, but all children have the same requirements for
learning. They learn when their minds and their bodies are active. They learn when
they socialize with other children. They can do these things during school time or
during play time. It doesn't matter when or where they do these things. It only
matters that they do them.*

*Children can learn a lot from formal education and they can learn a lot
from play. Parents need to make sure that the time their children spend in school
is quality time. They need to make sure that the time their children spend at play is
also quality time. Then they can feel assured that their children are getting the
experiences they need to learn and grow.*

Essay Organization

Theme:	Children can learn at school and at play if they are active participants.
Point 1: **Examples:**	Children can be either passive or active at school. Sit quietly and memorize Participate in learning activities Interact with other children
Point 2: **Examples:**	Children can be either passive or active at play. Watch TV or play video games Participate in physical activities Interact with other children Use the imagination
Point 3: **Examples:**	All children have the same requirements for learning. Mentally active Physically active Socialize with other children

Matrix

The matrix is useful for categorizing and classifying qualities. It can be used for all topics.

1. Read the topic.   (**Topic 119**) Do you agree or disagree with the following statement? People behave differently when they wear different clothes. Do you agree that different clothes influence the way people behave? Use specific examples to support your answer.

2. Identify the task.   Agreeing or disagreeing

3. Write a thesis.   Clothes make people behave differently because of other people's reactions.

4. Add general ideas.

	Reaction	
	Friend	Stranger
Office Setting		
Non-office		

5. Add supporting details.

	Reaction	
	Friend	Stranger
Office Setting	Business dress/ uniform	Business dress/ uniform
Non-office	Casual/formal	Neat and clean/ Old and dirty

Essay Topic 119

Compare the matrix with this essay.

You Aren't What You Wear

People behave differently depending on what they are wearing. The reason is not because they have changed, but because people's reactions to them have changed. Strangers react to your appearance because it is all they know about you. A friend may be influenced by your dress also, if it is inappropriate for a situation. In addition, appearance is almost always important at work.

Strangers can only judge you by the clothes you wear. Once I was wearing an old army coat. I went into a fancy candy shop to buy some chocolates. The woman saw my coat and was very suspicious of me. Because of the woman's negative reaction to me, I acted more politely than usual. The woman reacted to my clothes and that made me behave differently.

With friends clothes are less important because friends know more about you. However, friends can also react to you because of your clothes. Imagine you arrive at a friend's party. Everyone is wearing formal clothes and you are wearing casual clothes. You might have a good reason for this mistake, but your friend will still be disappointed. You will probably feel uncomfortable all evening because you disappointed your friend and because you are dressed differently from everyone else.

Certain clothes are appropriate for certain jobs. For example, business clothes are appropriate for some jobs, uniforms are appropriate for others. If you are not dressed appropriately for your job, clients and co-workers take you less seriously. You might begin to take yourself less seriously also, and your work could suffer. On the other hand, if you are wearing the right clothes, people will have confidence that you are the right person for the job, and you will feel this way, too.

Clothes don't change you into a different person, but they can make you behave differently. If you are dressed inappropriately for a situation, people will react to you in a different way. This reaction can, in turn, change your behavior. If you want good reactions from people, make sure to dress appropriately for every situation.

Essay Organization

Theme:	Clothes make people behave differently because of other people's reactions.
Point 1: **Example:**	Strangers react to your clothes. Experience of wearing an old coat in a fancy store
Point 2: **Example:**	Friends sometimes react to your clothes. Casual clothes at a formal party
Point 3: **Examples:**	Appearance is important at work. Inappropriate dress Appropriate dress

NPR

NPR is like a matrix and is also useful for categorizing and classifying qualities. It is most appropriate for making an argument. NPR stands for Now (topic the way things are now); Proposed (what we propose to change); and Reason (why we make this proposition).

1. Read the topic. (Topic 147) Your school has received a gift of money. What do you think is the best way for your school to spend this money? Use specific reasons and details to support your choice.

2. Identify the task. Making an argument

3. Write a thesis. New equipment is needed.

N — Now	P — Proposed	R — Reason
4. Add general ideas. Old school	New Equipment	Better environment
5. Add supporting details. Old classroom fixtures Shortage of desks	More desks, chairs, chalkboards, bookshelves, cabinets	Improved learning Long-lasting Attractive for community

Essay Topic 147

Compare the NPR concept map with this essay.

Our school has many needs, but I think the best way to spend a gift of money is on new classroom equipment. Our school is old. We don't have enough desks and chairs for all the students and our classroom furniture is out of repair. If we buy new equipment, the students will feel better and want to work hard. The community will take pride in our school. New equipment will last a long time, so we will feel the benefit of the gift for many years.

It is hard for students to study when there aren't enough chairs in the classroom. It is hard for them to use old, broken blackboards. It is hard when there aren't good bookshelves and cabinets to organize the classroom supplies. With new equipment students will feel like school is a nice place to be. They will feel like the teachers care about them. They will be motivated to study harder and do the best job they can.

It is hard for the community to feel proud of a school that looks old and broken. If members of the community visit the school and see new classroom equipment, they might feel better about the school. They might say, "This school has improved, and we can improve it more." They might be motivated to contribute money and volunteer time to further improve the school. Every school is better when community members become involved. New equipment can help motivate them.

We could spend the gift money on educational trips for the students. We could spend it on supplies like paper and pencils or on books. All these things are important for education, but they don't last. Students this year will benefit, but students five years from now won't. Classroom equipment, on the other hand, lasts many years. If we spend the money on equipment, students will benefit for many years to come.

New classroom equipment will motivate both students and community members to improve their participation in school. Everyone will benefit from new equipment now and in the future as well. Therefore, I think this is one of the best ways we can spend a gift of money to our school.

Essay Organization

Theme:	New classroom equipment is the best way to spend a gift of money to our school.
Point 1: **Examples:**	New equipment will motivate students to study harder. Old equipment makes it hard to study New equipment makes the students feel comfortable and important
Point 2: **Examples:**	New equipment will motivate community members to be involved in the school. They are embarrassed by an old, broken school They want to contribute to an improved school
Point 3: **Examples:**	Classroom equipment will provide a lasting benefit. The school can benefit from field trips and supplies for only a short time The school can benefit from classroom equipment for many years

Practice 3

Look at the concept map. Read the essay. Complete the missing parts of the map.

1. Read the topic.   You have been asked to suggest improvements to a park that you have visited. This might be a city park, a regional park, or a national park. What improvements would you make? Why? Use specific reasons and examples to support your recommendations.

2. Identify the task.   Making an argument

3. Write a thesis.   Improve the city park to encourage community members to use it.

	N – Now	P – Proposed	R – Reason
4. Add general ideas.	Decay	Repair	Community feeling
5. Add supporting details.	playground benches (5.1) _weeds_	new swings, picnic (5.2)_____, and benches new flowers	(5.3)_____ fun relaxing

Essay

Compare the NPR with this essay.

City Park for the City

Forty years ago people left the city and moved to the suburbs. They left behind what was once a green oasis in the center of the city, City Park. Where children used to play, there is now broken glass. Where their parents gossiped and watched their children play, there are now decayed benches. Where flowers bloomed every season, there are now just weeds. I want to bring this park back to life and encourage people to return to the city again to enjoy it.

The improvements I would propose are simple and relatively inexpensive. First, we have to clean up the park. Volunteer groups can bring rakes and brooms and pick up the trash that litters the playgrounds and the grass.

Second we have to add things that will make the park a place to come to. Swings and sandboxes for the children. Picnic tables and benches for families. Perhaps we can encourage food vendors to open a snack bar.

Third, we need to make the park beautiful again. Our volunteer groups can bring their trowels and their hoes. They can plant flowers and trim shrubs. They can cut the grass and pull the weeds. When more people return to use the park, the city can take over these chores.

People are returning to live in the city. We need to provide them a place that is safe, fun, and relaxing. We need the park to give us a sense of community.

Essay Organization

Theme:	Improving the park will encourage community members to use it.
Point 1: Example:	Community volunteers can clean up the park. Pick up the trash
Point 2: Examples:	New equipment will make it nicer to use the park. Swings and sandboxes Picnic tables Snack bar
Point 3: Examples:	Community volunteers can make the park beautiful. Plant flowers Cut grass Pull weeds

Practice 4

Look at the concept map. Read the essay. Complete the missing parts of the map.

1. Read the topic.   (Topic 118) Some people enjoy change, and they look forward to new experiences. Others like their lives to stay the same, and they do not change their usual habits. Compare these two approaches to life. Which approach do you prefer? Explain why.

2. Identify the task.   Stating a preference

3. Write a thesis.   Your routine is determined by your circumstances.

When I was young	Now I have a family	Advantages of routine
Enjoy change	Routine	Security
no responsibilities (5.1)_____ take off with friends day-to-day decisions	8 p.m.: bathe children put in pajamas (5.3)_____ 9 p.m.: put to sleep	friends know schedule; (5.4)_____ security
(5.2)_____ meet new and interesting people, and learn a lot about life		

4. Add general ideas.

5. Add supporting details.

Essay Topic 118

Compare the matrix with this essay.

My Routine

It is true that some people prefer things to stay the same while others prefer change. My preference is to establish a routine and follow it, although this has not always been true of me. My circumstances have changed since I was young.

When I was younger, I enjoyed change. During school vacations I was free from responsibility. I would travel, go away with friends at a moment's notice, and make decisions from day to day. In this way, I could have lots of new experiences, meet new and interesting people, and learn a lot about life.

These days, I enjoy following a routine. It makes my life easier because I am the mother of two small children. Their lives are happier if I don't upset their schedules too much. For example, we give the children a bath every night at 8:00, put them in their pajamas, read them stories, and put them to bed by 9:00. It is not always convenient to do this, but everyone in the family is happier when we follow our routine. In addition, our friends know when we are free, which makes visiting easier.

In conclusion, my preferences have changed with the circumstances of my life. Now, my family's needs force me to have a routine. The stability of a household routine is better for me now, even though I preferred the excitement and adventure of change when I was young. I think the people you spend your time with often dictate your lifestyle.

Essay Organization

Theme:	My routine has changed with my circumstances.
Point 1: Examples:	When I was young, I liked change. Travel with friends at moment's notice Have new experiences Meet new people Learn about life
Point 2: Examples:	Now I prefer routine. My children need routine It is easier to see friends

Practice 5

Look at the concept map. Read the essay. Complete the missing parts of the maps.

1. **Read the topic.**   When choosing a place to live, what do you consider most important: location, size, style, number of rooms, types of rooms, or other features? Use reasons and specific examples to support your answer.

2. **Identify the task.**   Giving an explanation

3. **Write a thesis.**   The most important thing for me is location.

4. **Add general ideas.**

5. **Add supporting details.**

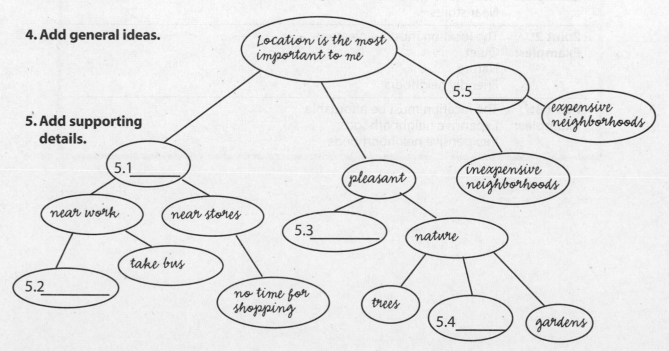

Essay

Compare the web concept map with this essay.

House Hunting

When choosing a place to live, I look at several things. I need to consider price, size, and type of housing. However, the most important thing of all is location. I look for a house in a convenient and pleasant neighborhood that has rents I can afford to pay.

My apartment must be conveniently located. I don't have a car, so I want to live near my job. I want to be able to walk or take the bus to work. I don't have a lot of time for shopping, so I want to live near stores, too.

I want to live in a pleasant neighborhood. I like quiet areas with little traffic. I like to have nature around me, so I prefer a neighborhood with a lot of trees, gardens, and maybe even a park. Most of all, I want to have friendly neighbors.

Some neighborhoods are more expensive than others. I have to look for my apartment in neighborhoods that aren't too expensive. Some neighborhoods are very beautiful, but if the rents are too high, I can't afford to live there. If I only look in areas of the city that have affordable rents, I won't be disappointed.

The size of my apartment or the style of the building aren't important to me. I don't care if my apartment is small or if the building is old and in need of repair. If I can find an affordable place to live in a convenient and pleasant location, then I will have everything I need.

Essay Organization

Theme:	The most important thing for me is location.
Point 1: **Examples:**	The location must be convenient. Near work Near stores
Point 2: **Examples:**	The location must be pleasant. Quiet Nature Friendly neighbors
Point 3: **Examples:**	The location must be affordable. Expensive neighborhoods Inexpensive neighborhoods

Practice 6

Look at the concept map. Read the essay. Complete the missing parts of the maps.

1. Read the topic. (**Topic 1**) People attend college or university for many different reasons (for example, new experiences, career preparation, increased knowledge). Why do **you** think people attend college or university? Use specific reasons and examples to support your answer.

2. Identify the task. Giving an explanation

3. Write a thesis. The three most common reasons are to prepare for a career, to have new experiences, and to increase their knowledge of themselves and the world around them.

4. Add general ideas.

5. Add supporting details.

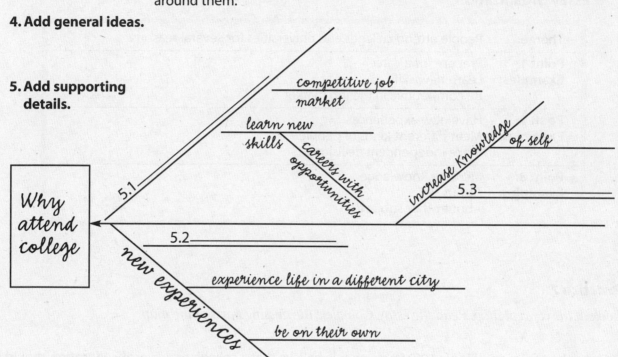

Essay Topic 1

Compare the fish bone with this essay.

Three Reasons People Attend College

People attend college for a lot of different reasons. I believe that the three most common reasons are to prepare for a career, to have new experiences, and to increase their knowledge of themselves and of the world around them.

Career preparation is probably the primary reason that people attend college. These days, the job market is very competitive. Careers such as information technology will need many new workers in the near future. At college, students can learn new skills for these careers and increase their opportunities for the future.

Students also go to college to have new experiences. For many, it is their first time away from home. At college, they can meet new people from many different places. They can see what life is like in a different city. They can learn to live on their own and take care of themselves without having their family always nearby.

At college, students have the opportunity to increase their knowledge. As they decide what they want to study, pursue their studies, and interact with their class-mates, they learn a lot about themselves. They also, of course, have the opportunity to learn about many subjects in their classes. In addition to the skills and knowledge related to their career, college students also have the chance to take classes in other areas. For many, this will be their last chance to study different subjects.

Colleges offer much more than career preparation. They offer the opportunity to have new experiences and to learn many kinds of things. I think all of these are rea-sons why people attend college.

Essay Organization

Theme:	People attend colleges and universities for several reasons.
Point 1: **Examples:**	Prepare for a career Learn new skills Be competitive in the job market
Point 2: **Examples:**	Have new experiences Meet different kinds of people Make independent decisions
Point 3: **Examples:**	Increase knowledge About self About other subjects

Practice 7

Look at the concept map. Read the essay. Complete the missing parts of the map.

1. Read the topic. (Topic 107) Some people believe that a college or university education should be available to all students. Others believe that higher education should be available only to good students. Discuss these views. Which view do you agree with? Explain why.

2. Identify the task. Stating a preference

3. Write a thesis. Higher education should be available to all students.

4. Add general ideas.   *cost*   *time*

5. Add supporting details.   *Not for poor*   *Open to all*

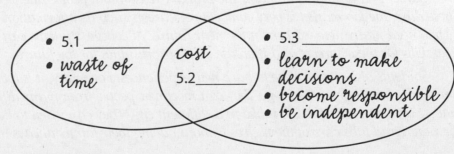

- 5.1 _____
- *waste of time*

cost
5.2 _____

- 5.3 _____
- *learn to make decisions*
- *become responsible*
- *be independent*

Essay Topic 80

Compare the Venn Diagram with this essay.

Higher Education: Open to All Students or Not?

Some people believe that only the best students should go to a college or university, but I don't. Academics are not the only purpose of a university education. Another important goal is to learn about yourself. When you are separated from your parents, you have to learn to be independent and make decisions about your future. I believe every student should have the opportunity to have this kind of experience.

I can understand why some people think that a college or university education should be available only to good students. Higher education is very expensive. It might seem like a waste of money to send a mediocre student to college. If a better student will learn more, why not send only the better student to college? Higher education is also a big investment of time. Maybe a mediocre student could spend his or her time in a better way, by getting a job or going to trade school.

I don't agree with this position. I think higher education should be available to all students. It is true that it is expensive and takes a lot of time, but I think every student deserves the opportunity to try it. People change. A student who didn't like school as a teenager may start to like it as a young adult. Also, having the opportunity to make independent decisions is part of a good education. A student may try college for a while and then decide that trade school is a better place for him or her. Or a student may decide, "I will work hard now because I want a good future." At a college or university students have the opportunity to make changes and decisions for themselves.

Every student who wants to should be given the chance to go to a college or university. In college they will have the opportunity to learn independence and to make adult decisions about their future. This is a basic part of education and an experience every student should have.

Essay Organization

Theme:	Higher education should be available to all students.
Point 1:	Some people think higher education should be available only to good students.
Examples:	Money
	Time
Point 2:	Higher education is good for all students.
Examples:	People change
	Opportunity to make decisions

Practice 8

Look at the concept map. Read the essay. Complete the missing parts of the map.

1. Read the topic. (Topic 136) Do you agree or disagree with the following statement? Playing a game is fun only when you win. Use specific reasons and examples to support your answer.

2. Identify the task. Giving an explanation

3. Write a thesis. I have fun playing all games because it gives me time to be with friends, learn new things, and work with others as a team.

4. Add general ideas.

5. Add supporting details.

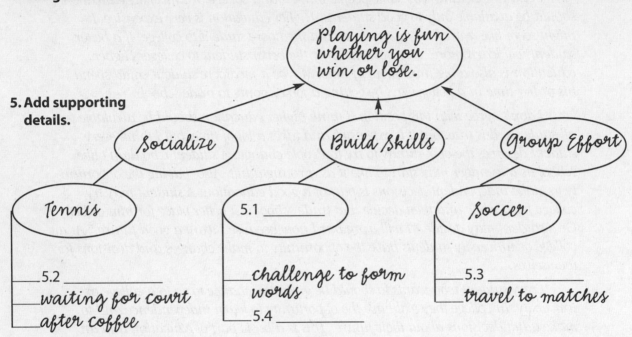

Essay Topic 136

Compare the web concept map with this essay.

Playing to Have Fun

I agree with the old saying, "It's not whether you win or lose, it's how you play the game." I have fun playing all games because they give me time to be with my friends, learn new things, and work as a team.

Tennis is one game that I enjoy. It's a great opportunity to socialize. First, I have to talk to my partner in order to arrange a time to play a game. We also talk about other things at the same time. We have another opportunity to talk while we are waiting for the tennis court to be free. After the game, we almost always go out for coffee and talk some more. We often don't even talk about tennis. The game is just an excuse for us to get together.

The board game Scrabble provides a good opportunity to build my language skills. It's a challenge to try to form words from the letters that are in front of me. I always learn new words from my opponents, too. Often we don't even keep score when we play the game. We just enjoy being together and improving our English.

The game of soccer gives me the chance to be on a team. I like traveling with the group when we go to other schools to play games. I like learning how to play as a team. Our coach tells us that the most important thing is to play well together. It's also important to have fun. Winning is secondary.

I play games because they are fun. Playing games gives me the opportunity to do things that I enjoy and be with people that I like. You can't win every time, but you can always have fun.

Essay Organization

Theme:	Playing games is fun because I can socialize, learn new things, and work as a team.
Point 1: Examples:	Socialize/Tennis Arranging a time to play Waiting for the court Going out after game
Point 2: Examples:	Build skills/Scrabble Form words Learn new words from friends
Point 3: Examples:	Team/soccer Travel with friends Play as a team

Free Practice

Identify the tasks for the following topics. Create a concept map for each. On a separate sheet of paper, write an essay using the concept map as your guide. Compare your essays with those essays in the Model Essay *section.*

1. **(Topic 11)** Do you agree or disagree with the following statement? Universities should give the same amount of money to their students' sports activities as they give to their university libraries. Use specific reasons and examples to support your opinion.

   Task: _____

   Thesis statement: _____

   Concept Map:

2. (Topic 9) Some people prefer to live in a small town. Others prefer to live in a big city. Which place would you prefer to live in? Use specific reasons and details to support your answer.

Task: _____

Thesis statement: _____

Concept Map:

3. (Topic 7) How do movies or television influence people's behavior? Use reasons and specific examples to explain your answer.

Task: _____

Thesis statement: _____

Concept Map:

4. (Topic 149) Imagine that you have received some land to use as you wish. How would you use this land? Use specific details to explain your answer.

Task: _____

Thesis statement: _____

Concept Map:

5. (**Topic 124**) Do you agree or disagree with the following statement? It is more important for students to study history and literature than it is for them to study science and mathematics. Use specific reasons and examples to support your opinion.

Task: _____

Thesis statement: _____

Concept Map:

6. (**Topic 154**) In some countries, people are no longer allowed to smoke in many public places and office buildings. Do you think this is a good rule or a bad rule? Use specific reasons and details to support your position.

Task: _____

Thesis statement: _____

Concept Map:

SELF-TEST ESSAY #2

Write on the same topic as Self-test Essay #1. Plan, write, and revise an essay on that topic within 30 minutes. Use the space provided. Do NOT write in the shaded areas.

Divide your time like this.

PLAN	5 minutes	30:00 – 25:00
WRITE	20 minutes	25:00 – 05:00
REVISE	5 minutes	05:00 – 00:00

Topic Number: _____

PLAN

Concept Map

Thesis Statement

General Ideas

Supporting Details

WRITE

REVISE

Proofing Checklist

Reread your essay. Use this checklist as a guide.

✓	CONTENT
	Is there a thesis statement or introduction?
	Is there a topic sentence for each paragraph?
	Are there supporting details for each topic statement?
	Is there a conclusion?
✓	CLARITY
	Are there run-on sentences or sentence fragments?
	Are there misplaced modifiers or dangling modifiers?
	Are the structures parallel?
	Are there transition words?
	Are the sentences and paragraphs cohesive?
✓	PUNCTUATION AND SPELLING
	Are the paragraphs indented?
	Are there punctuation marks such as periods at the end of each sentence?
	Do all sentences begin with capital letters?
	Are all the words spelled correctly?

3

Writing the Essay

DEVELOPING THE TOPIC

STEP 6: WRITE THE TOPIC SENTENCE FOR EACH PARAGRAPH

In the chapter on *Planning the Essay*, we learned about a thesis statement. A thesis statement tells the reader what the essay will be about. A topic sentence tells the reader what a paragraph will be about. A topic sentence can introduce the paragraph, or it can summarize what has been said in the paragraph. A topic sentence can be at the beginning, the middle, or the end of a paragraph.

When people start writing an essay without planning what they will say, the introduction usually has nothing to do with the essay. Some people write the body of an essay first; once they know what they have said, they go back and write the introduction. You don't have that time. You must plan in advance.

If you write a sentence for each of the general ideas in your concept map, you will have three to five topic sentences. These topic sentences will be used in the body of your essay and will be summarized in the introduction and conclusion. Learning to write a good topic sentence is important. If you think about the topic sentences that you want for each paragraph, your writing will be more coherent, and you will be able to write more quickly.

You must provide specific reasons to support the ideas in your essay. These phrases will often appear in the TOEFL Essay topic.

KEY PHRASES
Use specific reasons and examples to support your answer.
Use specific reasons and examples to support your opinion.
Use specific reasons and examples to develop your essay.
Use specific reasons and examples to explain your choice.
Give specific details to support your position.

All paragraphs contain a topic sentence supported by specific details. A topic sentence is usually a generalization.

Topic sentence:	Physical training is good for you.
Supporting details:	Physical activity improves blood circulation.
	The brain needs oxygen to function.
	You will be more alert in class.

The generalization is likely to be your opinion on the topic. You will need to support your opinion with details. Specific details give substance to your essay. They make it interesting and pertinent.

Topic sentence: I support the plan to build a new movie theater in my neighborhood.

Supporting details: The nearest movie theater is two miles away.

Restaurants will be built up around the theater.

Look at these examples.

Example from Topic 172

A school administrator should give new students a complete orientation to their school. She or he should take them on a tour of the school, showing them the classrooms, gym, computer lab, band room, and cafeteria. She or he should tell them about the history of the school, its academic achievements, its seven athletic and debating teams. The administrator can talk to the students about what's expected of them in the classroom and what rules the school has.

Topic sentence:	A school administrator should give new students a complete orientation to their school.
Supporting details:	take students on tour of school
	tell about history of school
	talk to them about what's expected

In the above paragraph the topic sentence is about the school administrator's job to give an orientation to new students. The orientation includes a tour of the school, its history, and a discussion of what is expected of students.

Example from Topic 182

Everyone, children as well as senior citizens, can have important relationships with pets. Children who have dogs have the opportunity to learn responsibility while caring for them. The elderly, who often feel lonely as they get older, are able to feel needed because they are caring for a dog that needs them.

Topic sentence:	Everyone, children as well as senior citizens, can have important relationships with pets.
Supporting details:	teaches children responsibility
	elderly take care of dogs who, in turn, need them.

Example from Topic 121

One should spend time getting to know people before judging them. I know that I do not always make the best first impression, even when I truly like the people I am with. We all have bad days, and I wouldn't want to lose a job or a new friend simply because I picked out the wrong clothing or said the wrong thing.

Topic sentence:	One should spend time getting to know people before judging them.
Supporting details:	I don't always make the best first impression.
	We all have bad days.
	We all pick out the wrong clothing or say something wrong.

Practice 1

Read the following paragraphs. Write the topic sentence and the supporting details for each paragraph. You may have more or fewer than three supporting details.

1. **Paragraph from Topic 148**
   Playing games also teaches us how to deal with other people. We learn about teamwork, if the game involves being on a team. We learn how to divide and assign tasks according to each person's skills. We learn how to get people to do what we want, and we learn that sometimes we have to do what other people want.

Topic sentence:	1.1
Supporting details:	1.2
	1.3
	1.4
	1.5

2. **Paragraph from Topic 13**
   Cooking takes a lot of time. While the food might not actually be on the stove for very long, you also have to consider the time that is spent shopping for the food, cleaning and chopping it, and cleaning up the kitchen after it is cooked.

Topic sentence:	2.1
Supporting details:	2.2
	2.3
	2.4

3. Paragraph from Topic 7

Watching movies and television can be good for us. One thing they do is help us understand the world more. For example, seeing movies can expose us to people of different races and cultures that we don't see often. We can then overcome some prejudices more easily. Recently there have been more handicapped people in films, and this also helps prevent prejudice.

Topic sentence:	3.1
Supporting details:	3.2
	3.3
	3.4

4. Paragraph from Topic 29

Our planet gives us everything we need, but natural resources are not endless. Strip mining destroys whole regions, leaving bare and useless ground. Deforestation removes old growth trees that can't be replaced. Too much fishing may harm fish populations to the point where they can't recover.

Topic sentence:	4.1
Supporting details:	4.2
	4.3
	4.4

5. Paragraph from Topic 4

The most important lessons can't be taught; they have to be experienced. No one can teach us how to get along with others or how to have self-respect. As we pass from childhood into adolescence, no one can teach us the judgement we need to decide on how to deal with peer pressure. As we leave adolescence behind and enter adult life, no one can teach us how to fall in love and get married, or how to raise our children.

Topic sentence:	5.1
Supporting details:	5.2
	5.3
	5.4

STEP 7: WRITE THE INTRODUCTION

You need two things to write a good introduction. You need to have an opinion on the topic and you need to have topic sentences for each of the paragraphs. Your opinion will tell the reader what you think about the subject; the summary of the topic sentences will guide your reader through your essay.

Stating Your Opinion

The introduction to your essay should tell the reader what your opinion is on the topic. The TOEFL Essay is a personal essay. Your ideas on a topic are important. The readers are interested in what you have to say. There is, however, no right or wrong opinion. The readers look to see how you express your opinion whatever it is.

   You can express your opinion by using set phrases or by varying the verbs, adjectives, and adverbs you use. On the TOEFL Essay, you must show semantic and syntactic variety in your language to score high. This section will help you give your writing more variety.

Set Phrases

KEY WORDS	
In my opinion	It is my opinion that
According to me	I believe
To my way of thinking	I think
In my view	It seems to me that
To me	It appears that
From my point of view	To my mind

Examples

   In my opinion, university students must attend classes.
   According to me, one must change with the times.
   To me, there is nothing more important than good health.

   It is my opinion that one learns by example.
   It seems to me that a good neighbor is one who respects your privacy.
   It appears that all the information one needs is available on computer.

Practice 2

Give your opinion about these topics. Use the phrases suggested.

1. People's lives (are/are not) easier today.

    In my opinion *people's lives are easier today.*

2. Most people (prefer/do not prefer) to spend their leisure time outdoors.

    It seems to me that_____

3. An apartment building (is/is not) better than a house.

    To my mind _____

4. It (is/is not) good that English is becoming the world language.

From my point of view_____

Verbs

You can use different verbs to show how strongly you feel about something. *Believe* and *think* are the most common verbs used to express a personal opinion.

KEY WORDS	
Agree	Infer
Believe	Realize
Guess	Suppose
Hope	Think
Imagine	Understand

Examples

I agree that studying science is more important than studying literature.

I hope that people remember the special gifts I gave them.

I infer from their actions that most youth feel they have nothing to learn from older people.

I understand why people like to work with their hands.

Practice 3

Give your opinion about these topics. Use the verbs suggested.

1. High schools (should/should not) allow students to study what they want.

I believe that _____

2. It is better to be a (leader/member) of a group.

I guess that _____

3. People (should/should not) do things they do not enjoy doing.

I agree that _____

4. I would rather have the university (assign/not assign) me a roommate.

I suppose that _____

Adjectives

You can use different adjectives to show how strongly you feel about something.

KEY WORDS	
Certain	Positive
Convinced	Sure

Examples

I am certain that movies influence people's behavior.
I am convinced that having a pet can contribute to a child's development.

Practice 4

Give your opinion about these topics. Use the adjectives suggested.

1. Children (should/should not) spend a great amount of time practicing sports.

   I am sure that _____

2. A shopping center in my neighborhood (will/will not) be a benefit to our community.

   I am positive that _____

Adverbials

You can use different adverbials to qualify your opinion. These adverbials show how strongly you feel about something.

KEY WORDS		
Seemingly	Maybe	Almost
Conceivably	Probably	Doubtless
Possibly	Presumably	No doubt
Perhaps	Certainly	Definitely

Examples

Seemingly, playing games can teach us about life.
Daily exercise definitely should be a part of every school day.
Doubtless, helping a child to learn to read is important.
Individual sports are possibly better than team sports for some students.

Practice 5

Give your opinion about these topics. Use the adverbials suggested.

1. A zoo (has/does not have) a useful purpose.

   No doubt _____

2. Growing up in the countryside (is/is not) better than growing up in the city.

   Perhaps_____

3. Our generation (is/is not) different from that of our parents.

   Certainly, _____

4. A sense of humor can sometimes be (helpful/detrimental) in a difficult situation.

   Conceivably_____

You can use different adverbials to make a general statement about how you feel about something.

KEY WORDS		
All in all	Basically	Generally
All things considered	By and large	In general
Altogether	Essentially	On the whole
As a rule	For the most part	Overall

Examples

All in all, it is better to learn from a teacher than on your own.
As a rule, it is better for students to wear uniforms to school.
For the most part, countries are more alike than different.
On the whole, higher education should be available to all.

Practice 6

Give your opinion about these topics. Use the adverbials suggested to make a general statement.

1. The family (is/is not) the most important influence on young adults.

   All things considered,_____

2. Parents (are/are not) the best teachers.

   In general, _____

3. People (are never/are sometimes) too old to attend college.

   By and large, _____

You can use different adverbials to qualify your opinion. These adverbials show an idea is not completely true.

KEY WORDS	
Almost	So to speak
In a way	For all intents and purposes
More or less	To some extent
practically	Up to a point

Examples

Up to a point, people succeed because of hard work, not because of luck.
For all intents and purposes, television has destroyed communication among family members.

Practice 7

Give your opinion about these topics. Use the adverbials suggested to show an idea is not completely true.

1. It is better to make a wrong decision than to make no decision.

   or

   It is better to make no decision than to make a wrong decision.

   In a way, _____

2. Watching movies (is/is not) more enjoyable than reading.

   To some extent, _____

3. You (can/cannot) learn as much by losing as winning.

   More or less, _____

GUIDING THE READER

The introduction to your essay should also tell the reader how you plan to develop your topic. The topic sentences that you developed from your concept maps can be summarized in the introduction.

Compare these introductions.

Introduction to Topic 1

Version A

I believe that people attend college for many different reasons. These reasons are personal to them.

Version B

> *People attend colleges or universities for a lot of different reasons. I believe that the three most common reasons are to prepare for a career, to have new experiences, and to increase their knowledge of themselves and the world around them.*

Comment

Version A starts with the writer's opinion, but it does not tell us much. What are these reasons? We need to know the basic reasons so we can prepare ourselves to find supporting details in the body of the essay.

Version B gives three specific reasons that the writer believes are the most important ones: to prepare for a career, to have new experiences, and to increase their knowledge of themselves and the world around them. From this introduction I will expect to see a paragraph on each of these reasons.

Introduction to Topic 6

Version A

> *I think there are changes necessary in my hometown. It is always the same. There has to be something different.*

Version B

> *If I could change one thing about my hometown I think it would be the fact that there's no sense of community here. People don't feel connected, they don't look out for each other, and they don't get to know their neighbors.*

Comment

Version A starts with the writer's opinion but doesn't say what changes are necessary. We need some guidance.

Version B narrows in on the topic and talks about the sense of community. The writer says that "People don't feel connected, they don't look out for each other, and they don't get to know their neighbors." From this introduction, I will expect to see a paragraph on each of these reasons.

Introduction to Topic 13

Version A

> *I believe that some people like to eat at food stands, and some like to eat in restaurants. There are different reasons for this.*

Version B

> *Some people like to eat out at food stands and restaurants, while others like to prepare food at home. Often it depends on the kind of lifestyle people have. Those with very busy jobs outside the house don't always have time to cook. They like the convenience of eating out. Overall, though, I think it is cheaper and healthier to eat at home.*

Comment

In *Version A*, the writer does not share what these reasons are. There are no general statements.

In *Version B*, the writer tells us that the choice depends on a person's lifestyle. The writer will probably give us more details about the reasons of convenience, costs, and health.

Practice 8

Read the following introductions and tell us what the writer believes and the focus of each paragraph. You may not have three paragraphs for all introductions.

1. **Introduction to Topic 111**

   We all need to have friends, and I think the more friends we have the better. Friendship helps us learn how to trust others, it helps us know what to expect from others, and it helps us profit from experiences. I want to have a lot of friends around me so I can learn more about myself from different people.

   Opinion: *I think the more friends we have the better*

   Paragraph focus: *learn how to trust others*

   Paragraph focus: *learn what to expect from others*

   Paragraph focus: *helps us profit from experiences*

2. **Introduction to Topic 148**

   Almost everyone, from little children to adults, loves games. The types of games may change as we grow up, but our enjoyment never changes. I believe that playing games is both fun and useful, because it teaches us the skills we need in life. Games teach us there is a cause-effect relationship; teach us about teamwork; and teach us to follow rules.

   Opinion: _____

   Paragraph focus: _____

   Paragraph focus: _____

   Paragraph focus: _____

3. **Introduction to Topic 114**

   Although friends make an impression on your life, they do not have the same influence that your family has. Nothing is as important to me as my family. From them, I learned everything that is important. I learned about trust, ambition, and love.

   Opinion: _____

   Paragraph focus: _____

   Paragraph focus: _____

   Paragraph focus: _____

4. Introduction to Topic 110

If I had to choose between spending time alone or spending time with my friends, I'd rather be alone. Being with friends can be fun and can help you get through hard times. However, it's the time alone that forms you as a person. I need time alone to pursue solitary activities such as reading and writing. I need time alone to get to know myself better. I need time alone to reenergize my mind and spirit.

Opinion: _____

Paragraph focus: _____

Paragraph focus: _____

Paragraph focus: _____

5. Introduction to Topic 44

Traveling alone is the only way to travel. If you take someone with you, you take your home with you. When you travel alone, you meet new people, have new experiences, and learn more about yourself.

Opinion: _____

Paragraph focus: _____

Paragraph focus: _____

Paragraph focus: _____

DEMONSTRATING FACILITY WITH ENGLISH

STEP 8: WRITE THE BODY PARAGRAPHS

Once you have stated your opinion and shown the reader how you plan to develop your essay, the rest is easy. You simply turn the supporting details in your concept maps into sentences. Of course, you must make sure your sentences have semantic and syntactic variety. Look how these concept maps turned into paragraphs.

Examples

Paragraph 3 from Topic 141

The foreign language program should be staffed with well-trained instructors. The current teachers in the program don't speak the language well enough. In our classes teachers frequently make errors that the students repeat. If the teachers were well-trained, they would be good models for the students.

Now	Proposed	Result
Don't speak the language well enough	well-trained teachers	teachers provide good model

Paragraph 2 from Topic 128

Another issue is economic. Many schools simply do not have the money to provide gym facilities, playing fields, and athletic equipment for their students. Other schools are located in cities where that kind of space just isn't available. A few schools would rather keep money for academic purposes.

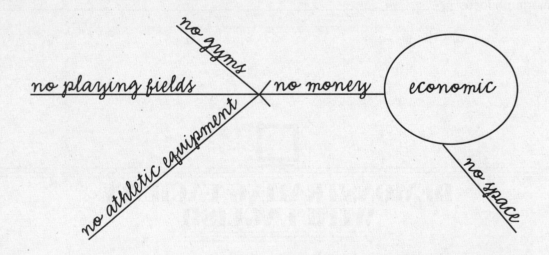

Practice 9

Read the following paragraphs and complete the concept maps for the paragraphs.

1. **Paragraph 3 from Topic 13**
   Eating at home is better for you. Meals at restaurants are often high in fat and calories, and they serve big plates of food—much more food than you need to eat at one meal. If you cook food at home, you have more control over the ingredients. You can use margarine instead of butter on your potatoes, or put less cheese on top of your pizza. At home, you can control your portion size. You can serve yourself as little as you want. At a restaurant you might eat everything on a big plate of food "because you paid for it."

Restaurant   Healthier   Home

High in fat
and calories   ingredients
1.1 _____   portions   1.2 _____

1.3 _____

2. Paragraph 2 from Topic 39

The internet and the world wide web have opened every major library and database to students around the world. Information comes not only in print form, but also in multimedia. You can get audio and video data. You can get information about events in the past as well as events that unfold as you watch your computer monitor.

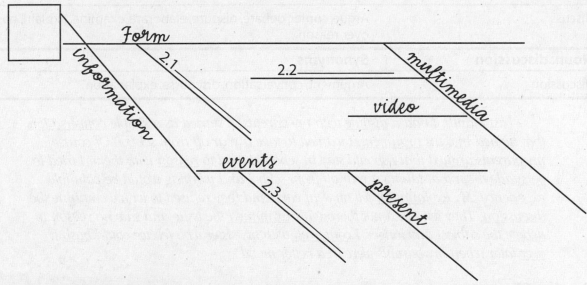

3. Paragraph 5 from Topic 14

In class, students receive the benefit of a teacher's knowledge. The best teachers do more than just go over the material in the class textbook. They draw their students into discussion of the material. They present opposing points of view. They schedule guest speakers to come, give the students additional information, or show documentary films on the subject.

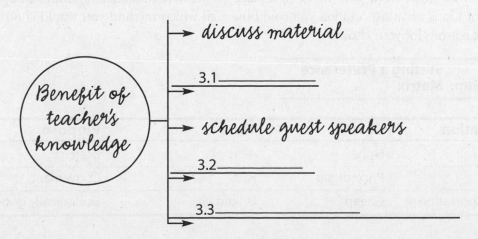

Using Semantic Variety

In order to be a good essay, your essay must interest the reader. One way to do this is to vary your vocabulary. Learning different ways to express similar ideas (synonyms) and different ways to help the reader move from one idea to the next will help you develop semantic variety.

Synonyms

When you are writing on one topic, you don't want to repeat the same verb or adverb, noun or adjective in every sentence. You should try to use words that are similar in meaning, and that will carry the meaning of the sentence. Synonyms are important because they help you link closely related words or ideas. Synonyms provide coherence in your essay.

Read the paragraph below. Look for these synonyms of *discuss* and *discussion*.

Verb: discuss	Synonyms
discuss	Argue, confer, debate, dispute, elaborate, examine, explain, hash over, reason

Noun: discussion	Synonyms
discussion	Argument, conversation, discourse, explanation

Last month, I had a <u>dispute</u> with my parents. It started as a simple <u>conversation</u> that turned into an <u>argument</u>. I wanted to take a year off from school. Of course, my parents <u>argued</u> that I should stay in school. I tried to <u>reason</u> with them; I tried to <u>persuade</u> them that taking a year off from school and working would be valuable experience. My <u>explanation</u> fell on deaf ears, and they refused to let me continue the <u>discussion</u>. They felt I had not thoroughly <u>examined</u> the issue and saw no reason to <u>debate</u> the subject any longer. I <u>conferred</u> with my sister who felt we could <u>hash</u> it <u>over</u> later when my parents were in a better mood.

Practice 10

Read the following topic and study the concept map. Then read the essay.

Topic 106

You need to travel from your home to a place 40 miles (64 kilometers) away. Compare the different kinds of transportation you could use. Tell which method you would choose. Give specific reasons for your choice.

Task: **Stating a Preference**
Concept Map: **Matrix**

Transportation	Cost	Time	Purpose
Bike	None	4 hrs	Exercise
Car	Price of gas	Fast	Convenient
Public transportation	Cheap	Unknown	Ecologically good

Essay (Topic 106)

When I choose a method of transportation to go 40 miles, I have three common choices: my bike, my parent's car, or public transportation. When I choose among them, I think about how much it will cost, how long it will take, and why I need to go from point A to point B.

My bike is a less expensive alternative. The only cost is my manual labor to pedal from my home to a place 40 miles away. This method, however, is extremely time consuming. I imagine it would take me all day. Biking is excellent exercise so if my only goal was to burn calories and strengthen my muscles, I should go by bike.

Public transportation is another alternative that is inexpensive. The cost is minimal and is shared by everyone on the bus or train. Where I live, you cannot depend on public transportation. It might take me all day to go by public transportation when I include the waiting time. However, using public transportation is good for the earth. By sharing the resources, we waste less.

Taking a private car is the most expensive. For me, especially, since I don't own a car and I must borrow one from my parents. They want me to pay for my own gas, which is a lot and I must also pay for parking the car when I get to my destination. A car is the most dependable way to go if I need to get there fast. When convenience is your goal, you should pick a car.

When I consider these points, I must confess that I am spoiled. I prefer the convenience of the car over the exercise of a bike and the virtues of public transportation. I like to go and come when I want without waiting even if it costs me more.

Essay Organization

Theme:	Choice of transportation method depends on time and cost.
Point 1: Examples:	Bike No cost Time consuming Good exercise
Point 2: Examples:	Public transportation Economical Unpredictable Ecologically good
Point 3: Examples:	Car Gas is expensive Dependable Convenient

The highlighted words in the essay could be replaced with a word from this synonym list. Write the synonym that matches the highlighted word.

Synonym List

admit	driving	purpose
choice	favor	quickly
count on	options	transit

Highlighted Words in Essay (Topic 106)

choices	1	*Options*
alaternative	2	
depend on	3	
transportation	4	
taking	5	
fast	6	
goal	7	
confess	8	
prefer	9	

Practice 11

Read the following topic and study the concept map. Then read the essay.

Topic 117

Some people choose friends who are different from themselves. Others choose friends who are similar to themselves. Compare the advantages of having friends who are different from you with the advantages of having friends who are similar to you. Which kind of friend do you prefer for yourself? Why?

Task: **Giving an Explanation**
Concept Map: Stating a Preference

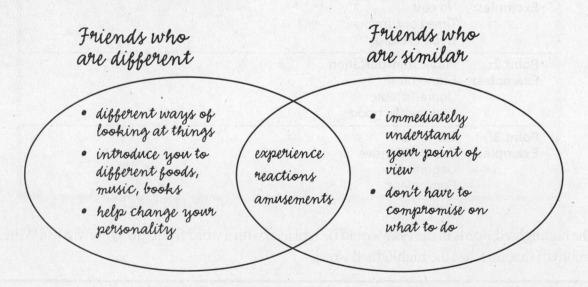

Friends who are different
- different ways of looking at things
- introduce you to different foods, music, books
- help change your personality

experience reactions amusements

Friends who are similar
- immediately understand your point of view
- don't have to compromise on what to do

Essay Topic 117

My Friends

There are a lot of advantages to having friends who are different from you.
They can introduce you to new food, books, and music. They can present you with
a different way of looking at the world. However, there are times when you need a
friend who really understands you. That is why I enjoy having all kinds of friends—
both those who are different from me and those who are similar.

Someone who is different from you can show different ways of looking at
things. If you tend to be a spontaneous person, a scheduled person can help you be
more organized. And you can help that person loosen up a bit at times, too. If you
are impatient, a patient friend can help you calm down. If you are a little bit timid,
an assertive friend can help you develop more self-confidence.

Someone who has different tastes from you can introduce you to new things.
A friend might persuade you to read a book that you thought you wouldn't like. A
friend might get you to try new kinds of food. You can share your different tastes
and interests with your friend, too. Together you can dare to try new things.

There are times, however, when you really need a friend who is similar to you.
Sometimes you get tired of compromising on what you want to do. You want to be
with someone who has the same tastes as you. A friend who is similar to you probably has the same reactions to situations as you do. Therefore, if you feel unhappy, a
friend who is similar to you can understand just why you feel that way.

Friends who are different from you have a lot to offer. Friends who are similar
offer something else. That is why it is important to know all kinds of people.

Essay Organization

Theme:	It's good to have both similar and different friends.
Point 1: **Examples:**	See a different point of view Spontaneous vs. scheduled Impatient vs. patient Timid vs. assertive
Point 2: **Examples:**	Learn about new things New books New kinds of food
Point 3: **Examples:**	Need similar friends, too Tired of compromising Have the same reactions

The highlighted words in the essay could be replaced with a word from this synonym list. Write the
synonym that matches the highlighted word.

Synonym List

are apt	a number of	relax	trade off
benefits	shy	restless	confident
introduce to	impulsive	response	

Highlighted Words in Essay (Topic 117)

a lot of	1	_____
advantages	2	_____
present with	3	_____
tends	4	_____
spontaneous	5	_____
loosen up	6	_____
impatient	7	_____
timid	8	_____
assertive	9	_____
compromising	10	_____
reaction	11	_____

Transition Words

Transitional words and phrases will help your reader follow your ideas from sentence to sentence and from paragraph to paragraph. Without transitional words and phrases, your ideas will stand alone, unrelated to the thesis of your essay.

In this section, you will learn to use transition words that show time; degree; comparison and contrast; and cause and effect. You will also learn transition words that let you add more information and transition words like pronouns that let you make connections to previously mentioned subjects.

Time

When you are explaining the sequence of events, you may want to use these expressions.

before	next	then	often
after	during	always	sometime
since	at the same time	while	meanwhile

Example

The school counselors should help students who are new to a school. *Before the first day* of school, they should give an orientation to the building. *On the opening day*, they should introduce the students to the teachers. *After* the students have gotten used to their classes, the counselors should find out about the student's hobbies and recommend some extracurricular clubs. *Sometime during* the first month, the counselor should invite the parents to visit the school so they can meet the teachers and administrators.

Degree

When you are explaining why one thing is more or less important than another thing, you may want to use these expressions.

most important	first	primarily	essentially
less important	second	secondary	principally
basically	subordinate	lesser	chiefly

Example

One of the *most important* gifts we can give to a child is an animal. *Above all*, an animal will help a child learn responsibility. A *lesser* reason, but an important one, is that a pet will return the child's love. But *essentially*, a child needs to learn how to take care of something that is dependent on the child.

Comparison and Contrast

When you are explaining how two or more things are similar or how they are different, you may want to use these expressions.

To compare			
similar to	similarly	like, alike	either/or
correspondingly	resemble	almost the same as	at the same time as
as	just as	in a like manner	in the same way
common in	than	also	neither/nor

To contrast			
differ from	however	otherwise	still
nevertheless	even do	different from	less than
more than	unlike	in contrast to	on the other hand
although	while yet	but	instead

Example

Although my friend chose to buy a car with his gift, I would have gone on vacation. He said he needed the car to go to work, *but* I think he should take the bus. He also wanted the car for convenience. *However*, a taxi is *just as* convenient and doesn't have to be serviced. We are *both alike* in that *neither* of us knows how to drive. *Otherwise*, I might have bought a car, *too*.

Cause and Effect

When you are explaining how something caused a change in something else, you may want to use these expressions.

so	thus	consequently	therefore
for this reason	as a result	because, because of	owing to
since	due to	although	so that

Example

Effective advertising wants to change people's behaviors. Some public service ads show coffins of people who died of lung cancer; *as a result* many people have quit smoking. Other ads show glamorous people smoking; *consequently* young people start to smoke. *Owing to* the influence of advertising on youth, many cigarette ads are not allowed near schools or on TV. *Although* these rules have been in effect a long time, the number of young smokers has increased. If this is not *due to* advertising, what is the reason?

Explanation

If you are explaining what something is by giving an example or if you are restating something for emphasis, you may want to use these expressions.

in other words	to clarify	to explain	to paraphrase
as	like	that is	for example
such as	for instance	to illustrate	namely

Example

People are never to old to attend college. *For example*, there are many women who stayed at home to raise their families and now have time to return to school. There are other examples *such as* retired people who move to a college town just so they can take occasional classes or even working people in their sixties, *for instance*, who want to take some night classes. *In other words*, you are never to old to learn.

Adding More Information

If you are adding more information to make your point stronger, you may want to use these expressions.

in addition	besides	furthermore	as well as
moreover	similarly	also	what's more

Example

Besides the fact that English is the international language of business, it is *also* becoming the language of social interaction. Because of the Internet, many people correspond in English by e-mail. *Moreover*, much of the information on the World Wide Web is in English *as well as* in the language of the web host. *In addition*, English is the language of diplomacy.

Pronouns

If you are describing someone or something, you may use some of these pronouns to refer to the person or thing you are describing.

Pronouns that replace a subject			
he	she	it	they
this	that	those	
Pronouns that replace an object			
his	her	them	
this	that	those	
Pronouns that replace a possessive			
his	her	its	their

Example

My community should hire a health worker. I worked in a rural area one summer with a community health worker and saw the wonderful ways *she* helped the people in the area. She worked with mothers teaching *them* how to keep *their* children healthy. She worked with school teachers helping *them* recognize early signs of illness. She worked with restaurant personnel showing *them* proper food handling techniques. A community needs help in many ways. *This* is one way *its* citizens can make *it* healthier.

NOTE: *This* in the last sentence refers to the whole paragraph. *This* equals *hiring a health worker*.

Practice 12

Read the paragraphs below. Choose the appropriate transition words or phrases to complete the thought.

1. **Paragraph from Topic 99**

   If I chose my own roommate, I'd ___(1)___ pick some candidates from the list supplied by the university. ___(2)___ I'd write to them and they'd write back. Through our letters, we'd find out if ___(3)___ shared common interests, ___(4)___ sports or movies. ___(5)___ we'd find out if we had similar habits. ___(6)___ my investigation, I'd probably find someone compatible with me.

we	next	first	as a result of	in addition to	such as

2. **Paragraph from Topic 30**

   ___(1)___ the traffic immediately ___(2)___ and after the school day, there also would be traffic ___(3)___ there was a sporting event ___(4)___ a basketball or football game at the school. Would there be enough parking in the school lot for everyone attending those events? Probably not. ___(5)___, those extra cars would end up in ___(6)___ neighborhood.

whenever	before	consequently	in addition to	our	such as

3. **Paragraph from Topic 109**

   ___(1)___ of adapting to life in a new country is learning that country's language. Children learn the language in school and use it all day ___(2)___ going to class and playing with other children. Adults, ___(3)___, don't have time for formal language classes. Their ___(4)___ priority is getting a job. ___(5)___, they have contacts in the new country—family or friends—who help them find employment. ___(6)___ all their co-workers come from the same country and speak the same language, then they don't have the opportunity to use the new language at work.

if	first	while	on the other hand	usually	a major part of

4. **Paragraph from Topic 134**

   In the past in America, children were valuable workers. ___(1)___, they helped on the farm or in the family business ___(2)___ bring in money. Just a few generations ___(3)___, attitudes have changed. Now children are ___(4)___ expected to do any work at all. Modern children often don't ___(5)___ do household chores. This is sad because ___(6)___ miss something if they don't help out at home. Sharing in household tasks benefits children of all ages.

even	later	they	hardly	for example	in order to

5. **Paragraph from Topic 129**

   ___(1)___, an agricultural research center would help all people. No country can survive without adequate food production. ___(2)___ the United States is able to produce enough food now, this may not remain true in the future. The erosion of natural resources ___(3)___ and the closing of many American farms may reduce its food supply. The farmers situation could improve ___(4)___ they start to build stronger networks across the country, ___(5)___ businessmen already have.

on the contrary	if	much as	as well as	even though

Using Syntactic Variety

On the TOEFL Essay you must not only demonstrate your command of vocabulary; you must also show your command of grammar. You cannot write only simple sentences. Your essay must show syntactic variety.

- **Paragraph with simple sentences**

  Television is bad for children. Television shows are too violent. Children are influenced by television. Television shows should not be so violent.

- **Paragraph with syntactic variety**

  Since many television shows are violent, many child psychologists believe that watching television is not good for children. As children are easily influenced, we should limit violence on television.

You will develop variety in your prose by using parallel structures, making your paragraphs cohesive, and writing sentences that vary in type, length, subject, and voice.

Parallel Structures

Parallelism gives your essay rhythm. It makes it easier to read and understand. Your structures, however, must be parallel. That is, the subjects, verbs, adjectives, adverbs, and gerunds must be parallel. Look at these examples of parallelism.

Parallel Subjects

> <u>Work</u> and <u>play</u> should be more evenly divided in my day.

Both *work* and *play* are the same kind of nouns. The subjects are parallel.

> <u>Working</u> and <u>play</u> should be more evenly divided in my day.

Here *working* is a gerund. It is not incorrect to use it here, but it sounds awkward. The subjects are not parallel.

> <u>Working</u> and <u>playing</u> should be more evenly divided in my day.

Here both *working* and *playing* are gerunds. The subjects are parallel.

Parallel Verbs

> We <u>press</u> a button, <u>wait</u> a short time, and <u>remove</u> the food from the microwave.

All three verbs are in the present tense. The verbs are parallel.

> We <u>press</u> a button, <u>wait</u> a short time, and <u>can remove</u> the food from the microwave.

The third verb uses the auxiliary *can*. It is not incorrect, but it sounds awkward. The verbs are not parallel.

> We *can press* a button, *wait* a short time, and *remove* the food from the microwave.

Here *can* precedes the first verb. This makes all three verbs parallel.

Parallel Adjectives

> I found the movie *long* and *boring*.

The adjectives are both parallel.

> I found the movie *long* and *it bored me*.

The sentence is not wrong, but it is not parallel.

Parallel Adverbs

> Athletes often move *gracefully*, *easily*, and *powerfully*.

The three adverbs all end in *-ly*. They are all parallel.

> Athletes often move with *grace*, *easily* and *powerfully*.

The first description is a prepositional phrase. The adverbs are not parallel.

> Athletes often move *gracefully*, *carefully*, and *powerfully*.

The second adverb *easily* was replaced with another adverb *carefully*. The meanings of *easily* and *carefully* are not the same, but *carefully* could be used to describe how an athlete moves. In this sentence, *carefully* adds to the rhythm of the sentence since the suffix *-fully* is used three times.

> Athletes move with *grace*, *ease*, and *power*.

This sentence can also be made parallel by using three prepositional phrases. The objects of the preposition *with* are all parallel nouns: *grace*, *ease*, and *power*.

Parallel Gerunds

> I enjoy *shopping* and *keeping* up with the latest styles, but not *paying* the bills.

Shopping, keeping up, and *paying* are gerunds. The gerunds are parallel.

> I enjoy *shopping* and to *keep up* with the latest styles, but not to *pay* the bills.

To keep up and *to pay* not only are not parallel with *shopping*, they are incorrect. The verb *enjoy* must be followed by a gerund, not an infinitive.

Parallel Sentences

> *While there are advantages and disadvantages to both machine-made, and hand-made products, I prefer machine-made products. While hand-made products are generally high quality, I find them expensive. While I appreciate high-quality products, I can't afford them.*

These three sentences are parallel. They all begin with an adverb clause introduced by *While*. The subject of the independent clause in all three sentences is *I*. Each sentence after the first one takes an idea from the previous sentence and carries it forward using the same construction. There is a nice rhythm to these sentences. Be careful though. There is a narrow line between rhythmic parallels and boring repetitions.

> *While there are advantages and disadvantages to both, given my type of personality, I prefer machine-made products. While hand-made products are generally high quality, they are also very expensive. While I do appreciate high quality, my status as a student makes me appreciate low cost as well.*

In this version, the basic parallel construction remains. The last two sentences have been changed. In these two sentences, the parallelism is within the sentences as well as between the sentences.

> *Hand-made products are high quality.*

> *Hand-made products are very expensive.*

> *I appreciate high quality.*

> *I appreciate low cost.*

The writer draws a similarity between adjectives *high quality* and *very expensive*, and contrasts the products with the adjectives *high quality* and *low cost*.

Practice 13

Read the sentences and decide if the underlined word or phrase should be changed. Some underlined words are incorrect; others are grammatically correct, but not well written. If the word should be changed, rewrite it.

1. Dogs provide older people an important chance to learn or <u>maintaining</u> social skills. *maintain*

2. My parents didn't have time to analyze their feelings or <u>thinking</u> about themselves.

3. I believe zoos are useful both in terms of educating the general public as well as <u>they can advance</u> scientific research.

4. I prefer a combination of living <u>at</u> a small, suburban town and working in a big city.

5. Agricultural research improves individual citizens' lives, whereas successful businesses <u>to improve</u> a country's economy.

6. Heated debate is interesting, and <u>interest</u> things are easier to learn about.

7. <u>One</u> might think that it is a waste of time to go out to see a movie when you can watch DVDs at home.

8. Teachers can instruct tomorrow's leaders; doctors can make those leaders healthier; and <u>engineering</u> can guarantee that future generations have good housing.

9. I could see the house where my grandmother grew up and my cousins still live in that <u>house</u>.

10. Many people want to travel abroad to see new places and things; people also want to travel abroad <u>so that they can</u> improve their educational opportunities.

Coherence

Transition words help the reader see the relationship between sentences and ideas. They are one way to provide coherence in an essay. There are two other ways to provide coherence: repeating words and rephrasing ideas.

Repeating

Repeating words can provide a rhythm to a paragraph. In the example below, notice how the phrase *She worked with* is repeated three times to show ways a community health worker helped people.

Example

She *worked with* mothers teaching *them* how to keep *their* children healthy. She *worked with* school teachers helping *them* recognize early signs of illness. She *worked with* restaurant personnel showing *them* proper food handling techniques. A community needs help in many ways.

Repeating words can also link ideas that may be several sentences apart. Look at the Pronoun example on page 95. The second sentence in the example ends with *she helped the people in the area*. The next to the last sentence, *A community needs help in many ways*, emphasizes the need of the community for *help*.

Rephrasing

We learned the words to use to introduce a statement that has been restated or rephrased for emphasis. We can also rephrase words to provide coherence in the essay. Rephrasing gives the reader a second chance to understand your thesis. Synonyms are one way to rephrase.

Example

The countryside where I grew up is very *isolated*. You can drive for miles without seeing another car. It seems in all directions you look at a *breathtaking vista*. The *scenery near the ocean* is especially *dramatic, with giant dark* cliffs rising out of the water.

Such a *secluded, remote* environment is a perfect place to relax. The *spectacular views* bring out the artist in me. I often take my paints and a canvas and try to capture the exciting *feel of the shoreline*.

Notice the ideas that are rephrased:

The countryside where I grew up is very *isolated*. You can drive for miles without seeing another car.

Such a *secluded, remote* environment is a perfect place to relax.

It seems in all directions you look at a *breathtaking vista*.

The *spectacular views* bring out the artist in me.

The *scenery near the ocean* is especially *dramatic, with giant dark* cliffs rising out of the water.

I often take my paints and a canvas and try to capture the exciting *feel of the shoreline*.

Practice 14

Choose which phrase or sentence best completes the thought and makes the paragraph cohesive.

1. An effective advertisement matches images and music to its product and _____(1)_____. For instance, if it's selling cars to young men, it uses the image of speed and rock music. If it's selling cars to families, it uses the image of practicality and pleasant melodies. _____(2)_____.

   1.1
   (A) its market
   (B) the market it wants to reach
   (C) to those who will buy the product

   1.2
   (A) If it's trying to sell a more expensive car, it uses classical music to suggest elegance and comfort.
   (B) If the car is for the rich, advertisers will want to emphasize elegance and wealth.
   (C) If it's selling cars to wealthy executives, it uses the image of wealth and classical music.

2. Our parents studied grammar, a subject that a lot of schools don't teach today. They studied penmanship, a skill that today few people have mastered. _____(1)_____. They didn't have to learn advanced mathematics, but _____(2)_____ how to do basic math without the help of a calculator.

2.1

(A) A foreign language, which is optional today, was a required subject.

(B) They were taught to communicate in a foreign language.

(C) They studied a foreign language, something that is not a requirement in many schools today.

2.2

(A) they had to learn

(B) it was important to learn

(C) they felt they should know

3. The contributions scientists make to society are more obvious. The cars we drive, the computers we use at home and at work,_____(1)_____—all of these come from the ideas and hard work of scientists. Because of scientific contributions, we're living longer and more healthful lives. Scientists also _____(2)_____ the arts. Movies are the result of science, as are television, radio, and compact discs.

3.1

(A) and the stove and cleaning machine

(B) the appliances we have to help us cook our meals and clean our houses

(C) the cooking and cleaning inventions

3.2

(A) contribute to

(B) help fund

(C) support

Practice 15

Which option rephrases the word, phrase, or sentence taken from the paragraph. There may be more than one correct answer.

1. Zoos are also important for the research opportunities they provide. Because zoos are controlled environments, research is safer and easier to conduct. Scientists can feel safe in the confined area of the zoo. They may not be as safe in the wild. For example, while conducting a medical experiment in an open field, scientists have to worry about both the animal they are working with, and also other animals nearby in the bush. In zoos, however, they need only worry about the research subject.

1.1 zoos are controlled environments

(A) Zoos are also important for the research opportunities they provide.

(B) Scientists can feel safe in the confined area of the zoo.

(C) …while conducting a medical experiment in an open field

1.2 in the wild

(A) in an open field

(B) in the bush

(C) In zoos

2. Teachers have been trained to teach their students in whatever way helps students learn the most about the subject. For instance, some students learn better by discussing a topic; others by writing about it. Teachers can help students learn in the way that's best for each student. A textbook can only give you one way of learning something. But a teacher can adapt her teaching to your needs as a student.

> **2.1 whatever way helps students learn**
> (A) some students learn better by discussing a topic
> (B) others by writing about it
> (C) in the way that's best for each student

3. Both art and music help students express themselves. Students who have never drawn a picture or thought about making a sculpture will be pleasantly surprised when they get their hands in the clay or start using the pencils. It is always satisfying to try something new, even if you find you don't like it.

> **3.1 express themselves**
> (A) get their hands in the clay
> (B) handling a pencil
> (C) find themselves surprised

Sentences

The TOEFL Essay wants you to demonstrate syntactic variety. You can vary the types of sentences you use, the length of the sentences, the subject of the sentences, and the voice of the sentences.

Type

There are four types of sentences: simple, compound, complex, and compound-complex.

- **Simple sentence**

  A simple sentence has one subject and one verb.

  Television <u>commercials</u> <u>are</u> the most effective form of advertising.
                   subject   verb

- **Compound sentence**

  A compound sentence has two or more simple sentences linked by the conjunctions *and*, *or*, and *but*.

  <u>Newspaper ads are often ignored</u>, and <u>radio ads are quickly forgotten.</u>
     simple sentence 1   conjunction   simple sentence 2

- **Complex sentence**

  A complex sentence is made up of a simple sentence (independent clause) and one or more subordinate clauses.

  <u>Most people listen to radio</u>   <u>when they're driving to work.</u>
         simple sentence   subordinate clause

- **Compound-complex sentence**

  A compound-complex sentence has two or more simple sentences (independent clauses) and one or more subordinate clauses.

  <u>Although families may listen to a radio during the day</u>, <u>the parents listen only for news reports</u>, and <u>the children use it for background noise.</u>

Length

Some students think they have to use compound-complex sentences to show they are very proficient in English. This makes the essay very heavy and very difficult to read. It is better to mix up the type of sentences you use. For example, a complex sentence followed by several simple sentences can be very effective.

Example

As the number of pets increase, the amount of money being spend on pets is also increasing. Pet owners buy special toys for their pets. They order them special clothes. They put them in day care centers. They treat them like children.

Practice 16

Label the sentences by their type in the following essay.

Simple = S	Complex = Cx
Compound = C	Compound-Complex = C-Cx

Topic 12

1. S
2. ____
3. ____
4. ____
5. ____

Why People Visit Museums

People visit museums for a number of reasons. They visit museums when traveling to new places because a museum tells them a lot about the culture of those places. They also go to museums to have fun. People also are usually interested in museums that feature unusual subjects. It's impossible to get bored in a museum.

6. ____
7. ____
8. ____
9. ____
10. ____
11. ____
12. ____

When visiting someplace new, you can find out about the culture of that place by going to a movie or a place of worship or a nightclub. Another option is to sit in the park and listen to the people around you. The easiest way to learn about a place, though, is by visiting its museums. Museums will show you the history of the place you're visiting. They will show you what art the locals think is important. If there aren't any museums, that tells you something, too.

13. ____
14. ____
15. ____
16. ____

Museums are fun. Even if you're not interested in art or history, there is always something to get your attention. Many museums now have "hands-on" exhibits. These exhibits usually involve activities like pushing a button and hearing more about what you're looking at, or using similar materials to create your own work of art, or trying on clothes like those on the models in the museum.

17. _____ 18. _____ 19. _____ 20. _____	*People also enjoy museums about unusual subjects. For instance, in my hometown there's a museum devoted to the potato. This museum has art made out of potatoes, tells all about the history of the potato, and sells potato mementos, like key chains and potato dolls. People enjoy this museum because it's so unusual.*
21. _____ 22. _____ 23. _____	*People everywhere like museums. They like learning about interesting and unusual things. No matter who you are or what you like, there is a museum that will amaze and interest you.*

Essay Organization

Theme:	People visit museums for a number of reasons.
Point 1: Examples:	Learn about the culture of a place History Art Lack of museums
Point 2: Example:	Have fun Hands-on exhibits
Point 3: Example:	Learn about unusual subjects Potato museum

Subject

Not all sentences should have the same subject. You will want to vary the subjects that you use. Notice in the example in the section *Sentence Length*, the subject of the last four sentences is the same: *Pet owners* and the pronoun *they*. In this case, there is a rhythm to the paragraph, and the sentences do not seem monotonous. These last four sentences are essentially a list; they tell you on what four things pet owners are spending money.

Compare these two versions of the same paragraph.

Topic 174

Every generation of people is different in important ways. How is your generation different from your parents' generation? Use specific reasons and examples to explain your answer.

Version A

> *My parents' generation has strict standards about acceptable behavior. My parents' generation has a difficult time accepting other standards of behavior. My parents' generation is still very concerned about what other people think of them. My parents' generation grew up in small communities where everyone knew everybody.*

Version B

> *My parents' generation has strict standards about acceptable behavior. Consequently, they have a difficult time accepting other standards of behavior. Since my parents' generation grew up in small communities where everyone knew everybody, they are still very concerned about what other people think of them.*

By combining sentences and rearranging the order, you can provide variety to the paragraph and not repeat the same subject in every sentence.

Practice 17

Choose the subject that best completes the blank.

1. High school students can't decide alone what they need to study. ___(1)___ need the guidance of experts in the field of education. However, they also need the freedom to follow their curiosity and interests. ___(2)___ should have the freedom to choose some courses, and should be required to take others.

   1.1

   (A) They

   (B) We

   (C) Secondary school attendees

   1.2

   (A) One

   (B) You

   (C) They

2. English is a difficult language to learn. Its pronunciation is erratic, and so is its spelling. Why are "though," "through," and "thought" pronounced differently? Why do many English words have two different spellings? ___(1)___ is very idiomatic, too. Everywhere you travel in an English-speaking country, ___(2)___ find different expressions for the same thing, and different pronunciations for the same word.

   2.1

   (A) Spelling

   (B) Pronunciation

   (C) English

   2.2

   (A) you'll

   (B) travelers

   (C) there'll

3. A good neighbor respects your property and asks your permission before doing something that might affect it. This means ___(1)___ doesn't put in a driveway that takes up part of your lawn. Or build a fence that cuts off part of your backyard. A good ___(2)___ works with you to decide where to put the fence, and maybe the two of you could share the cost.

3.1

    (A) he or she

    (B) they

    (C) it

3.2

    (A) fence builder

    (B) friend

    (C) neighbor

Voice

There are two voices in English: active and passive. The active emphasizes the doer of the action; the passive emphasizes the action itself.

- **Active voice**

  <u>Parents</u> must teach their children computer skills.
    doer

- **Passive voice**

  Children must be <u>taught</u> computer skills by their parents.
        action

Some students think they should write only in the passive voice because it sounds more impressive. The active voice is a very direct way of writing and is often clearer and easier to read than the passive voice. Again, you should vary the use of voice in your essay.

Practice 18

Underline the verbs in the following essay and tell whether they are active or passive.

    Topic 5

1. *active*	***No Factory!***
2. _____	*People like factories because they <u>bring</u> new jobs to a community. In my*
3.1. _____	*opinion, however, the benefits of a factory are outweighed by the risks. Factories*
3.2. _____	*cause pollution and they bring too much growth. In addition, they destroy the*
4. _____	*quiet lifestyle of a small town. That is why I oppose a plan to build a factory near*
5. _____	*my community.*

6. _____

7.1. _____

7.2. _____

8. _____

9. _____

10. _____

11.1 _____

11.2 _____

Factories cause smog. If we build a new factory, the air we breathe will become dirty. Everything will be covered with dust. Factories also pollute rivers and streams. Our water will be too dirty to drink. The environment will be hurt and people's health will be affected.

12.1. _____

12.2. _____

13. _____

14. _____

15. _____

16. _____

17. _____

Some people will say that more jobs will be created by a factory. However, this can have a negative result. Our population will grow quickly. Many new homes and stores will be built. There will be a lot of traffic on the roads. Fast growth can cause more harm than good.

18. _____

19. _____

20. _____

21. _____

22.1. _____

22.2. _____

23. _____

Our city will change a lot. It is a pleasant place now. It is safe and quiet. Everybody knows everybody else. If a factory brings growth to the city, all of this will change. The small-town feel will be lost.

24.1. _____

24.2. _____

25. _____

26. _____

A factory would be helpful in some ways, but the dangers outweigh the benefits. Our city would be changed too much by a factory. I cannot support a plan to build a new factory here.

Essay Organization

Theme:	The benefits of a factory are outweighed by the risks.
Point 1: Examples:	Factories would harm the environment. Smog Pollution
Point 2: Examples:	The city will be harmed by fast growth. More homes and stores will be built There will be a lot of traffic
Point 3: Examples:	The small town feel will be lost. Now it is safe and quiet Now everybody knows everybody else

Practice 19

Choose the active sentence that correctly carries the meaning of the passive sentence.

1. Our lives have been dramatically improved by changes in food preparation.

   (A) Changes in food preparation have dramatically improved our lives.

   (B) Our lives are changing dramatically and
   so have changes in food preparation.

   (C) Our food preparation improvements
   have been dramatic changes.

2. Young people will be helped to overcome the fear of aging by associating with older people.

   (A) Our fear of associating with older people
   can overcome young people.

   (B) Young people can associate with older
   people who fear aging.

   (C) Association with older people will help
   young people overcome the fear of
   aging.

3. I do not like the fact that these products are made by machines.

   (A) I do not like the fact that these are
   machine-made products.

   (B) Products made by machine are not liked;
   it's a fact.

   (C) It's not a fact that these products were
   made by machines.

4. Large sums of money are earned by entertainers who do little to contribute to society.

   (A) Society earns a little from entertainers'
   contributions.

   (B) Entertainers earn large sums of money
   yet contribute little to society.

   (C) Money is contributed to society by entertainers who earn a lot.

5. If an agricultural research station were established, our community would profit.

(A) The agricultural research station would profit from our community.

(B) The community would be profitable if an agricultural research station were established.

(C) We would benefit from the establishment of an agricultural research station.

Free Practice

Do either or both of the following activities on your own or in a group. There are no answers provided.

1. Read the essays in the Model Essay section. Identify the use of syntactic and semantic variety.

2. In the essays in the Model Essay section, underline and label all parallel structures,

transition words, and examples of coherence. Identify the types of sentences, the subjects of the sentences, and the voice of the sentences.

CONCLUDING THE TOPIC

STEP 9: WRITE THE CONCLUSION

A good essay should have a good conclusion. A conclusion is a few sentences that support your thesis and remind the reader of your intentions. There are a few different ways to write a conclusion. Look at these conclusions from the essays in this book. You can review the complete essay in the Model Essay section.

Restatement

You can end your essay by restating your thesis and/or restating your topic sentences.

Conclusion from Topic 134

Children should not work all the time. A happy life needs balance. If children can successfully handle tasks at home, they will handle life better, too. They will know the satisfaction of doing a good job, be involved in family life, and become more confident and responsible adults.

Generalization

You can use all the information you provided and make a generalization about it.

Conclusion from Topic 117

All things considered, I think I'd like to have a lot of acquaintances who are different and a few close friends who are similar to me. That seems to be the best of both worlds.

Prediction

You can summarize the information you provided and point the reader toward the next logical step.

Conclusion from Topic 26

I believe that a new movie theater is a fine idea. I support it because of the changes it will bring to our citizens and our town. I believe that the reduction in crime, the increase in employment, and the improved infrastructure will make our town a nicer place to live.

Question

You can conclude with a question that does not need an answer. This is called a rhetorical question. The answer is contained in the question.

Conclusion from Topic 2

The most important thing to realize is that we all have many teachers in our lives. Where we would be without our parents, teachers, and our peers to guide us? What would we do without books, newspapers, and television to inform us? All of them are very valuable.

Recommendation

You can urge your readers to do something with the information you provided.

Conclusion from Topic 13

Both eating at restaurants and cooking at home can be satisfying. Both can taste good and be enjoyed with family and friends. I prefer cooking at home, because of the money and health issues. I encourage my friends to eat out less, but it's up to them to make the choice that fits their lifestyles best.

Practice 20

What kind of a conclusion is each of these sentences or paragraphs? Refer to the whole essay, given at the end of the book, to help you decide.

1. **Conclusion from Topic 40**

   If you give up you might as well die. My advice is to always look for another opportunity, another goal, or another option. There is always something else. Don't give up.

   (A) Restatement

   (B) Generalization

   (C) Prediction

   (D) Question

   (E) Recommendation

2. **Conclusion from Topic 119**

   Clothes don't change you into a different person, but they can make you behave differently. If you are dressed inappropriately for a situation, people will react to you in a different way. This reaction can, in turn, change your behavior. If you want good reactions from people, make sure to dress appropriately for every situation.

   (A) Restatement

   (B) Generalization

   (C) Prediction

   (D) Question

   (E) Recommendation

3. **Conclusion from Topic 25**

   On the whole, though, I think my neighborhood should support having a shopping center built here. It would bring more variety to our shopping, give us the opportunity to amuse ourselves at movie theaters and restaurants, and bring more jobs into the area.

   (A) Restatement

   (B) Generalization

   (C) Prediction

   (D) Question

   (E) Recommendation

4. **Conclusion from Topic 121**

   If we all based our final opinion of others on first impressions, it would be hard to get to know anyone. We would probably miss many opportunities to make good friends. Isn't it important to give everyone the chance to show us who they really are? And don't you want other people to do the same for you?

   (A) Restatement

   (B) Generalization

   (C) Prediction

   (D) Question

   (E) Recommendation

5. Conclusion from Topic 31

The more I moved the more I would experience change. I would meet new people in every place I lived; I could move to sample countries with four seasons or even a continent like Antarctica, which only has two. Wherever I lived, I would experience living in housing particular to that area. I would then be a citizen of the world, wouldn't I? Could you call me a foreigner if I called every-place my home?

(A) Restatement

(B) Generalization

(C) Prediction

(D) Question

(E) Recommendation

Practice 21

Read the essay. Underline the topic sentences. Double underline the words in the introduction that guide the reader. Circle the eight words or phrases that indicate a personal opinion.

Topic 40

Learning about the past has no value for those of us living in the present. Do you agree or disagree? Use specific reasons and examples to support your answer.

People often say, "Those who don't understand history will repeat the mistakes of the past." I totally disagree. I don't see any evidence that people have made smart decisions based on their knowledge of the past. To me, the present is what is important. I think that people, weather, and politics determine what happens, not the past.

People can change. People may have hated each other for years, but that doesn't mean they will continue to hate each other. Look at Turkey and Greece. When Turkey had an earthquake, Greece sent aid. When Greece had an earthquake, Turkey sent aid. These two countries are cooperating now. No doubt, if we had looked at the past, we would have believed this to be impossible. But people change.

The weather can change. Farmers plant certain crops because these crops have always grown well in their fields. But there can be a long drought. The crops that grew well in the past will die. The farmers need to try a drought-resistant crop. If we had looked at the past, we wouldn't have changed our crop. Weather changes.

Politics can change. If politicians looked only at the past, they would always do the same thing. If we looked at the past in the United States, we would see a lot of discrimination against races, women, and sexual orientation. On the whole, people now are interested in human rights, and the government protects these rights. Politics change.

As a rule, it is important to follow the mood of today. It doesn't help us to think about the past. People, the weather, and politics can change in any direction. The direction of this change, in my opinion, cannot be predicted by studying the past.

Essay Organization

Theme:	People, politics, and weather determine what happens, not the past.
Point 1: Example:	People can change. Greece and Turkey
Point 2: Example:	The weather can change. Droughts affect farmers
Point 3: Example:	Politics can change. Human rights

Practice 22

Read the essay. Underline the topic sentences. Double underline the words in the introduction that guide the reader. Circle the eight words or phrases that indicate a personal opinion.

Topic 133

Do you agree or disagree with the following statement? A person's childhood years (the time from birth to 12 years of age) are the most important years of a person's life. Use specific reasons and examples to support your answer.

I think I'd have to agree that a person's childhood years are the most important. These are the years that form us. During these years we learn about relationships, begin our formal education, and develop our moral sense of right and wrong.

No doubt, the early years are the time when we learn about relationships, first with our family, then with the rest of the world. We learn how to respond to others based on the way others treat us. If we're loved, then we learn how to love. If we're treated harshly, then we learn to treat others in the same way. We also form our ideas about self-worth based on the way others treat us during these years. They can teach us that we're worthless, or they can show us that we deserve love and respect.

These are the years when we begin our formal education. In school we learn the basic skills of reading, writing, and working with numbers. These are skills that we will use throughout our lives. We also learn how to analyze and use information. This is perhaps the most important thing we learn during these years. Presumably, these are skills that will always be useful.

Most important, from my point of view, we develop our moral sense of right and wrong during these years. At first others teach us about good and bad. As we grow, we begin to decide for ourselves. During this time we also begin to develop self-discipline to live according to our morals.

I believe a person grows and changes throughout the many stages of life. However, the foundation is laid, by and large, in those first few years of life.

Essay Organization

Theme:	A person's childhood years are the most important.
Point 1: Examples:	We learn about relationships. How to treat others Our sense of self-worth
Point 2: Examples:	We begin our formal education. Learn basic skills Learn to analyze and use information
Point 3: Examples:	We develop our moral sense. Learn right and wrong Develop self-discipline

Practice 23

Read the essay. Underline the topic sentences. Double underline the words in the introduction that guide the reader. Circle the nine words or phrases that indicate a personal opinion.

Topic 131

Do you agree or disagree with the following statement? **Only** people who earn a lot of money are successful. Use specific reasons and examples to support your answer.

Many people believe that a large income equals success. I believe, however, that success is more than how much money you make. Some of those measures of success definitely include fame, respect, and knowledge.

Most people assume that famous people are rich people, but that isn't always true. For example, some day I would like to be famous in my field as a professor of English. I will still only make a professor's salary, which by U.S. standards will not mean that I am rich. Still, I will feel myself to be successful if I am well known. Additionally, there are many famous humanitarians who are not rich. Mother Theresa was one. Certainly, no one would say she was not successful.

I also believe that being respected by coworkers indicates success. Without that respect, money means little. For example, I once did some work for a top attorney in a law firm. He made a very good salary, but he wasn't a nice man. No one ever did work for him willingly. He ordered everyone around, and we didn't respect him. In contrast, however, I had a band director in high school who had to take extra jobs just to make enough money to support his family. His students had great respect for him and always listened to what he said. As a result, we were a very good band. In my opinion, my band director was more successful than the attorney was.

Finally, I think one of the most important indicators of success is knowledge. Wealthy people don't always know all the answers, and sometimes pay others to do work they can't do. Similarly, in the movie Good Will Hunting, *the only person who could solve some complex problems was the janitor. He knew a lot, and decided what he wanted to do with that knowledge rather than just think about money. In my opinion, he was extremely successful.*

When we think of history, there are few people that we remember simply because they were rich. Overall, we remember people who did something with their lives—they were influential in politics, or contributed to science or art or religion. If history is the ultimate judge of success, then money surely isn't everything.

Essay Organization

Theme:	Success is more than how much money you make.
Point 1: **Examples:**	Success can mean fame. Professor Mother Theresa
Point 2: **Examples:**	Success can mean respect. Attorney Band director
Point 3: **Examples:**	Success can mean knowledge. Wealthy people don't know everything Janitor in *Good Will Hunting*

Free Practice

Do either or both of the following activities on your own or in a group. There are no answers provided.

1. Read the essays in the Model Essay section. Identify the type of conclusion each contains.

2. Change the conclusion in any or all of the essays to another type of conclusion.

SELF-TEST ESSAY #3

Write on the same topic as Self-test Essay #1. Plan, write, and revise an essay on that topic within 30 minutes. Use the space on the following pages. Do NOT write in the shaded areas.

Divide your time like this.

PLAN	5 minutes	30:00 – 25:00
WRITE	20 minutes	25:00 – 05:00
REVISE	5 minutes	05:00 – 00:00

Topic Number: _____

PLAN

Concept Map

Thesis Statement

General Ideas

Supporting Details

WRITE

REVISE

Proofing Checklist

Reread your essay. Use this checklist as a guide.

✓	**CONTENT**
	Is there a thesis statement or introduction?
	Is there a topic sentence for each paragraph?
	Are there supporting details for each topic statement?
	Is there a conclusion?
✓	**CLARITY**
	Are there run-on sentences or sentence fragments?
	Are there misplaced modifiers or dangling modifiers?
	Are the structures parallel?
	Are there transition words?
	Are the sentences and paragraphs cohesive?
✓	**PUNCTUATION AND SPELLING**
	Are the paragraphs indented?
	Are there punctuation marks such as periods at the end of each sentence?
	Do all sentences begin with capital letters?
	Are all the words spelled correctly?

Revising the Essay

CHECKING THE CONTENT AND CLARITY

STEP 10: CHECK THE CONTENT

The Proofing Checklist advises you to check four things in your essay.

Is there a thesis statement or introduction?
Is there a topic sentence for each paragraph?
Are there supporting details for each topic statement?
Is there a conclusion?

These content items have been fully explained in the chapters on planning and writing your essay. You will get more practice in checking the content in the section on proofing that follows.

STEP 11: CHECK THE CLARITY

On the TOEFL Essay your computer will not have a grammar checker. Whether you type your essay or write by hand, you will have to proofread carefully to find your errors. Of course, it is better not to make errors. By thinking before you write, you can avoid common errors with sentences and modifiers.

Sentences

A sentence must have a subject and a verb. If a sentence is missing a subject or verb or both, it is called a sentence fragment. If a sentence has extra subjects and/or verbs (for example, two sentences written as one), it is called a run-on sentence.

Recognizing Sentence Fragments

The following examples of sentence fragments show how a subject and/or verb can be forgotten.

Example 1

Fragment   Gives us the big picture.

This sentence fragment is missing a subject. A possible subject is *History*.

Corrected   History gives us the big picture.

Example 2

Fragment   What they did learn, much more completely.

This sentence fragment *much more completely* is missing both a subject and a verb in the independent clause. The noun clause *What they did learn* is complete. The independent clause needs a subject and a verb such as *they learned*.

Corrected   What they did learn, they learned much more completely.

Example 3

Fragment   Means more than drawing or sculpting.

The verb *means* has no subject. A possible subject is *Studying art*.

Sentence   Studying art means more than drawing or sculpting.

Example 4

Fragment   It important to adapt to the customs of the country.

The sentence fragment is missing a verb. A possible verb is *is*.

Corrected   It is important to adapt to the customs of the country.

Practice 1

Tell which of the following from Topic 125 are sentence fragments. There are 8 sentence fragments. Choose a possible subject and/or verb from this box to complete the sentence.

study	who	you	It
help	who	is	am

1. I agree that all students should art and music in high school.

2. Young children who study those subjects in grade school do better in other subjects.

3. I assuming that this is true of teenagers.

4. All high school students must take physical education because it good for their physical health.

5. Well, studying art and music is good for their mental health.

6. Both art and music are interesting and students to express themselves.

7. Students have never drawn a picture will be surprised when they start to draw.

8. It is always satisfying to try something new, even if you find don't like it.

9. There's a reason cave dwellers drew on the walls and made music with drums.

10. The desire for self-expression is a natural human inclination.

11. Gives us an avenue for our emotions and fears.

12. The teacher taught me how to play the piano was very inspiring.

13. It shouldn't matter if the end result is mediocre.

Recognizing Run-on Sentences

The following examples of run-on sentences show how two sentences can be incorrectly written together.

Example 1

Run-on sentence   We all make decisions we can learn from them.
We all make decisions.
We can learn from them.

Corrected   We all make decisions that we can learn from.

Example 2

Run-on sentence   A movie is more vivid you're seeing it on a large screen.
A movie is more vivid.
You're seeing it on a large screen.

Corrected   A movie is more vivid because you're seeing it on a large screen.

Example 3

Run-on sentence   We can conduct research on Earth this is less costly than in space.
We can conduct research on Earth.
This is less costly than in space.

Corrected   Conducting research on Earth is less costly than in space.

Example 4

Run-on sentence   English is a difficult language to learn its spelling is irregular.
English is a difficult language to learn.
Its spelling is irregular.

Corrected   English is a difficult language to learn because its spelling is irregular.

Practice 2

Decide if these sentences are run-on sentences. There are six run-on sentences. In these six, underline the first sentence and double underline the second sentence in the run-on sentences below.

1. The most important decision I made in my life was to major in computer science.

2. This taught me important professional skills this assured me a successful career.

3. I was in college, computer science was relatively new.

4. None of my friends understood what I was doing all day.

5. They were learning how to be teachers, journalists, and economists I was learning how to write computer programs.

6. I graduated I had eight very good job offers.

7. My choice of college major gave me a lucrative career it helped in my married life.

8. I married a Naval officer through the years we've moved six times.

9. Each time, no matter where we've lived, I've been able to find a job with my computer programming skills.

10. In fact, by moving I learned about various computer technologies that I wouldn't have learned by staying with one company.

Correcting Sentences

Both sentence fragments and run-on sentences can be fixed by combining them correctly. Some of the ways sentences can be combined are shown below. For more practice, you should study the Grammar Review section in the current edition of Pamela Sharpe's *How to Prepare for the TOEFL*, Barron's Educational Series.

You can combine two simple sentences to make a compound sentence.

> *I want to buy a house, but I don't have enough money.*

You can add a dependent clause to a simple sentence to make a complex sentence.

> *I want to buy a house that has three bedrooms.*

You can add an independent clause to a complex sentence to make a compound-complex sentence.

> *I want to buy a house that has three bedrooms, but I don't have enough money.*

To combine two simple sentences, you can use coordinating conjunctions.

and	but	or
nor	then	yet

Sentence Fragment	I prefer to study in the morning. My sister to study in the evening.
Combination	I prefer to study in the morning, *and* my sister prefers to study in the evening.
Run-on Sentence	People exercised more years ago they called it work, not exercise.
Combination	People exercised more years ago, *but* they called it work, not exercise.

To combine a dependent clause with a sentence, you need subordinating conjunctions. There are a variety of subordinating conjunctions with different purposes. The following conjunctions are used to indicate contrast, manner, time, relationship, and reason.

CONTRAST			
although	even though	though	much as
while	in spite of	despite	whereas

Sentence Fragment   Teenagers should have jobs. While they are students.

Combination   Teenagers should have jobs *while* they are students.

Run-on Sentence   Not everyone can get the best health care everyone can get basic health care and advice.

Combination   *Although* not everyone can get the best health care, everyone can get basic health care and advice.

MANNER				
as	as if	as though	like	the way

Sentence Fragment   We can understand other cultures through their music. As we can through their art.

Combination   We can understand other cultures through their music *as* we can through their art.

Run-on Sentence   The Spanish-speaking population is increasing, the English-speaking population is remaining at the same level.

Combination   The Spanish-speaking population is increasing, *even as* the English-speaking population is remaining at the same level.

TIME			
after	as	as soon as	before
once	since	the minute	until
when	while	the moment	the second

Sentence Fragment   We should earn money. Before we spend it.

Combination   We should earn money *before* we spend it.

Run-on Sentence   Poor people need help they can manage on their own.

Combination   Poor people need help *until* they can manage on their own.

RELATIONSHIP		
that	which	who
whom	whose	where

Sentence Fragment   We should eat more fruits. Now available year-around

Combination   We should eat more fruits, *which* are now available year-around

Run-on Sentence   Food contains a lot of preservatives they aren't good for us.

Combination   Food contains a lot of preservatives, *which* aren't good for us.

REASON		
what	why	how

Sentence Fragment   The teacher asked me. Why he wasn't here.

Combination   The teacher asked me *why* he wasn't here.

Run-on Sentence   Doctors know more now about reasons what causes disease and how to cure it.

Combination   Doctors know more now about *what* causes disease and *how* to cure it.

Practice 3

Combine the following to avoid sentence fragments or run-on sentences. Use the subordinate conjunctions suggested.

1. **Reason *why***
   Students wonder. Teachers are critical.
   Students wonder why teachers are critical.

2. **Time *when***
   A birdbath is a source of water for birds the weather is hot.

3. **Relationship *where***
   I'd like to have a garden I could grow vegetables.

4. **Contrast *Even though***
   We have all we need, we want more.

5. **Manner *As***
   Our population ages we will need more services for the elderly.

Modifiers

Earlier we saw how you can combine sentences using conjunctions. You can combine sentences by taking words or phrases from the second sentence and inserting them in the first as modifiers.

Original

Sentence 1   I want to live in a townhouse.

Sentence 2   The townhouse should be <u>renovated.</u>

Revised

Sentence 1+2   I want to live in a <u>renovated</u> townhouse.

This is a simple, straightforward combination. An adjective *renovated* describing *townhouse* in the second sentence is placed in front of the noun *townhouse* in the first.

You must be careful when you combine participial phrases or prepositional phrases in other sentences. There are two problems that can occur here: a misplaced modifier and a dangling modifier. Look at these examples.

Misplaced modifier

Sentence   I had difficulty finding a parking space <u>searching for an apartment</u>.

Original

Sentence 1   I had difficulty finding a parking space.

Sentence 2   I was searching for an apartment.

Revision

Sentence 1+2   <u>Searching for an apartment</u>, I had difficulty finding a parking space.

The parking space is NOT searching for an apartment. A person is searching. You must place the participial phrase *near* the noun it modifies.

Dangling modifier

Sentence   <u>To live within my budget</u>, a place should be convenient.

Original

Sentence 1   I need to live within my budget.

Sentence 2   I need a convenient place.

Revision

Sentence 1+2   <u>To live within my budget</u>, I need a place that is convenient.

A place cannot "live within a budget." The person *I* that the prepositional phrase modifies is missing.

Practice 4

Combine these sentences as directed.

1. There would be more money for schools.

    There would be more money for libraries.

    There would be more money for other community needs.

Combine with *and*

_____

_____

2. Once the buildings were completed, the jobs would be those on the campus itself. The jobs would include teachers, office workers, custodians, and librarians.

Combine with *and*

_____

_____

3. Our community is a place.
It is a place where everyone knows everyone else.

Combine by deleting *It is a place.*

_____

_____

4. Playing sports is a wonderful way to learn discipline.
Playing sports should not be the focus of a university education.

Combine by adding *Although* to the first sentence. Use a pronoun as the subject for cohesion.

_____

_____

5. Immigrant children learn their new language while playing with other children.
They also learn while going to school.

Combine with *and*

_____

_____

Practice 5

Rewrite these sentences to place the modifiers correctly.

1. A child has exciting places to visit in the city growing up.

_____

_____

2. Children do better in all subjects who study art.

_____

_____

3. Reading fiction is more enjoyable than watching a movie such as novels and short stories.

_____

_____

4. English is the language of diplomacy which is very idiomatic.

_____

_____

5. Looking for a rewarding career computer science attracts many young people.

_____

_____

CHECKING THE PUNCTUATION AND SPELLING

STEP 12: CHECK THE PUNCTUATION AND SPELLING

It is beyond the scope of this book to provide activities to improve your spelling. Remember that there is no spell checker on the computer that you use with the TOEFL Essay. When you read, pay close attention to words. This will help you understand English spelling patterns.

Also when you read, pay attention to punctuation. This will help you when writing your essay. There are four important things to remember about punctuation on the TOEFL Essay.

- **Indent each paragraph.**
  This will help the reader determine when you are starting a new idea.

- **Capitalize the first word of a sentence.**
  This will help the reader determine when you are starting a new sentence.

- **Put a period or question mark at the end of a sentence or question.**
  This will help the reader determine when you are ending a sentence or question.

- **Start each paragraph on a new line.**
  This will help the reader determine when you are starting a new topic.

Here are some other forms of punctuation that will make your essay easier to read.

Comma

Use a comma in a list of three or more things. It is optional to put a comma before the *and*.

> *I want to have a kitchen, living room and bedroom.*
>
> *I want a large, airy, inexpensive house.*

Use a comma between a noun and any following descriptions.

> *My favorite area, Orchard Hill, was developed by John Bartle, an entrepreneur.*

Use a comma to separate adjectives or participles that are not part of the sentence or were added for emphasis.

> *The apartment was expensive, very expensive.*
>
> *Excited, I signed the lease without reading the fine print.*

Use a comma to separate a non-restrictive relative clause.

> *All the neighbors, who are very friendly, keep their houses very tidy.*

Use a comma after a subordinate clause at the start of the sentence.

> *Once I've chosen an area, I decide whether I want to live in a house or an apartment.*

Semicolon

Use a semicolon to separate closely related sentences.

> *I wanted a renovated townhouse; none was available.*

Colon or Dash

Use a colon or dash in front of a list or explanation.

> *I looked at these kinds of apartments: studio, one-bedroom, and two-bedroom.*
>
> *My needs are simple—a swimming pool and a two-car garage.*

Practice 6

Punctuate the following essay. The corrected essay follows it.

Topic 21

Why People are Living Longer

people are living to be much older these days than ever before. the main reasons for this are greater access to health care improved health care and better nutrition.

basic health care is available to more people now. when someone is seriously ill he or she can go to a public hospital. there are also more clinics and doctors than there used to be Years ago, health care wasn't available to everyone. some people didn't live near a doctor or hospital and others couldn't pay for the care they needed.

people also live longer because the quality of health care has improved. doctors now know more about diseases and cures Years ago, people died young because of simple things like an infection or a virus. now we have antibiotics and other medicines to help cure infections

The quality of nutrition has improved also We eat more healthfully than we used to. we know that eating low-fat food can prevent heart disease and we know that eating fruits and vegetables can prevent cancer.

Improved health care and healthy eating habits allow us to live longer Now we need to make sure that everyone in the world has these benefits

Corrected Essay

Why People Are Living Longer

People are living to be much older these days than ever before. The main reasons for this are greater access to health care, improved health care, and better nutrition.

Basic health care is available to more people now. When someone is seriously ill, he or she can go to a public hospital. There are also more clinics and doctors than there used to be. Years ago, health care wasn't available to everyone. Some people didn't live near a doctor or hospital and others couldn't pay for the care they needed.

People also live longer because the quality of health care has improved. Doctors now know more about diseases and cures. Years ago, people died young because of simple things such as infection or a virus. Now we have antibiotics and other medicines to help cure infections.

The quality of nutrition has improved also. We eat more healthfully than we used to. We know that eating low-fat food can prevent heart disease, and we know that eating fruits and vegetables can prevent cancer.

Improved health care and healthy eating habits allow us to live longer. Now we need to make sure that everyone in the world has these benefits.

Essay Organization

Theme:	People are living longer these days for several reasons.
Point 1: **Examples:**	Health care is available to more people now. Public hospitals More clinics and doctors
Point 2: **Examples:**	The quality of health care has improved. More knowledge about diseases and cures Antibiotics and other medicines
Point 3: **Examples:**	The quality of nutrition has improved. Low-fat food prevents heart disease. Fruits and vegetables prevent cancer.

Free Practice

Do any or all of the following activities on your own or in a group. There are no answers provided.

1. Read the essays in the Model Essay section. Identify all the subjects and verbs.

2. Read the essays in the Model Essay section. Identify the coordinate and subordinate conjunctions.

3. Read the essays in the Model Essay section. Underline all modifying expressions.

4. Read the essays in the Model Essay section. Circle all the punctuation.

5. Review all of the essays you have written. Check the sentences, clauses, modifiers, and punctuation.

USING THE PROOFING CHECKLIST

HOW TO REVISE

It is very easy to make clean, precise revisions when you use the computer. If you make corrections on your handwritten essay, you must do so very neatly. Here are some ways to make your revisions clear to your reader.

Delete a word or phrase.   Cross out the word completely.

Insert a word or phrase.   Use the caret (^) symbol to indicate where something should be inserted.

Student evaluations of teachers ^also *makes students feel* ^as if ~~like~~
they have a say in what happens in ^their *schools.*

If you write your essay by hand, you might want to leave extra space between the lines in case you need to insert a change.

Proofing Checklist

You will not be able to take this list into the testing room, but soon it will be second nature to you. As you proof the practice essays in this book and proof your own practice essays, you will become familiar with the four areas of this checklist.

✓	**CONTENT**
	Is there a thesis statement or introduction?
	Is there a topic sentence for each paragraph?
	Are there supporting details for each topic statement?
	Is there a conclusion?
✓	**CLARITY**
	Are there run-on sentences or sentence fragments?
	Are there misplaced modifiers or dangling modifiers?
	Are the structures parallel?
	Are there transition words?
	Are the sentences and paragraphs cohesive?
✓	**PUNCTUATION AND SPELLING**
	Are the paragraphs indented?
	Are there punctuation marks such as periods at the end of each sentence?
	Do all sentences begin with capital letters?
	Are all the words spelled correctly?

Practice 7

Proof the following essay by answering the questions that follow.

Which activity is most important?
• reducing pollution in your neighborhood
• helping a child learn to read
• visiting an elderly person regularly

Explain your choice using reasons and details.

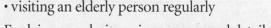

Helping a child learn to read is important.

opens up new world

forms a child's personality

feeds a child's creativity

- other times, cultures
- other ways to view situation
- leaves options

- logical or fanciful
- sympathetic or judgmental

- different ways to describe things
- increases vocabulary

Helping a Child to Read

The children of today will be the citizens of tomorrow. They will control the world we live in. For that reason, they must have the best education possible. We must prepare them for their role in our future. I think the most important preparation is helping a child learn to read.

Reading opens up a whole new world to a child. It lets them travel to other countries, other centuries, and to cultures that are different. It teaches them about the way people different from themselves think about things. They learn that there are another ways to view situations.

Reading helps to form a child's personality. Does the child prefer fantasy stories, adventure stories, or nonfiction. is she sympathetic to the characters' difficulties, or does she think the characters' problems are there own fault? Children learn how to form preferences and make judgments when they're reading.

A childs creativity is fed by reading. It shows them there are many different ways to describe the same thing. It increases their vocabulary which will help them learn subjects in school more quickly.

Many ways to make a difference in a community. Learning to read, I believe that the activity brings hope to the future.

Essay Organization

Theme:	The most important activity is helping a child learn to read.
Point 1: Examples:	Opens up new worlds. "Travel" to other countries, centuries, and cultures Learn how different people think about things
Point 2: Examples:	Helps form a child's personality. Develop preferences for different types of stories Make judgments of the characters' situations
Point 3: Examples:	Feeds creativity. See different ways to describe things Increase vocabulary

Answer the questions.

1. Which of the following sentences is the thesis statement for this essay?

   (A) They learn that there are other ways to view situations.

   (B) I think the most important preparation is helping a child learn to read.

   (C) They will control the world we live in.

   (D) None of the above.

2. Which of the following sentences is the topic sentence for paragraph 3?

   (A) Does the child prefer fantasy stories, adventure stories, or nonfiction?

   (B) Children learn how to form preferences and make judgments when they're reading.

   (C) Reading helps to form a child's personality.

   (D) None of the above.

3. Which of the following sentences supports this statement: Reading opens up a whole new world to a child.

   (A) There are many ways to make a difference in a community

   (B) We must prepare them for their role in our future.

   (C) It teaches them about the way people different from themselves think about things.

   (D) None of the above.

4. In which paragraph is there a sentence fragment? Correct it.

   (A) Paragraph 1   (B) Paragraph 3   (C) Paragraph 5

   _____

   _____

5. In which sentence is there a dangling participle? Correct it.

   (A) Sentence 4, paragraph 1   (B) Sentence 1, paragraph 4   (C) Sentence 2, paragraph 5

   _____

   _____

6. Which sentence is not parallel with the others in paragraph 2? Correct it.

(A) Sentence 1   (B) Sentence 2   (C) Sentence 3

_____

_____

7. Which topic sentence is not parallel with the others? Correct it.

(A) Sentence 1, paragraph 2   (B) Sentence 1, paragraph 3   (C) Sentence 1, paragraph 4

_____

_____

8. Which object in sentence 2, paragraph 2 is not parallel with the others? Correct it.

(A) other countries   (B) other centuries   (C) to cultures that are different

_____

_____

9. In paragraph 1, the transition phrase *For that reason* connects which two ideas?

(A) control of world and education

(B) trite and true

(C) children and preparation

_____

_____

10. Which paragraph is not indented?

(A) Paragraph 1   (B) Paragraph 3   (C) Paragraph 4

11. Which sentence does not end with the correct punctuation? Correct it.

(A) Sentence 2, paragraph 2   (B) Sentence 2, paragraph 3   (C) Sentence 1, paragraph 4

_____

_____

12. Which sentence does not begin with a capital letter?

(A) Sentence 5, paragraph 1   (B) Sentence 2, paragraph 2   (C) Sentence 3, paragraph 3

13. Which word is not spelled correctly in this essay? Correct it.

(A) *lets* in sentence 2, paragraph 2

(B) *there* in sentence 3, paragraph 3

(C) *ways* in sentence 2, paragraph 4

_____

_____

14. Which word is not used correctly in this essay? Correct it.

(A) *must* in sentence 4, paragraph 1

(B) *another* in sentence 4, paragraph 2

(C) *learn* in sentence 4, paragraph 4

_____

_____

Practice 8

Proof the following essay by answering the questions that follow.

Your community has enough money to hire one new employee. Which one of the following (three choices will be presented in the actual test) should your community hire? • a community health worker • a counselor • an emergency medical technician • a firefighter • a judge • a landscaper • a police officer • a recreation center director • a teacher. Use specific reasons and details to develop your essay.

Now	Proposed	Reason
poor recreation areas	more park areas	bring community together socially
areas not useful	more bicycle paths/hiking	encourage exercise
not enough shade	plant trees	cooler, better appearance
entrance to community poorly defined	plantings around entranceway	recognition as community pride

A Landscaper for Our Community

Since our community has only enough money to hire one new employee, the townspeople have been debating which specialty would be the best. After considering alot of possibilities, I believe that hiring a landscaper would be most beneficial to us.

Right now, we don't have a community recreation area but we have empty land that isn't used. These areas could be made attractive and useful. They could be used as parks. For example, a landscaper could put in gardens and benches. a landscaper could design bike and walking paths. Everyone would enjoy these things, and they would bring the community together.

Our community doesn't have enough shade. A landscaper suitable to the area could plant trees. Every year our community would become shadier, cooler, and it will be more attractive. Property values would increase, too.

We need a more noticeable and attractive entrance to our community. we have a sign at the entrance, but guests and delivery people drive by all the time the entrance difficult to see. A landscaper could plant flowers and bushes around the entrance to make it more noticeable. Flowers and bushes would also make the entrance more attractive and create pride in our neighborhood.

We all want a community that is a safe, pleasant place four families and children to live. Our next step should be to make our neighborhood more beautifully and functional by hiring a professional landscaper.

Essay Organization

Theme:	Our community should hire a landscaper.
Point 1: **Examples:**	We need to make empty land attractive and useful. Gardens and benches Bike and walking paths
Point 2: **Examples:**	We need to plant shade trees. Improve appearance Increase property value
Point 3: **Examples:**	We need a better entrance. Noticeable Attractive

Answer the questions.

1. Which of the following sentences is the thesis statement for this essay?

    (A) I believe that hiring a landscaper would be most beneficial to us.

    (B) Everyone has been debating which specialty would be the best.

    (C)) Our community has only enough money to hire one new employee.

    (D) None of the above.

2. Which of the following sentences is the topic sentence for paragraph 4?

    (A) We need a more noticeable and attractive entrance to our community.

    (B) We have a sign at the entrance.

    (C) A landscaper could plant flowers and bushes around the entrance.

    (D) None of the above.

3. Which of the following sentences supports this statement: These areas could be made more attractive and useful.

    (A) Our community doesn't have enough shade.

    (B) They could be used as parks.

    (C) We have empty land that isn't used.

    (D) None of the above.

4. In which paragraph is there a run-on sentence? Correct it.

    (A) Paragraph 1   (B) Paragraph 2   (C) Paragraph 4

    _____

    _____

5. In which sentence is there a misplaced modifier? Correct it.

    (A) Sentence 2, paragraph 1   (B) Sentence 1, paragraph 2   (C) Sentence 2, paragraph 3

    _____

    _____

6. Which modifier is not parallel in paragraph 5? Correct it.

(A) safe   (B) beautifully   (C) professional

_____

_____

7. Which adjective in sentence 4, paragraph 3 is not parallel with the others? Correct it.

(A) shadier   (B) cooler   (C) it will be more attractive

_____

_____

8. In paragraph 5, the transition phrase *Our next step* connects which two ideas?

(A) We don't have a recreation area./We should hire a landscaper.

(B) We don't have shade./We don't have trees.

(C) We need an attractive entrance./Our neighborhood is safe.

9. In paragraph 3, which words provide cohesion?

(A) shade/shadier

(B) community/landscaper

(C) attractive/values

10. Which words provide cohesion?

(A) In paragraph 1, *Since*

(B) In paragraph 2, *For example*

(C) In paragraph 4, *all the time*

11. Which paragraph is not indented?

(A) Paragraph 1   (B) Paragraph 2   (C) Paragraph 5

12. Which sentence is not correctly punctuated? Correct it.

(A) Sentence 1, paragraph 2   (B) Sentence 2, paragraph 3   (C) Sentence 3, paragraph 4

_____

_____

13. Which sentences do not begin with a capital letter?

(A) Sentence 2, paragraph 1

(B) Sentence 5, paragraph 2

(C) Sentence 2, paragraph 4

14. Which word is not spelled correctly in this essay? Correct it.

(A) *be* in sentence 2, paragraph 1

(B) *by* in sentence 2, paragraph 4

(C) *four* in sentence 1, paragraph 5

_____

_____

15. Which word is not used correctly in this essay? Correct it.

 (A) *enough* in sentence 1, paragraph 1

 (B) *alot* in sentence 2, paragraph 1

 (C) *get us* in sentence 3, paragraph 4

_____

_____

Practice 9

Proof the following essay by answering the questions that follow.

Topic 167

Your school has enough money to purchase either computers for students or books for the library. Which should your school choose to buy—computers or books? Use specific reasons and examples to support your recommendation.

Now	Proposed	Reason
out-of date reference material	use Internet	get current information on the Internet
students might not know computer skills	give every student a computer	students will learn computer skills
slow access to info	get information instantly	find information quickly on Internet

Buy Computers

Our school already has books in its library and it already has computers. however, I think buying more computers is more important than buying more books. Computers provide access to more information than books, and they provide it more quickly. Also, in this modern world, every student needs to learn how to use computers skillfully. We need computers more than we need books.

Computers, unlike books, provide access up-to-date information. Right now, the books reference in our library are very outdated. If we buy new books today, they will become old very quickly. Computers, on the other hand, provide the ability to access the latest information on the Internet. They are the best tool available.

Computers also provide information more quickly. Just type in a keyword and many sources of information appear instantly on the screen. It takes much longer to watch information in a book, and often the book you want is not immediately available. You have to wait for somebody to return it or one has to order it from another library.

Computers are an important tool in the modern world, so students have to learn how to use them. If students do all their schoolwork on computers, they will develop the computer skills that they will need in the future. Therefore, we need to have a computer for every student in the school.

If we buy more computers for our school, all the students will have access to the latest information. They will be able to do their work more quickly and important skills will be learned, to. For these reasons, I feel that purchasing computers will benefit us more than buying books.

Essay Organization

Theme:	Our school should buy more computers instead of more books.
Point 1: Examples:	Computers provide access to the latest information. Books become old quickly. The latest information is on the Internet.
Point 2: Examples:	Computers provide information more quickly. You can get information instantly on a computer. It takes a long time to find information in a book.
Point 3: Examples:	Students need to learn computer skills. Computer skills are important in the modern world. Students learn computer skills by using computers daily.

Answer the questions.

1. Which of the following sentences is the thesis statement for this essay?

   (A) Our school already has books in its library and it already has computers.

   (B) Computers provide access to more information than books.

   (C) Every student needs to learn how to use computers skillfully.

   (D) None of the above.

2. Which of the following sentences is the topic sentence for paragraph 2?

   (A) If we buy new books today, they will become old very quickly.

   (B) Right now, the books in our library are very outdated.

   (C) Computers, unlike books, can access up-to-date information.

   (D) None of the above.

3. Which of the following sentences supports this statement: "Computers also provide information more quickly."

   (A) You have to wait for somebody to return it.

   (B) It takes much longer to look up information in a book.

   (C) Many sources of information appear instantly on the screen.

   (D) None of the above.

4. In which paragraph is there a sentence fragment? Correct it.

   (A) Paragraph 1   (B) Paragraph 4   (C) Paragraph 5

   _____

   _____

5. In which sentence is there a misplaced modifier? Correct it.

   (A) Sentence 4, paragraph 1

   (B) Sentence 2, paragraph 2

   (C) Sentence 3, paragraph 4

   _____

   _____

6. In which sentence in paragraph 3 could parts be made parallel? Correct it.

(A) Sentence 2   (B) Sentence 3   (C) Sentence 4

_____

_____

7. Which sentence in paragraph 5 could parts be made parallel? Correct it.

(A) Sentence 1   (B) Sentence 2   (C) Sentence 3

_____

_____

8. In paragraph 2, sentence 5, the pronoun *They* refers to which antecedent?

(A) books   (B) students   (C) computers

9. Which word provides cohesion between paragraphs 2 and 3?

(A) provide   (B) access   (C) available

10. Which words provide cohesion?

(A) In paragraph 2, *up-to-date* and *latest*

(B) In paragraph 3, *appear* and *return*

(C) In paragraph 4, *important* and *develop*

11. Which paragraph is not indented?

(A) Paragraph 1   (B) Paragraph 3   (C) Paragraph 5

12. Which sentence does not begin with a capital letter?

(A) Sentence 2, paragraph 1

(B) Sentence 3, paragraph 3

(C) Sentence 2, paragraph 5

13. Which word is not spelled correctly in this essay? Correct it.

(A) *than* in sentence 5, paragraph 1

(B) *Therefore* in sentence 3, paragraph 4

(C) *to* in sentence 2, paragraph 5

_____

_____

14. Which word is not used correctly in this essay? Correct it.

(A) *However* in sentence 2, paragraph 1

(B) *unlike* in sentence 1, paragraph 2

(C) *watch* in sentence 3, paragraph 3

_____

_____

Practice 10

Proof the following essay. Use the Proofing Checklist as a guide.
  The type and number of errors are identified.

Proofing Checklist

✓	**CONTENT**
1	**Is there a thesis statement or introduction?**
✓	**Is there a topic sentence for each paragraph?**
✓	**Are there supporting details for each topic statement?**
✓	**Is there a conclusion?**
✓	**CLARITY**
2	**Are there run-on sentences or sentence fragments?**
1	**Are there misplaced modifiers or dangling modifiers?**
1	**Are the structures parallel?**
✓	**Are there transition words?**
✓	**Are the sentences and paragraphs cohesive?**
✓	**PUNCTUATION AND SPELLING**
✓	**Are the paragraphs indented?**
2	**Are there punctuation marks such as periods at the end of each sentence?**
1	**Do all sentences begin with capital letters?**
1	**Are all the words spelled correctly?**

Topic 2

Do you agree or disagree with the following statement? Parents are the best teachers. Use specific reasons and examples to support your answer.

Not the Best Teachers

Parents shape their children from the beginning of their children's lives. They teach their children values. They share their interests with them. They develop close emotional ties with them. Parents can be very important teachers in their children's lives;

Parents may be too close to their children emotionally. For example, may limit a child's freedom in the name of safety. A teacher may organize an educational trip to a big city, but a parent may think this trip is too dangerous. A school may want to take the children camping, but a parent may be afraid of the child getting hurt.

Another problem that parents sometimes expect their children's interests to be similar to their own. if the parents love science, they may try to force their child to love science too. But what if the child prefers art. If the parents enjoy sports, they may expect their child to participate on different teams. But what if the child prefers to read?

Parents want to pass on there values to their children. However, things change. The children of today are growing up in a world different from their parents' world. Sometimes parents can't keep up with rapid social or technological changes, especially older ones. A student who has friends of different races at school may find that his parents have narrower views. A student who loves computers may find that her parents don't understand or value the digital revolution.

Parents are important teachers in our lives, but they aren't always the best teachers. Fortunately, we have many teachers in our lives. Our parents teach us, our teachers teach us, and we learn from our peers. Books and newspapers also teach us. All of them are valuable

Essay Organization

Theme:	Parents aren't always the best teachers.
Point 1: **Examples:**	They may be close emotionally. Trip to a big city Camping.
Point 2: **Examples:**	They may expect similar interests. Science vs. art Sports vs. reading
Point 3: **Examples:**	Values change Friends of different races Computers

Write the error, its location (sentence/paragraph), and its correction.

ERROR	LOCATION	CORRECTION
CONTENT		
1. Thesis statement	paragraph 1 sentence 5+	Parents can be very important teachers in their children's lives; however, they are not always the best teachers.
GRAMMAR		
2.		
3.		
4.		
5.		

PUNCTUATION

6.

7.

8.

SPELLING

9.

Practice 11

Proof the following essay. Use the Proofing Checklist as a guide. Use the concept map to help you identify the content.

The type and number of errors are identified.

Proofing Checklist

	CONTENT
✓	
1	Is there a thesis statement or introduction?
✓	Is there a topic sentence for each paragraph?
1	Are there supporting details for each topic statement?
✓	Is there a conclusion?
✓	**CLARITY**
1	Are there run-on sentences or sentence fragments?
1	Are there misplaced modifiers or dangling modifiers?
1	Are the structures parallel?
✓	Are there transition words?
✓	Are the sentences and paragraphs cohesive?
✓	**PUNCTUATION AND SPELLING**
5	Are the paragraphs indented?
1	Are there punctuation marks such as periods at the end of each sentence?
1	Do all sentences begin with capital letters?
1	Are all the words spelled correctly?

Topic

Is it better for children to participate in team sports or individual sports? Why? Use specific reasons and examples to support your answer.

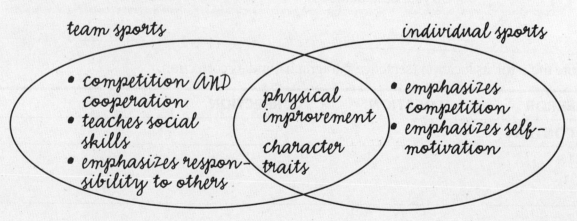

team sports

individual sports

- competition AND cooperation
- teaches social skills
- emphasizes responsibility to others

physical improvement

character traits

- emphasizes competition
- emphasizes self-motivation

Learning to Be a Team Player

Both individual and team sports help children to improve physically. Both types of sports help children develop social skills and a sense of responsibility, too.

Both individual and team sports emphasize competition, but team sports have an added benefit They also emphasize cooperation with teammates. All the players must work together to make the team win. Cooperation is important when throwing and to catch the ball. It is also important when planning a strategy. Without cooperation, the team cannot succeed.

Team sports teach social skills better than individual sports. Team players must learn to communicate with other players to succeed that is not true for individual sports. Team players must learn to get along with their teammates. in individual sports, on the other hand, there are no teammates to interact with.

Finally, teem sports help children learn to be responsible to others.

All sports teach skills important, but I believe that team sports players learn skills that will make them successful and happy throughout life. Thus, I always encourage young people to try a team sport.

Essay Organization

Theme:	It is better for children to participate in team sports.	
Point 1: **Examples:**	Learn cooperation Throwing and catching the ball Planning a strategy	
Point 2: **Examples:**	Learn social skills Communicate with teammates Get along with teammates	
Point 3: **Examples:**	Learn responsibility Show up on time Do your best for the team	

Write the error, its location (sentence/paragraph), and its correction.

ERROR	LOCATION	CORRECTION
CONTENT		
1.		
2.		

GRAMMAR

3.

4.

5.

PUNCTUATION

6.

7.

8.

9.

10.

11.

12.

SPELLING

13.

Practice 12

Proof the following essay. Use the Proofing Checklist as a guide. Use the concept map to help you identify the content.

The type and number of errors are identified.

Proofing Checklist

✓	**CONTENT**
✓	Is there a thesis statement or introduction?
✓	Is there a topic sentence for each paragraph?
✓	Are there supporting details for each topic statement?
1	Is there a conclusion?
✓	**CLARITY**
1	Are there run-on sentences or sentence fragments?
1	Are there misplaced modifiers or dangling modifiers?
3	Are the structures parallel?
✓	Are there transition words?
1	Are the sentences and paragraphs cohesive?
✓	**PUNCTUATION AND SPELLING**
1	Are the paragraphs indented?
✓	Are there punctuation marks such as periods at the end of each sentence?
1	Do all sentences begin with capital letters?
✓	Are all the words spelled correctly?

Topic 125

Do you agree or disagree with the following statement? All students should be required to study art and music in secondary school. Use specific reasons to support your answer.

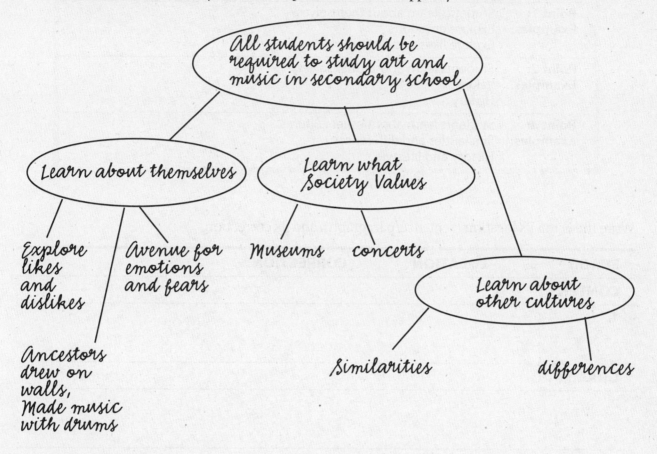

Yes to Music and Art in High School

I agree that all students should be required to study art and music in high school. Art and music can teach us many things. They can teach us about ourselves, about our society, and about the world we live in.

By studying art and music, students can learn a great deal about themselves. Both natural forms of self-expression. Just as our ancestors in caves drew on the walls and made music with drums, people today use art and music to explore their emotions. Students also explore their likes and dislikes when they choose the music they want to learn, or when they decide which subjects they want to draw. The process of making music or making art is a process of self-exploration.

Studying art and music means more than drawing or playing an instrument. Students go to museums and concerts, too. By studying pictures in museums, or when they listen to the selections in a musical program, students learn about their own culture. We learn about what our society values. They also learn about the history of their society and how lifestyles and values have changed over time.

By studying art and music from other cultures, students learn about other people around the world. they learn about what is important in other societies. They learn about similarities and differences between cultures. They learn about the history and lifestyles of other places. New worlds are opened up to them.

Essay Organization

Theme:	Studying art and music teaches students many things.
Point 1: Examples:	Students learn about themselves. Explore emotions Explore likes and dislikes
Point 2: Examples:	Students learn about their society. Values History
Point 3: Examples:	Students learn about other cultures. Similarities and differences History and lifestyle

Write the error, its location (sentence/paragraph), and its correction.

ERROR	LOCATION	CORRECTION
CONTENT		
1.		
GRAMMAR		
2.		
3.		
4.		
5.		
6.		
PUNCTUATION		
7.		
8.		

Free Practice

Do the following on your own or in a group. There are no answers provided.

1. Exchange essays with your friends and proof them following the Proofing Checklist.

SELF-TEST ESSAY #4

Write on the same topic as Self-Test Essay #1. Plan, write, and revise an essay on that topic within 30 minutes. Use the space on the following pages. Do NOT write in the shaded areas.

Divide your time like this.

PLAN	5 minutes	30:00 – 25:00
WRITE	20 minutes	25:00 – 05:00
REVISE	5 minutes	05:00 – 00:00

Topic Number: _____

PLAN

Concept Map

Thesis Statement

General Ideas

Supporting Details

WRITE

REVISE

Proofing Checklist

Reread your essay. Use this checklist as a guide.

✓	**CONTENT**
	Is there a thesis statement or introduction?
	Is there a topic sentence for each paragraph?
	Are there supporting details for each topic statement?
	Is there a conclusion?
✓	**CLARITY**
	Are there run-on sentences or sentence fragments?
	Are there misplaced modifiers or dangling modifiers?
	Are the structures parallel?
	Are there transition words?
	Are the sentences and paragraphs cohesive?
✓	**PUNCTUATION AND SPELLING**
	Are the paragraphs indented?
	Are there punctuation marks such as periods at the end of each sentence?
	Do all sentences begin with capital letters?
	Are all the words spelled correctly?

Appendix

MODEL ESSAYS

The 185 topics on the following pages may appear on your actual TOEFL. You should become familiar with the list before you take the TOEFL. Remember that when you take the test you will NOT have a choice of topics. You must write only on the topic that is assigned to you.

The 185 topics are classified according to their type. Remember this classification is not always precise. *Giving an Explanation* can also be called *Making an Argument* in some cases. Both tasks are very similar. These classifications are to guide you only.

TOEFL Topics			
MA	Making an Argument	63	34%
AD	Agreeing or Disagreeing	54	29%
PR	Stating a Preference	39	21%
EX	Giving an Explanation	29	16%

As you study these topics and the essays, look for the organizational patterns. Can you find the three main points and the supporting details in each essay?

1	EX	People attend college or university for many different reasons (for example, new experiences, career preparation, increased knowledge). Why do **you** think people attend college or university? Use specific reasons and examples to support your answer.

People attend college for a lot of different reasons. I believe that the three most common reasons are to prepare for a career, to have new experiences, and to increase their knowledge of themselves and of the world around them.

Career preparation is probably the primary reason that people attend college. These days, the job market is very competitive. Careers such as information technology will need many new workers in the near future. At college, students can learn new skills for these careers and increase their opportunities for the future.

Students also go to college to have new experiences. For many, it is their first time away from home. At college, they can meet new people from many different places. They can see what life is like in a different city. They can learn to live on their own and take care of themselves without having their family always nearby

At college, students have the opportunity to increase their knowledge. As they decide what they want to study, pursue their studies, and interact with their classmates, they learn a lot about themselves. They also, of course, have the opportunity to learn about many subjects in their classes. In addition to the skills and knowledge related to their career, college students also have the chance to take classes in other areas. For many, this will be their last chance to study different subjects.

Colleges offer much more than career preparation. They offer the opportunity to have new experiences and to learn many kinds of things. I think all of these are reasons why people attend college.

▼

2	AD	Do you agree or disagree with the following statement? Parents are the best teachers. Use specific reasons and examples to support your answer.

Parents shape their children from the beginning of their children's lives. They teach their children values. They share their interests with them. They develop close emotional ties with them. Parents can be very important teachers in their children's lives; however, they are not always the best teachers.

Parents may be too close to their children emotionally. For example, they may limit a child's freedom in the name of safety. A teacher may organize an educational trip to a big city, but a parent may think this trip is too dangerous. A school may want to take the children camping, but a parent may be afraid of the child getting hurt.

Another problem is that parents sometimes expect their children's interests to be similar to their own. If the parents love science, they may try to force their child to love science too. But what if the child prefers art? If the parents enjoy sports, they may expect their child to participate on different teams. But what if the child prefers to read?

Parents want to pass on their values to their children. However, things change. The children of today are growing up in a world different from their parents' world. Sometimes parents, especially older ones, can't keep up with rapid social or technological changes. A student who has friends of different races at school may find that his parents have narrower views. A student who loves computers may find that her parents don't understand or value the digital revolution.

Parents are important teachers in our lives, but they aren't always the best teachers. Fortunately, we have many teachers in our lives. Our parents teach us, our teachers teach us, and we learn from our peers. Books and newspapers also teach us. All of them are valuable.

▼

3	EX	Nowadays food has become easier to prepare. Has this change improved the way people live? Use specific reasons and examples to support your answer.

Food is a basic part of life, so it follows that improved methods of food preparation have made our lives better. Nowadays we can prepare meals much faster than we could in the past. We can also enjoy a greater variety of food and eat more healthfully, all because of modern methods of food preparation.

Microwave ovens have made it possible to prepare delicious food quickly. People these days rarely have time to shop and prepare meals the old-fashioned way. We live very fast lives. We are busy working, caring for our families, traveling, playing sports, and many other things. Because of microwave ovens, we have time to enjoy a good meal with our family and then play soccer, go to a movie, study, or do anything else we want to afterwards.

Modern methods of preserving food have made it possible to enjoy a wide variety of food. Because of refrigerators, freezers, canning, and freeze-drying, we can eat fruits and vegetables that come from far away places. We can prepare a meal one day and save the leftovers in the refrigerator or freezer to eat at another time. We can keep different kinds of food in the refrigerator or on the shelf. It's easy to always have food available and to be able to eat completely different meals every day.

Healthful eating is easier now than it ever was. Because of modern transportation methods, fresh fruits and vegetables are available all year round. Modern kitchen appliances make it easy to prepare fruits and vegetables for cooking. Bread machines make it possible to enjoy healthful, home-baked bread whenever we like. We can eat fresh and healthful food everyday because modern methods have made preparation easy.

Our lifestyle is fast, but people still like good food. New food preparation methods have given us is more choices. Today we can prepare food that is more convenient, healthier, and of greater variety than ever before in history.

▼

4	PR	It has been said, "Not everything that is learned is contained in books." Compare and contrast knowledge gained from experience with knowledge gained from books. In your opinion, which source is more important? Why?

"Experience is the best teacher" is an old cliché, but I agree with it. We can learn a lot of important things from books, but the most important lessons in life come from our own experiences. Throughout the different stages of life, from primary school to university to adulthood, experience teaches us many skills we need for life.

As children in primary school, we learn facts and information from books, but that is not all we learn in school. On the playground we learn how to make friends. In our class work, we learn how it feels to succeed and what we do when we fail. We start to learn about the things we like to do and the things we don't. We don't learn these things from books, but from our experiences with our friends and classmates.

In our university classes, we learn a lot of information and skills we will need for our future careers, but we also learn a lot that is not in our textbooks. In our daily lives both in class and out of class, we learn to make decisions for ourselves. We learn to take on responsibilities. We learn to get along with our classmates, our roommates, and our workmates. Our successes and failures help us develop skills we will need in our adult lives. They are skills that no book can teach us.

Throughout our adulthood, experience remains a constant teacher. We may continue to read or take classes for professional development. However, our experiences at work, at home, and with our friends teach us more. The triumphs and disasters of our lives teach us how to improve our careers and also how to improve our relationships and how to be the person each one of us wants to be.

Books teach us a lot, but there is a limit to what they teach. They can give us information or show us another person's experiences. These are valuable things, but the lessons we learn from our own experiences, from childhood through adulthood, are the most important ones we learn.

▼

5	PR	A company has announced that it wishes to build a large factory near your community. Discuss the advantages and disadvantages of this new influence on your community. Do you support or oppose the factory? Explain your position.

People like factories because they bring new jobs to a community. In my opinion, however, the benefits of a factory are outweighed by the risks. Factories cause pollution and they bring too much growth. In addition, they destroy the quiet lifestyle of a small town. That is why I oppose a plan to build a factory near my community.

Factories cause smog. If we build a new factory, the air we breathe will become dirty. Everything will be covered with dust. Factories also pollute rivers and streams. Our water will be too dirty to drink. The environment will be hurt and people's health will be affected by a factory.

Some people will say that more jobs will be created by a factory. However, this can have a negative result. Our population will grow quickly. Many new homes and stores will be built. There will be a lot of traffic on the roads. Fast growth can cause more harm than good.

Our city will change a lot. It is a pleasant place now. It is safe and quiet. Everybody knows everybody else. If a factory brings growth to the city, all of this will change. The small-town feel will be lost.

A factory would be helpful in some ways, but the dangers outweigh the benefits. Our city would be changed too much by a factory. I cannot support a plan to build a new factory here.

▼

6	MA	If you could change one important thing about your hometown, what would you change? Use reasons and specific examples to support your answer.

If I could change one thing about my hometown, I think it would be the fact that there is no sense of community here. People don't feel connected, they don't look out for each other, and they don't get to know their neighbors.

People here don't feel connected to the community. They come and go a lot. They change jobs frequently and move on. This means that they don't put down roots in the community. They don't join community organizations and they don't get involved in community issues. They don't participate in the schools or try to beautify the neighborhoods. They don't feel like community members.

People don't try to support others around them. They don't watch out for each others' children or check in on elderly neighbors. They may not know if a neighbor loses a loved one. There's not a lot of community support for individuals.

Neighbors don't get to know each other. When neighbors go on vacation, no one watches their house for them. When neighbors' children ride their bikes through someone's garden, there's no casual, friendly way of mentioning the problem. A simple problem becomes a major disagreement.

My hometown is a nice place to live in many ways, but it would be much nicer if we had that sense of community.

▼

7	EX	How do movies or television influence people's behavior? Use reasons and specific examples to support your answer.

Television is a big influence in the lives of most of us. We spend hours every week watching television programs, so of course this will affect our behavior. Unfortunately, the effect of television is usually negative. Television makes people more violent, more inactive, and less imaginative.

Many programs and movies on television are violent. The more we see violence on television, the less sensitive we become to it. Eventually violence doesn't seem wrong. This is especially true because violence on television doesn't seem to have consequences. Actors can be killed and come back for another movie. Sometimes we confuse that with reality and we forget that killing someone is permanent.

Watching television makes us less active. The act of watching television requires almost no activity on the part of the watcher. We just turn it on and change the channels. In addition, all the time that we spend in front of the television is time that we are not spending moving around, playing a sport, or taking a walk.

When we watch television, we don't exercise our imagination. All the stories are told for us. We don't even have to imagine what a character or a place looks like because everything is shown to us. When we have television, we don't have to invent a way to spend a few free moments. We just turn on the television and watch.

Television is a big influence in modern life and it can be a valuable educational tool. The other side of television, however, is that it has a strong negative effect on our behavior, encouraging us to accept violence and to be inactive and unimaginative.

▼

8	AD	Do you agree or disagree with the following statement? Television has destroyed communication among friends and family. Use specific reasons and examples to support your opinions.

Some people believe that television has destroyed communication among friends and family. In my opinion, however, the opposite is true. Television can increase communication. News and other information we see on TV gives us things to discuss with our friends and family. TV also helps us understand each other better because we all have access to the same TV programs. Finally, TV can help us share our interests with other people.

Television programs give us things to think and talk about. These days it is always possible to hear up-to-the minute news every time we turn on the television. We hear about things happening all around the world that directly affect our lives. Everybody has opinions about these things and everybody wants to discuss their opinions with other people. So, TV news and information programs encourage us to discuss our ideas with our friends and family.

No matter what city you live in, you have access to the same TV programs as people in other parts of the country. When you go to a new city to work, study, or take a vacation, you will already have something in common with the people there. When you meet new people, you will probably be familiar with at least some of the same TV programs. This gives you something to talk about and a way to begin new friendships.

Most people use TV as a way to pursue their interests. People who play sports usually like to watch sports on TV. People who like to cook watch cooking shows. If your friends and family watch some of the same programs as you do, they can learn more about the things that interest you. This is an excellent form of communication that helps people understand each other better.

TV is a tool that gives us access to information, entertainment, and education. When we watch programs that interest us, we want to share this interest with other people. That is why I believe TV encourages communication among people.

▼

9	PR	Some people prefer to live in a small town. Others prefer to live in a big city. Which place would you prefer to live in? Use specific reasons and details to support your answer.

I grew up in a small town and then moved to a big city. I didn't think I would like living here, but I was wrong. I think life is much better in a big city. Transportation is much more convenient, everything is more exciting, and there is a greater variety of people. I can't imagine ever living in a small town again.

Transportation is easier in a city. In a small town, you have to have a car to get around because there isn't any kind of public transportation. In a city, on the other hand, there are usually buses and taxis, and some cities have subways. Cities often have heavy traffic and expensive parking, but it doesn't matter because you can always take the bus. Using public transportation is usually cheaper and more convenient than driving a car, but you don't have this choice in a small town.

City life is more exciting than small town life. In small towns usually nothing changes. You see the same people every day, you go to the same two or three restaurants, everything is the same. In a city things change all the time. You see new people everyday. There are many restaurants, with new ones to choose from all the time. New plays come to the theaters and new musicians come to the concert halls.

Cities have a diversity of people that you don't find in a small town. There are much fewer people in a small town and usually they are all alike. In a city you can find people from different countries, of different religions, of different races—you can find all kinds of people. This variety of people is what makes city life interesting.

Life in a city is convenient, exciting, and interesting. After experiencing city life, I could never live in a small town again.

▼

| 10 | AD | "When people succeed, it is because of hard work. Luck has nothing to do with success." Do you agree or disagree with the quotation above? Use specific reasons and examples to explain your position. |

When people succeed, it is because of hard work, but luck has a lot to do with it, too. Luck is often the final factor that turns years of working hard into success. Luck has helped people invent and discover things, it has helped people become famous, and it has helped people get jobs.

Many people have discovered or invented things with the help of luck. Columbus worked hard for years to prepare for his trip around the world. Many thought he was crazy, but still he was able to get support for his endeavor. He worked hard to be able to make his trip to India, but it was because of luck that he actually found the Americas.

Luck can help people become famous. Consider movie stars. Many work hard to learn how to act. They take acting classes. They work at small, low-paying jobs in order to gain experience. Then one day a lucky actor may be given a certain part in a movie, and he gets noticed for it. Or he meets a movie director at the right time and place. Years of hard work bring him close to success, but that one lucky chance finally helps him succeed.

Because of luck, many people find jobs. A person may spend weeks writing and sending off résumés, looking at help wanted ads, and going on job interviews. But often it is because of luck that a job hunter meets the person who will give him or her a job, or hears of an opportunity that isn't advertised in the newspaper. Being in the right place at the right time is often what gets a person a job, and that is all about luck.

It is certainly difficult to be successful without hard work, but hard work also needs to be helped by a little luck. Luck has helped many people, both famous and ordinary, become successful. I think that luck and hard work go hand in hand.

▼

| 11 | AD | Do you agree or disagree with the following statement? Universities should give the same amount of money to their students' sports activities as they give to their university libraries. Use specific reasons and examples to support your opinion. |

I disagree strongly with the idea that the same amount of money should go to university sports activities as to university libraries. Although playing sports is an important part of education, libraries are fundamental. Students cannot study without them and they require a lot of financial support to maintain up-to-date technology, to keep new books and magazines on the shelves, and to keep them operating.

Students need up-to-date library facilities to get a good education. They need computerized programs and access to Internet research databases. It costs money to have these things available, but they are fundamental to education. If a university offers its students only resources of a decade ago, it deprives those students of a tremendous amount of information.

Although we get a lot of information from computers and the Internet, university libraries still need to maintain a complete book and magazine collection. Every day new information is published on every subject, and every university wants to have this information available to its students. Again, this requires money.

It also costs money for universities to operate their libraries. University libraries are usually open for long hours and during this time they use heat and electricity. Most important, a university library needs a well-educated, knowledgeable staff. In order to be able to hire the best people, they have to be able to pay good salaries.

University students are only going to benefit from their education if they can get all the tools they need to learn. Sports are secondary to the resources that students need from university libraries. For this reason, libraries should always be better funded than sports activities.

▼

| 12 | EX | Many people visit museums when they travel to new places. Why do you think people visit museums? Use specific reasons and examples to support your answer. |

People visit museums for a number of reasons. They visit museums when traveling to new places because a museum tells them a lot about the culture of those places. They also go to museums to have fun. People also are usually interested in museums that feature unusual subjects. It's impossible to get bored in a museum.

When visiting someplace new, you can find out about the culture of that place in many ways. The easiest way to learn about a culture, though, is by visiting its museums. Museums will show you the history of the place you're visiting. They'll show you what art the locals think is important. If there aren't any museums, that tells you something, too.

Museums are fun. Even if you're not interested in art or history, there is always something to get your attention. Many museums now have what they call "hands-on" exhibits. These exhibits have activities such as pushing a button to hear more about what you're looking at, or creating your own work of art. Everyone, from child to adult, enjoys these hands-on activities in museums.

People also enjoy visiting museums about unusual subjects. For instance, in my hometown there's a museum devoted to the potato. This museum has art made out of potatoes. It also tells the history of the potato, and sells unusual items such as potato dolls. People enjoy visiting this museum because it is so unusual. There is no other place like it.

People everywhere like museums. They like learning about interesting and unusual things. No matter who you are or what you like, there is a museum that will amaze and interest you.

▼

| 13 | PR | Some people prefer to eat at food stands or restaurants. Other people prefer to prepare and eat food at home. Which do you prefer? Use specific reasons and examples to support your answer. |

Although many people prefer to eat at restaurants because it is easier than cooking at home, I prefer to prepare food at home. I believe it is much cheaper and healthier to eat at home, and it can be more convenient, too.

While eating in restaurants is fast, the money you spend can add up. When I have dinner at a restaurant, the bill is usually $25 or more. I can buy a lot of groceries with that much money. Even lunch at a food stand can easily cost seven or eight dollars. That's enough to feed the whole family at home.

Eating at home is better for you, too. Meals at restaurants are often high in fat and calories. When you cook at home, however, you can control what you eat. You can cook with low-fat and low-calorie ingredients. Restaurants also often serve big plates of food. You may eat a full plate of food at a restaurant "because you paid for it," while at home you can control your portion size. You can serve yourself as little as you want.

It may seem more convenient to eat at a restaurant because you don't have to shop, cook, or clean up. All you do is eat. Cooking at home, however, can actually be more convenient. There are lots of simple meals that don't take long to prepare. In addition, when you eat at home, you don't have to drive to the restaurant, look for a parking space, wait for a table, and wait for service.

People often choose to eat at restaurants because it seems more convenient. I find, however, that cooking at home is actually easier, and it is cheaper and healthier as well.

▼

14	MA	Some people believe that university students should be required to attend classes. Others believe that going to classes should be optional for students. Which point of view do you agree with? Use specific reasons and details to support your answer.

Some people believe that going to classes should be optional for university students, but I disagree. Students learn a lot more in classes than they can learn from books. In class they have the advantage of learning from the teacher, of interacting with their classmates, and of developing the responsibility it takes to be a good student.

When students attend class, they receive the benefit of the teacher's knowledge. The best teachers do more than just go over the material in the class textbook. They draw their students into discussion of the material. They present opposing points of view. They provide additional information by inviting guest speakers or showing documentary films.

Going to class also teaches students how to work with other people. In class, students have to present their ideas to their classmates. They have to defend their ideas if their classmates disagree with them, but still remain friendly when the discussion is over. They have to learn to work in groups to complete class projects.

Attending classes teaches students responsibility. Having to be at a particular place at a particular time prepares them for getting a job. Having to complete assignments on time also helps develop responsibility.

Anyone can get information from books, but students get a great many more advantages when they attend class. They get the benefit of the teacher's knowledge and experience, and even more than that, they learn how to work with others and to develop a sense of responsibility. These are not optional skills in life, so attending classes should not be optional at a university.

▼

15	MA	Neighbors are the people who live near us. In your opinion, what are the qualities of a good neighbor? Use specific details and examples in your answer.

There are several qualities that a good neighbor has. If you have a good neighbor, you are a lucky person. You have someone who is respectful of your property, who is helpful with the little day-to-day problems that arise, and who is supportive in times of crisis.

A good neighbor respects your property. This means she asks for your permission before doing something that may affect you. She doesn't plant a huge tree between your houses without asking you how you feel about it. If she wants to put up a fence, she tells you about her plans first.

A good neighbor is willing to lend a hand when you need a little help. He lends you some milk if you run out, or gives you a ride if your car breaks down. He lets your children stay at his house if you get stuck working overtime. You do the same for him. Both of you help make each other's lives easier.

When you go through a crisis, like a death in the family, a good neighbor volunteers to help in any way she can. She might do something small, like prepare a few meals for you. Or, she might do something big, like help you get through the sadness of a funeral.

A neighbor can be as close as a good friend, or more like a distant acquaintance. Either way, a good neighbor is someone who respects you and supports you as he can. We should all be lucky enough to have good neighbors.

▼

16	PR	It has recently been announced that a new restaurant may be built in your neighborhood. Do you support or oppose this plan? Why? Use specific reasons and details to support your answer.

II can see both advantages and disadvantages to having a new restaurant built in our neighborhood. I believe, however, that the disadvantages outweigh the advantages. A new restaurant would bring more traffic problems to the area. In addition, it could attract undesirable people. Most of all, I think there are other types of business that would be more beneficial to the neighborhood.

Traffic congestion is already a problem in our neighborhood. Our streets are too narrow for the traffic we have now. A new restaurant would just bring more traffic. In addition, it is difficult to find parking on our streets, especially on weekend evenings. Unless it had its own parking lot, a new restaurant would make it even harder for residents to find places to park their cars.

I'm also concerned about the type of patrons the new restaurant would bring into our neighborhood. If the restaurant serves drinks and has dancing, there could be problems. The restaurant would stay open late and people leaving the restaurant might be drunk. They could be noisy too. This is not the kind of thing I want to see in my neighborhood.

Finally, there are other types of businesses that we need in our neighborhood more. We already have a restaurant and a couple of coffee shops. But we don't have a bookstore or a pharmacy, and we have only one small grocery store. I would prefer to see one of these businesses established here rather than another restaurant. Any one of them would be more useful to the residents and would maintain the quiet atmosphere of our streets.

A new restaurant could disrupt the quiet lifestyle of our neighborhood. It might bring jobs, but it would also bring traffic and noise, and it would use space that might be better used for another type of business. This is why I would oppose a plan for a new restaurant.

▼

17	PR	Some people think that they can learn better by themselves than with a teacher. Others think that it is always better to have a teacher. Which do you prefer? Use specific reasons to develop your essay.

Most people can learn to do something simple on their own with just a set of instructions. However, to learn about something more complex, it's always best to have a teacher. Teachers help you find the way you learn best. They help you stay focused on what you're learning. They provide you with a wider range of information than you might find on your own. In short, teachers provide you with a lot more support and knowledge than you can usually get by yourself.

Teachers can help students learn in the way that is best for each student because teachers understand that different people have different learning styles. For example, some students learn better by discussing a topic. Others learn more by writing about it. A teacher can help you follow your learning style, while a book can give you only one way of learning something.

Teachers help you focus on what you are learning. They can help keep you from becoming distracted. They can show you the most important points in a lesson that you have to understand. If you study on your own, it might be difficult to keep your attention on the material, or to know which parts are most important.

Teachers bring their own knowledge and understanding of the topic to the lesson. A book presents you with certain information, and the teacher can add more. The teacher might also have a different point of view from the book, and can provide other sources of information and ideas, as well.

There is nothing wrong with studying on your own. For the best possible learning, though, a teacher is the biggest help you can have.

▼

18	MA	What are some important qualities of a good supervisor (boss)? Use specific details and examples to explain why these qualities are important.

Even though job situations can be very different, there are several qualities that all good supervisors have in common. A good supervisor treats her employees fairly. She gives clear directions. Most important of all, she acts as a good example for her employees.

A good supervisor is fair. She treats all her employees with equal respect and doesn't have favorites. She uses the same set of criteria to evaluate each employee's performance. She doesn't let her personal feelings about an individual influence her treatment of him.

A good supervisor gives clear and understandable directions. She doesn't constantly change her mind about what she wants employees to do. She also doesn't get angry when an employee is confused and needs more explanation.

Finally, a good supervisor sets the standards for her employees by her own behavior. She works hard and acts responsibly and gets her work done on time. She can only expect her employees to act professionally if she acts professionally, too.

Employees are more likely to do the best job they can when they are treated fairly, given good directions, and have a good example in front of them. This is why good supervisors are so important to the success of any type of business.

▼

19	MA	Should governments spend more money on improving roads and highways, or should governments spend more money on improving public transportation (buses, trains, subways)? Why? Use specific reasons and details to develop your essay.

Governments should definitely spend more money on improving all forms of public transportation. The widespread use of private cars has contributed to some serious problems in society, including depletion of natural resources, increased pollution, and the loss of a sense of community. By encouraging the use of public transportation, governments can do a lot to counteract these problems.

Cars depend on oil and gasoline, which are nonrenewable resources. Once we have used them up, they are gone forever. Every time a person gets into a private car to go to work, to the store, or anywhere, gasoline is used up just to take one person to one place. The more people drive their cars, the more resources are used up. When people use public transportation, on the other hand, less oil and gasoline are used up per person.

Cars cause pollution. Every time a person drives his car somewhere, more pollution is put into the air. In many big cities, the high amount of air pollution causes health problems for the residents. Public transportation means fewer cars on the road, and that means less pollution.

Cars tend to isolate people from each other. When a person uses a private car, he is alone or only with people that he already knows. He doesn't have the opportunity to see other people or talk to them or feel that he is part of a larger community. When he uses public transportation, however, he is surrounded by neighbors and other fellow city residents. He has a chance to be with people he might not otherwise see, and maybe even to get to know them a little.

Environmental problems and increased isolation are some of the most serious problems of modern society. Encouraging the use of public transportation is one way governments can work against these problems and start creating a better world.

▼

| 20 | AD | It is better for children to grow up in the countryside than in a big city. Do you agree or disagree? Use specific reasons and examples to develop your essay. |

I have to disagree that it is better for children to grow up in the countryside. In the countryside, children have limited opportunities to see and learn about things. In the city, on the other hand, they are exposed to many different things. They see all kinds of different people every day. They have opportunities to attend many cultural events. They see people working in different kinds of jobs and therefore can make better choices for their own future. Growing up in the city is definitely better.

All different kinds of people live in the city, while in a small town in the countryside people are often all the same. City people come from other parts of the country or even from other countries. They are of different races and religions. When children grow up in this situation, they have the opportunity to learn about and understand different kinds of people. This is an important part of their education.

In the city, there are many opportunities to attend cultural events, whereas such opportunities are usually limited in the countryside. In the city there are movies and theaters, museums, zoos, and concerts. In the city children can attend cultural events every weekend, or even more often. This is also an important part of their education.

People in the city work in different kinds of jobs, while in the countryside there often isn't a variety of job opportunities. People in the city work at all different types and levels of professions, as well as in factories, in service jobs, and more. Children growing up in the city learn that there is a wide variety of jobs they can choose from when they grow up. They have a greater possibility of choosing a career that they will enjoy and do well in. This is perhaps the most important part of their education.

People usually move to the city because there are more opportunities there. Children who grow up in the city have these opportunities from the time they are small. The city is definitely a better place for children to grow up.

▼

| 21 | MA | In general, people are living longer now. Discuss the causes of this phenomenon. Use specific reasons and details to develop your essay. |

People are living to be much older these days for a number of reasons. The main reasons are greater access to health care, improved health care, and better nutrition.

Basic health care is available to more people now. When someone is seriously ill, he or she can go to a public hospital. There are also more clinics and doctors than there used to be. Years ago, health care wasn't available to everyone. Some people didn't live near a doctor or hospital and others couldn't pay for the care they needed.

People also live longer because the quality of health care has improved. Doctors now know more about diseases and cures. Years ago, people died young because of simple things such as an infection or a virus. Now we have antibiotics and other medicines to help cure infections.

The quality of nutrition has improved also. We eat more healthfully than we used to. We know that eating low-fat food can prevent heart disease, and we know that eating fruits and vegetables can prevent cancer.

Improved health care and healthy eating habits allow us to live longer. Now we need to make sure that everyone in the world has these benefits.

▼

| 22 | MA | We all work or will work in jobs with many different kinds of people. In your opinion, what are some important characteristics of a co-worker (someone you work closely with)? Use reasons and specific examples to explain why these characteristics are important. |

I've worked in several offices, and I've found there are certain characteristics that all good co-workers have in common. They tend to be cooperative people, they adapt well to changes, and they are helpful to others in the office. People who have these characteristics are easy to work with.

A good co-worker is very cooperative. She does her best to get along with others. She tries to do her part well because she knows that if one person doesn't get her work done, it affects everyone else. She also has a positive attitude that creates a pleasant working environment.

A good co-worker is adaptable. She is not stubborn about changes in schedules or routines. She doesn't object to having her job description revised. She has no problem with new procedures and welcomes changes when they come.

A good co-worker is helpful. She helps out when someone falls behind in his or her work. She is willing to change her schedule to accommodate another worker's emergency. She doesn't keep track of how often she has to take on extra work.

We spend more time with our co-workers during the week than we do with our family. Thus, it's important for our co-workers to be people we can get along with. When co-workers are cooperative, adaptable, and helpful, everyone gets along better and can get their job done well.

▼

| 23 | MA | In some countries, teenagers have jobs while they are still students. Do you think this is a good idea? Support your opinion by using specific reasons and details. |

I don't think it is a good idea for teenagers to have jobs while they are still students. It can interfere with their studies, it can disrupt their home life, and it takes away part of their childhood that they can never replace.

A job can interfere with a teenager's schoolwork. Education today is very complex and difficult. In order to learn and get good grades, a student must work very hard and concentrate. This means attending classes for most of the day, then doing research for projects, then going home and doing homework. It is very difficult to do all this and have a job, too.

Having a job can also disrupt a teenager's home life. If a teenager has a job to go to after school, he won't be home for dinner. He won't be home after dinner either, and may not get home until late at night. This means he doesn't have much time to spend with his family. Teenagers may be almost grown up, but they still need the companionship and support they get from their families.

The main drawback of a teenager having a job is that he misses out on the fun of being young. He has a whole lifetime ahead of him in which he'll have to earn a living. This is the last free time he'll have. It's the last chance he'll have to hang out with friends and just enjoy himself. Soon enough he'll have to start worrying about paying the rent and buying food.

Jobs bring money, but money isn't everything. For a teenager it is important to concentrate on his studies, spend time with his family, and enjoy being young. A teenager with a job gives up too much.

▼

24	EX	A person you know is planning to move to your town or city. What do you think that person would like and dislike about living in your town or city. Why? Use specific reasons and details to develop your essay.

A friend of mine from college is moving to my city. I think there are things she will like about living here, but there are also things she might dislike. I like living here because there are a lot of things to do, there are a lot of nice neighborhoods to live in, and we have beautiful parks. On the other hand, my friend might not like it because it's very crowded and expensive and we're far from beautiful places like the mountains and the beach.

Living in this city is very exciting because there are so many interesting things to do, although you pay a price for it. We have museums, art galleries, and lots of movie theaters. We have restaurants with food from all over the world. However, when you go to these places they are always very crowded. Also, there is almost always heavy traffic on the way and it is difficult to find parking once you arrive. I know my friend likes peace and quiet, so she may not enjoy the crowds in my city.

In this city we have many beautiful neighborhoods, although some of them are very expensive. We have neighborhoods of old houses with interesting architecture. We have more modern neighborhoods with new apartment buildings. We have lots of nice places to live, but it isn't always easy to find a place that you can afford. I know my friend doesn't earn a big salary, so she might not like this aspect of living here.

Even though we are far from the countryside, we have many beautiful, natural areas right here in the city. We have a big park where people go hiking and biking, and in the winter they go ice skating. We also have many small parks throughout the city and lots of trees and gardens. It is a pretty city and I know my friend will like that. However, we are far from the mountains and far from the beach. I know my friend likes to spend time in the countryside, so she might not like living far away from those places.

All in all, there are both advantages and disadvantages to living here. My friend will have to decide if she prefers excitement and crowds or quiet and nature before she makes her final decision about moving here.

▼

| 25 | PR | It has recently been announced that a large shopping center may be built in your neighborhood. Do you support or oppose this plan? Why? Use specific reasons and details to support your answer. |

There would be both advantages and disadvantages to having a shopping center built in my neighborhood. Overall, however, I think the advantages are greater. One important advantage would be convenience. In addition, a shopping center would give neighborhood residents more choices for shopping and entertainment and it would bring jobs to the area, too.

It would be very convenient to have a shopping center in the neighborhood. Shopping would be easier and faster because I wouldn't have to drive great distances to get to the stores. Also, all the stores would be together, so I would only have to go to one place.

A shopping center would mean more choices. There would be more stores selling different products. There would probably also be restaurants and food courts, so we would have a greater variety of places to eat. The shopping center might have a movie theater, too.

Having a shopping center built in the neighborhood would also mean more jobs for the community. Initially, these jobs would be in the building of the center. Later, the jobs would be in the stores, theaters, and food establishments.

I can see some disadvantages to building a shopping center here. On the whole, though, I think my neighborhood should support having a shopping center here. It would be a big convenience, it would give us variety in our shopping and entertainment, and it would create jobs for area residents.

▼

| 26 | PR | It has recently been announced that a new movie theater may be built in your neighborhood. Do you support or oppose this plan? Why? Use specific reasons and details to support your answer. |

Some people will say that a new movie theater in our neighborhood would be a bad thing. However, I fully support the plan to build one. I feel that a movie theater would provide more opportunities for entertainment, reduce teenage delinquency, and bring more business to our town.

A movie theater would provide a much needed source of entertainment to our area. Right now, there is little to do in my town. There is almost nowhere to go in the evenings, and the nearest place that has movie theaters and restaurants is thirty minutes away. If we build a movie theater here, we can enjoy evenings right in our own neighborhood.

A movie theater would reduce juvenile delinquency. Like everywhere else, teenagers here are bored. They need activities to keep them busy and out of trouble. A movie theatre would not only provide them with entertainment, it would also be a source of jobs for them. We need more businesses that want to employ young people, and a movie theater is the perfect sort of business for that.

A movie theater would attract more business to our town. People who come from other towns to use our movie theater would also shop in our stores. New stores and restaurants might open because there would be more customers for them. Our town could become more prosperous, and more interesting, too.

I believe our town would benefit greatly from a new movie theater. It would make life here more interesting and could make us more prosperous. I fully support the plan and hope that others in the neighborhood will join me to convince residents and local governments.

▼

27	AD	Do you agree or disagree with the following statement? People should sometimes do things that they do **not** enjoy doing. Use specific reasons and examples to support your answer.

I agree that people should sometimes do things that they don't enjoy doing. This is a basic part of life. There are many small things we have to do in both our personal and professional lives that we may not enjoy, but that are part of our responsibilities. In addition, sometimes by doing things we don't enjoy, we actually learn to like them.

Most people's personal lives are filled with tasks that they don't enjoy doing, but they do them anyway. Who likes going to the doctor or dentist, for example? But we do this because we know that it is important to take care of our health. I don't know many people who like changing the oil in their cars or mowing the lawn. We do these things, however, because we understand that we need to maintain our personal property.

Similarly, our professional lives are filled with tasks that are not fun, but that are necessary parts of our jobs. No one likes to do boring assignments or to work with someone who no one else likes. If we're in management, we may sometimes have to fire someone. No one likes to do things like these, but if they are part of our professional responsibilities, we have to do them.

On the other hand, sometimes doing something we don't enjoy can lead to enjoyment. Simply by trying it again, we may decide we like doing it. For instance, we may think we hate to dance. We agree to go to a club only to please someone else. Yet, for some reason, this time we enjoy dancing. The same can be true of trying new foods or going to a new type of museum.

Not everything in life is fun. Unpleasant or boring tasks are a necessary part of life. We don't like them, but we do them anyway. And sometimes they surprise us and turn into something enjoyable.

▼

28	AD	Do you agree or disagree with the following statement? Television, newspapers, magazines, and other media pay too much attention to the personal lives of famous people such as public figures and celebrities. Use specific reasons and details to explain your opinion.

I think the media pay too much attention to the private lives of famous people. They discover things that happened years ago and report them as if they still mattered. They publicize things about famous people's lives that are really private, personal matters. They put out information that could end up having a bad effect on a person's family and personal life. They do this just to entertain the public, but I don't find it entertaining at all.

The media like to dig up bad information about the past actions of famous people. They find out that a person took drugs when he was young, or that someone was a reckless driver and caused a bad accident. Then a person in her forties has to explain something that she did when she was fifteen. I don't understand how something that happened so long ago could have any interest or importance now.

The media says that the public has the right to know about the private actions of famous people. They say it is our right to know if someone had an extramarital affair or didn't pay back some money that he owed. I say these are personal matters. We respect the privacy of ordinary people and we should do the same for famous people.

The media seem to report these things without considering what might happen as a result. Reporting on a celebrity's personal affairs could have an effect on that person's family, especially the children. A celebrity's good name and credibility could be ruined before he or she can prove that the rumors are false. A person's entire career could be ruined by something that is reported in the media.

Having details of one's personal life reported in public can have all sorts of negative consequences on a person's life. Ordinary people don't have to suffer this sort of attention, and I see no reason why celebrities should either.

▼

| 29 | MA | Some people believe that the Earth is being harmed (damaged) by human activity. Others feel that human activity makes the Earth a better place to live. What is your opinion? Use specific reasons and examples to support your answer. |

The quality of human life has improved greatly over the past few centuries, but Earth is being harmed more and more by human activity. As we develop our technology, we use more and more natural resources and cause more and more pollution. As our population grows, we destroy more and more natural areas in order to expand towns and cities. The Earth is being harmed, and this harms people as well.

We often act as if we have unlimited natural resources, but this isn't true. If we cut down too many trees to build houses and make paper, not all the trees will grow back. If we catch too many fish, the fish population will get smaller and smaller. If we aren't careful about how we use our natural resources, we will lose many of them. We are already losing some.

We don't seem to pay attention to the amount of pollution human activity can cause. Our cars pollute the air. Our factories pollute both the air and the water. We throw our waste into rivers and streams. We act as if the air and water can clean themselves up, but they can't.

As urban populations grow, the cities grow too, taking over more and more land. New houses, stores, and office buildings are built all the time. Land that was once forest or farms is now parking lots and apartment buildings. We seem to act as if we have unlimited land, but we don't. We need to plan more carefully so that we use our limited land in the best way possible.

People need to respect the Earth and try to preserve it. If we don't, we will lose all the natural resources that we depend on for life. Then what will happen?

▼

| 30 | PR | It has recently been announced that a new high school may be built in your neighborhood. Do you support or oppose this plan? Why? Use specific reasons and details in your answer. |

I oppose having a new high school built in my neighborhood. I don't think there is a real need for one. I think it would cause traffic problems in our area, and it would mean that we would lose the use of our beautiful neighborhood park. I don't think a high school would be of any benefit to us at all.

First of all, there are very few teenagers in our neighborhood. Most of the residents here are either retired or are young couples with babies and small children. This means that most of the high school students would come from other parts of town, but that the majority of the people who live here would not benefit.

Second, a high school would cause a lot of traffic. Most of the students would live too far away to walk to school, so they would come by car or school bus. In addition to the traffic on regular school days, there would be even more traffic after school and on weekends for sports events, school drama productions, and other school activities. This would disrupt the quiet life style of our neighborhood.

Finally, everyone in the neighborhood would be upset by the loss of the park, which is the site that has been selected for the high school. Parents take their small children to the park every day to play. Older people like to walk there in the evenings after dinner. On weekends, people enjoy having picnics and playing games in the park. We would be sorry to lose our neighborhood park.

Our town may need a new high school, but our neighborhood is not the right place for it. We don't want our quiet lifestyle disrupted, and most people in this area have no need for a high school, anyway.

▼

| 31 | PR | Some people spend their entire lives in one place. Others move a number of times throughout their lives, looking for a better job, house, community, or even climate. Which do you prefer: staying in one place or moving in search of another place? Use reasons and specific examples to support your opinion. |

Even though I have lived in the same house, in the same neighborhood, in the same city my entire life, I know I would be happy living in a variety of places. Moving would expose me to new people, new weather, and new housing.

Even if I moved to another part of my own city, I would encounter new people. Each neighborhood has a distinct personality. If I moved to a new neighborhood, I would meet the shopkeepers and residents that shape that neighborhood's personality. It would be a new experience for me and I could become part of a new community.

If I want to experience a different kind of climate, I would have to move far from my city. Where I live now, it is the same temperature all year. I would like to go to a place where there are four seasons so I can experience really cold weather. I would like to walk in the snow and learn winter sports such as skiing.

Now I live with my parents in their house. It is a one-story house built around a courtyard where we spend a lot of time. If I could move to a different kind of house, I would like to live in an apartment on a very high floor so I could see all around me. I could also meet my neighbors on the elevator and we could get together for coffee in my apartment.

I like to have variety in my life. I like to have the opportunity to get to know different kinds of people and see new places. I can go far away to do this, or I can do it close to where I live now. Either way, I think it is important to experience a variety of places and people, and I want to do this while I am still young.

▼

32	MA	Is it better to enjoy your money when you earn it, or is it better to save your money for some time in the future? Use specific reasons and examples to support your opinion.

When I have a choice between spending money or putting it in my savings account at the bank, I always put it in the bank. I will have a lot of expenses in the future, like my education, travel, and unforeseen emergencies. I need to set money aside for these expenses.

Education is expensive. I can't depend on my parents to pay all my bills. I have tuition, room and board, books, and incidental expenses to pay for. My parents help me, but I have to pay part of it. If I spend my money now, I won't be able to pay for my education.

Travel is also very expensive. I don't mean vacation travel. I mean travel to and from school, because my school is far from home. First I have to get to school, then, of course, I want to return to my family for important festivals and family occasions. I need to save money for these trips.

Emergencies could arrive at any moment. I might have an unexpected illness while I am at school. One of my family members may need help and I will have to send them money. You can't predict emergencies like these, but you can be prepared. I need to save money for these emergencies.

When you are not rich, you cannot spend your money carelessly. You must plan ahead. I know I will have expenses for my schooling and for traveling to and from home. I know that I will also have unexpected expenses from time to time. I must be prepared. I need to save money for these events.

▼

| 33 | PR | You have received a gift of money. The money is enough to buy either a piece of jewelry you like or tickets to a concert you want to attend. Which would you buy? Use specific reasons and details to support your answer. |

The choice between spending money on tickets to a concert or spending money on jewelry is an easy one. Given this choice, I would buy jewelry. The reasons are obvious. Jewelry is an investment, it is permanent, and it is fashionable.

Jewelry is a very good investment. It is a good idea for everyone to own some gold jewelry because its value increases every year. In addition, if you have a financial problem, you can always sell your jewelry to get the money you need. You could not sell your used concert ticket.

Jewelry, unless you sell it, is permanent. You always have it to wear. Each time you put it on, you will remember the day you bought it. It will give you pleasure for years and years. You could not wear the ticket stub from the concert.

Jewelry is very fashionable. I would feel very smart wearing a beautiful gold bracelet or diamond pin. People would comment and tell me how much they love my jewelry. They would compliment me on my good taste.

I would feel very rich with my jewelry. I would have a good investment that is permanent and fashionable. Then, when someone invites me to a concert (and pays for my ticket), I will have something beautiful to wear.

▼

| 34 | AD | Businesses should hire employees for their entire lives. Do you agree or disagree? Use specific reasons and examples to support your answer. |

In some business cultures, it is the practice to hire workers when they are young and employ them until they retire. In other business cultures, companies hire people to do a job and then fire them when they are not needed. I agree with the latter position. In today's economy it is not important to hire employees for their entire lives. The important considerations for companies are an employee's performance, speed, and ability to change. Loyalty is not a consideration.

Today there is a lot of competition so we need to hire workers who can perform their jobs well. We need to find skilled workers who can do a job without a lot of extra training. We need to match the job to the worker, and if the job changes, we change the worker.

Because of competition, we also need to be able to produce our goods and services quickly. We need young people who are aggressive and will push themselves to do their job faster. We need young people who are willing to work long hours.

In order to compete, we have to be able to change to meet the changing demands of the market. By changing our workforce frequently, we can bring in new ideas. By hiring young workers, we get fresh points of view.

Although a feeling of loyalty between a company and its workers is a noble idea, it is not practical today. A company needs to keep up with the changing forces of the economy. In order to be able to do this, it needs to be able to change its workforce as necessary.

▼

35	AD	Do you agree or disagree with the following statement? Attending a live performance (for example, a play, concert, or sporting event) is more enjoyable than watching the same event on television. Use specific reasons and examples to support your opinion.

Some people think that attending a live performance is preferable to watching it on television. I say, however, that if you have a good TV, it is much better to watch a performance that way. It is much more convenient and comfortable, and it is cheaper, too. I almost never attend a live performance of anything.

It is much more convenient to stay home and watch a performance on TV. I don't have to go anywhere. I don't have to worry about leaving the house on time. I don't have to worry about traffic or parking. I don't have to stand on line for a ticket. I just turn on the television at the time the event begins, sit back, and enjoy myself.

It is much more comfortable to watch a performance at home. I can wear any clothes that I want to. I know I will have a good seat with a good view. I can get up and get a snack at any time. I can relax and enjoy myself in the comfort of my own home.

It is much cheaper to watch a performance on TV. I don't have to buy a ticket. I don't have to pay for parking or for dinner at a restaurant before the performance. I already own a TV, so watching a performance on it doesn't cost me anything. If it turns out I don't like the performance, I can just turn off the TV and go do something else. I haven't lost any money, or much time either.

Watching a performance on TV is so comfortable and convenient, I don't know why people attend live performances. It's much better to enjoy them at home.

▼

36	EX	Choose **one** of the following transportation vehicles and explain why you think it has changed people's lives. • automobiles • bicycles • airplanes Use specific reasons and examples to support your answer.

An airplane is a form of transportation that has changed people's lives. Thanks to the plane, our lives are now faster, more exciting, and more convenient than before.

You cannot deny that a plane is fast. The Concorde flew at supersonic speed. A businessperson could have left Paris at 11:00 A.M. and arrived in New York at 8:00 the same morning in time for the day's work. Many businesspeople in Europe fly to London for a noon meeting and then return home to Rome or Madrid for dinner.

It is always exciting to take a plane trip. When you travel by plane, you might cross time zones, oceans, and many countries. When you get off the plane, you could be in a place where the people speak a different language. You are in a completely different place from where you started.

Nothing can beat the convenience of a plane. You can go anywhere at any time you want. Other forms of transportation are not so convenient. Boats, for example, leave only on certain days of the week and they can't go everywhere. Planes give you the option to leave several times a day and they take you very close to your final destination.

Although other forms of transportation may be more comfortable, none has changed the way we do business and live our lives more than the plane. Thanks to the speed, excitement, and convenience of the plane, our lives are richer.

▼

37	AD	Do you agree or disagree that progress is always good? Use specific reasons and examples to support your answer.

Who would disagree with the statement "progress is good?" Without progress, there would be no change. Without progress there would be no improvements in our economy, our standard of living, or our health.

Progress is required to keep the economy moving forward. Without progress, new products wouldn't be developed and new services wouldn't be created. We would be living in the same way our grandparents and great grandparents lived and working at the same kind of jobs.

Progress is required to raise our standard of living. Our homes today are more efficient and use fewer resources thanks to improvement in home construction techniques. Our clothes are warmer and safer thanks to developments in textile manufacturing. Our educational system is better thanks to the use of modern computer technology.

Progress is required to improve the health of the world's population. Without progress, there would be no vaccines against terrible diseases like smallpox. Without progress, we would have high infant mortality rates. Without progress, we wouldn't have treatments for heart disease and cancer. Thanks to progress, our lives are longer and healthier.

Progress is a natural state. Without it, we would not evolve. Without it, our economy, our standard of living, and our health would deteriorate. Who could deny the necessity of progress?

▼

38	AD	Learning about the past has no value for those of us living in the present. Do you agree or disagree? Use specific reasons and examples to support your answer.

People often say, "Those who don't understand history will repeat the mistakes of the past." I totally disagree. I don't see any evidence that people have made smart decisions based on their knowledge of the past. To me, the present is what is important. I think that people, weather, and politics determine what happens, not the past.

People can change. People may have hated each other for years, but that doesn't mean they will continue to hate each other. Look at Turkey and Greece. When Turkey had an earthquake, Greece sent aid. When Greece had an earthquake, Turkey sent aid. These two countries are cooperating now. No doubt, if we had looked at the past, we would have believed this to be impossible. But people change.

The weather can change. Farmers plant certain crops because these crops have always grown well in their fields. But there can be a long drought. The crops that grew well in the past will die. The farmers need to try a drought-resistant crop. If we had looked at the past, we wouldn't have changed our crop. Weather changes.

Politics can change. If politicians looked only at the past, they would always do the same thing. If we looked at the past in the United States, we would see a lot of discrimination against races, women, and sexual orientation. On the whole, people now are interested in human rights, and the government protects these rights. Politics change.

As a rule, it is important to follow the mood of today. It doesn't help us to think about the past. People, the weather, and politics can change in any direction. The direction of this change, in my opinion, cannot be predicted by studying the past.

▼

39	AD	Do you agree or disagree with the following statement? With the help of technology, students nowadays can learn more information and learn it more quickly. Use specific reasons and examples to support your answer.

Technology has greatly improved the way we get information. Students can now get more information, get it more quickly, and get it more conveniently.

An amazing amount of information is available through the Internet. It has made every major library and database available to students around the world. You can get information about events in the past as well as about events that unfold as you watch your computer monitor.

Information comes through the Internet instantly. You can type a few words in your search engine, and in a matter of seconds the engine will search the entire World Wide Web to find information on that topic. You don't have to spend hours going through card catalogues in the library and looking at the shelves.

It is certainly convenient to sit at home and do research on the Internet with your computer. Your computer is open 24 hours a day, unlike a library or office. You can do research in your pajamas while you eat breakfast. What could be more convenient?

Technology, especially the Internet, has changed the quantity and quality of the information we get. The speed and convenience of a computer helps students learn more and learn it more quickly.

▼

| 40 | AD | The expression "Never, never give up" means keep trying and never stop working for your goals. Do you agree or disagree with this statement? Use specific reasons and examples to support your answer. |

"If at first you don't succeed, try, try again." These are wise words. One should never give up. There is always another opportunity, another goal, or another option.

Once I ran for president of my class. Unfortunately, I lost because I didn't promote myself enough. I looked at my mistakes and decided how to correct them. The following year, I ran for president again. This time I gave speeches, called voters on the phone, and handed out brochures. This time I won. Never give up. There is always another opportunity.

Once I wanted to study medicine. Unfortunately, I didn't like science. I failed all my science courses at school. Then I realized that what I liked about medicine was helping people. I changed my goal from healing people to helping people. Now I'm studying psychology. There is always another goal.

Once I wanted to talk with my friend. Unfortunately, his computer was down and I couldn't e-mail him. His phone line was busy so I couldn't call him. Since I really wanted to talk to him, I got on the bus and went across town to visit him. There is always another option.

If you give up, you might as well die. My advice is always look for another opportunity, another goal, or another option. There is always something else. Don't give up.

▼

| 41 | AD | Some people think that human needs for farmland, housing, and industry are more important than saving land for endangered animals. Do you agree or disagree with this point of view? Why or why not? Use specific reasons and examples to support your answer. |

Many animals are now extinct and many more are in danger of extinction. This is because their habitat is destroyed when people use land to build houses, factories, and farms. Does it matter? It certainly does. Our basic human needs, our quality of life, and the way we live are all affected when animals' habitats are destroyed.

Many animals affect our basic human needs even though we may not realize it. There is a delicate balance of nature. If one small part is removed, it will affect all the other parts. For example, if certain trees are cut down, bats will have no place to live. If there are no bats, there will be no animal to eat certain insects that destroy our crops. This will affect our basic need for food.

The loss of certain animals affects the quality of our lives. Certain flowers are pollinated by butterflies that migrate from Canada to Mexico. Some of the breeding grounds of these butterflies was destroyed. Now, these flowers are disappearing. We will no longer be able to enjoy their beauty, and we will no longer be able to enjoy the beauty of the butterflies. This is just one small example.

When animals' habitats are destroyed we may think that it only affects the animals, but it affects our way of life, too. Large parts of the Amazon rain forest have been cut down to make room for farms. This rain forest is an important part of the weather system all around the world. Weather patterns have been changing because of this. This will have a huge effect on how we live.

When animals' lives are endangered, our way of life is endangered, too. I would encourage humans to look for other alternatives for our farmlands, housing, and industries. We have alternatives; the animals do not.

▼

| 42 | MA | What is a very important skill a person should learn in order to be successful in the world today? Choose **one** skill and use specific reasons and examples to support your choice. |

I do not define success economically; I define success socially. Therefore, the one skill I would choose for success is tolerance. To succeed in society, we need to be tolerant of one another's background, opinions, and lifestyle.

People come from all different backgrounds. The world is becoming increasingly mobile. We are no longer able to work only with people who grew up in the same place we did, or who went to the same schools we went to. Now, we work with people whose backgrounds are completely different from ours. We all must be tolerant of these differences so we can work together amiably.

Different people have different opinions, but we cannot stop speaking to them just because of differences in opinion. We shouldn't start a war just because someone has a different idea. We have to find common ground, an idea we can agree on. We have to learn to respect the people we live and work around. We need to be tolerant of differences of opinion.

Different people live different lifestyles. Woman can live on their own, hold important jobs, and raise children alone. Men can stay home and take care of the family. Social roles can change and we must be tolerant of the different lifestyles that people choose.

To succeed socially, you must be able to adapt to differences. You must be tolerant of all people regardless of their background, their opinion, or their lifestyle.

▼

| 43 | MA | Why do you think some people are attracted to dangerous sports or other dangerous activities? Use specific reasons and examples to support your answer. |

Dangerous sports are interesting for most people to watch or read about. Only certain kinds of people, however, are attracted to participating in these sports. Often they are people who love risks, who seek a feeling of power, or who need a way to deal with some personal problems.

Dangerous sports attract risk takers. People often take risks in their lives. They take risks with their money, with their jobs, and in love. But these are ordinary risks. Nothing compares with the risk of putting your own life in danger. Risking one's life in a dangerous sport has a special thrill that is very attractive to some people.

Dangerous sports attract people who want a feeling of power. It is a great accomplishment to climb a difficult mountain or to learn how to skydive. When people do these things and still end up alive, they feel like they have conquered the forces of nature. What a feeling of power that must give them!

Finally, I think dangerous sports attract some unhappy people. People who don't like their jobs or who have problems with their family may turn to dangerous sports as a way of dealing with their problems. Learning how to do something difficult and dangerous can make them feel worthwhile. It can give them something interesting to focus their attention on.

Dangerous sports can be attractive for several reasons. They can attract people who like thrill, power, or who need a way to forget their problems. In my opinion, however, dangerous sports are never worth the risk.

▼

44	PR	Some people like to travel with a companion. Other people prefer to travel alone. Which do you prefer? Use specific reasons and examples to support your choice.

Traveling alone is the only way to travel. If you take someone with you, you take your home with you. When you travel alone, you meet new people, have new experiences, and learn more about yourself.

When I travel with a friend, I spend all my time with that friend. We do everything together. When I travel alone, I spend my time looking for new friends. I meet other tourists or local people. We have coffee together or share a meal and we become friends. It's easier to meet new people when I travel alone.

When I travel with a friend, my routine is predictable. We follow the same schedule that we do at home. When I travel alone, I adapt myself to the customs of the place. I might take a nap in the afternoon and eat dinner late at night. I might go to a club and dance all night. I am more open to new experiences when I travel alone.

When I travel with a friend, we take care of each other. When I am alone, I have to take care of myself. If I encounter a difficult situation, I have to find my own solution. Maybe I don't speak the language and I have to figure out how to make myself understood. Maybe the food looks strange and I have to decide what to eat. When I travel alone, I learn about how I react in new or strange situations.

I think it is always important to do things on your own. You can find new friends, have new experiences, and learn a lot about yourself, too. Isn't that the point of travel?

▼

45	PR	Some people prefer to get up early in the morning and start the day's work. Others prefer to get up later in the day and work until late at night. Which do you prefer? Use specific reasons and examples to support your choice.

I prefer getting up later in the day and staying up late at night. This routine fits my body's rhythm, my work schedule, and my social life.

I believe in following my body's natural rhythm. My body tells me to sleep until I am ready to get up and to go to bed when I am sleepy. This means I never get up early in the morning. My body tells me it likes to sleep until 10:00 or 11:00 in the morning.

Sleeping late also fits my work schedule. I prefer working in the afternoon. Since I don't have that much work to do, I can easily get it done between lunch and dinner. That's enough for me, because I need time to enjoy myself, too.

My active social life is another reason I prefer to sleep late. Who gets up early in the morning to have fun? No one. Anything amusing, such as concerts, dances, parties, or dinners, all happen at night. If I got up early in the morning, I would be too tired to enjoy myself in the evening.

I will maintain this pattern forever, I hope. I think it is always important to listen to your body. If your body tells you to stay in bed, that is what you should do. By listening to your body, you will never let work interfere with your social life.

▼

| 46 | EX | What are the important qualities of a good son or daughter? Have these qualities changed or remained the same over time in your culture? Use specific reasons and examples to support your answer. |

The qualities that parents wish their sons and daughters to have—obedience, loyalty, respect—have not changed. Any parent will tell you that, like their ancestors, they expect these qualities from their children. However, they do not always get what they expect.

Parents expect their children to obey them. Even when their sons and daughters grow up and get married, parents still expect obedience from them. At least, that's the way it was. Children these days still obey their parents when they are young. When they reach age 18 or 20, however, they want to make their own decisions. They want to follow their own ideas even if these ideas are against their parents' wishes.

Parents also expect loyalty from their children. If there is a dispute between families, parents expect their children to side with their own family. This is probably still very common. Most children today will support their family against others.

Parents, of course, demand respect. As children become introduced to non-traditional ways of doing things, however, this quality may not endure. Children sometimes see their parents as old-fashioned. They think their parents are too old to understand them. They lose respect for their parents.

Obedience, loyalty, and respect are virtues that are being challenged today. These days we tend to show these qualities to our parents less and less. I hope, though, that my children obey me, are loyal to me, and respect me.

47	PR	Some people prefer to work for a large company. Others prefer to work for a small company. Which would you prefer? Use specific reasons and details to support your choice.

I would prefer to work in a large company rather than a small one. A large company has more to offer in terms of advancement, training, and prestige.

In a large company, I can start at an entry-level position and work my way up to the top. I can start in the mailroom and, once I know the company, I can apply for a managerial position. In a small company, there would not be as much room to grow.

In a large company there is the opportunity to learn a variety of jobs. I could work in sales, in shipping, or in any department I applied for. I could be trained in a variety of positions and would have valuable experience. In a small company, there would not be the same opportunity.

In a large company, there would be more prestige. I could brag to my friends that I worked for one of the biggest companies in the world. I would always have something to talk about when I met strangers. If I worked for a small company, I would always have to explain what the company did.

Working for a small company would not give me the same opportunities for advancement or training as working for a larger company would. Nor would I be as proud to work for a small company—unless the small company was my own.

48	EX	People work because they need money to live. What are some **other** reasons that people work? Discuss one or more of these reasons. Use specific examples and details to support your answer.

Although people work to earn money, money is not the main reason people stay in their jobs. They also work because they like to be with other people, they want to contribute something to society, and they feel a sense of accomplishment.

Many people enjoy going to work because they like being with other people. They like to interact with their coworkers and clients. They like to help people solve problems or get a product, and they like to make friends.

People also enjoy their jobs because it gives them a chance to contribute to society. Teachers educate our future generations. Doctors and nurses heal people. Manufacturers produce things that people need to use. Through work, each individual is able to do his or her part in this world.

A lot of people like to work because it gives them a sense of accomplishment. For example, people who work in factories take pride in the car they produce or the television they assemble. When they see a car on the street, they can feel a sense of accomplishment. They helped make that car.

Money is nice, but it is not the only reason people get up and go to work each day. I believe that people work because it gives them the opportunity to be with other people, to contribute to society, and to feel that they have accomplished something.

▼

| 49 | AD | Do you agree or disagree with the following statement? Face-to-face communication is better than other types of communication, such as letters, e-mail, or telephone calls. Use specific reasons and details to support your answer. |

I would have to agree that face-to-face communication is the best type of communication. It can eliminate misunderstandings immediately, cement relationships, and encourage continued interaction.

When you talk to someone directly, you can see right away if they don't understand you. A person's body language will tell you if they disagree or if they don't follow your line of thought. Then you can repeat yourself or paraphrase your argument. When you send an e-mail, the receiver may misinterpret what you want to say. He or she could even be insulted. Then you have to waste time explaining yourself in another e-mail.

When you talk face to face, you communicate with more than words. You communicate with your eyes and your hands. You communicate with your whole body. People can sense that you really want to communicate with them. This energy bonds people together. Your relationship with a person can grow much stronger when you communicate in person.

When you meet someone face to face, the interaction tends to last longer than other forms of communication. An e-mail lasts a second; a telephone call, a few minutes. When you meet someone face to face, however, you've both made an effort to be there. You will probably spend longer talking. The longer you talk, the more you say. The more you say, the stronger your relationship will be.

In summary, if you want to establish a relationship with another human being, the best way is talking face to face. When you communicate directly, you can avoid misunderstandings that may occur in writing. You can communicate on levels other than just words and you can spend more time doing it.

▼

| 50 | PR | Some people like to do only what they already do well. Other people prefer to try new things and take risks. Which do you prefer? Use specific reasons and examples to support your choice. |

I am not a risk taker. I like to do just those things that I am proficient at. I don't want to waste my time doing things that I don't do well. I always feel better when I do something well, and other people have a better impression of me. I don't see a good reason to try something new that I don't know how to do at all.

I don't have time to waste doing things that I don't really know how to do. For example, I don't know how to sew. I could spend a whole day trying to make a dress, and at the end of the day I still wouldn't have a dress to wear. It would be better to spend an hour buying a dress at the store. Then I could spend the rest of the day doing other things that I know I can do.

I feel good when I do a good job, but I feel terrible when I do something poorly. Once, I decided to figure my income taxes myself. But I am not an accountant and I made many mistakes. I felt very bad about it. Finally, I realized I could pay a professional accountant to do it for me. Then I could spend my time feeling good about other things that I know how to do.

When I do something well, I make a better impression on other people. If I tried to cook a meal for you, you would not have a good impression of me at all. I am a terrible cook. But I can change the oil in your car for you and I can tune up the engine. When you see me do a good job at that, you see me as a competent, accomplished mechanic instead of as a sorry cook.

Some people like to take risks and try doing new things, but I am not one of those people. When I do something that I really don't know how to do, I just end up feeling bad and I give other people a bad impression. I don't see the point of wasting my time this way.

▼

51	EX	Some people believe that success in life comes from taking risks or chances. Others believe that success results from careful planning. In your opinion, what does success come from? Use specific reasons and examples to support your answer.

I think that we must all take risks in our lives, but they must be calculated risks. If we look at the great explorers and scientists of history, we see that their successes were usually a combination of both risk taking and planning. Like the great thinkers, we must plan carefully, seize all opportunities, and reevaluate our plans when necessary.

It is hard to be successful without careful planning. In his search for a new route to India, Columbus drew maps, planned his route carefully, and gathered the necessary support and supplies. Madame Curie worked long hours in her laboratory and recorded every aspect of her experiments. Neither of them could have made their achievements without this planning.

Even with a careful plan, changes occur. Columbus was looking for India, but he ended up in the Caribbean instead. Lewis and Clark were looking for a river passage west, but they discovered much more. You have to be ready to take advantage of new things as they occur.

When things go against plan, you must be ready to change direction. Columbus didn't bring back spices from the East Indies, but he did bring back gold from the Americas. It is important to make your mistakes work for you and change your plans when necessary.

You will never succeed in life if you don't take chances. But before you start, you must plan carefully so that you are ready to take advantage of every opportunity and change your plans as required.

▼

| 52 | MA | What change would make your hometown more appealing to people your age? Use specific reasons and examples to support your opinion. |

I think that people my age would like to have a place to go after school. They could go there to socialize, have meetings, and just relax.

In my town, there are a few teahouses, but these are reserved for our fathers and their friends. Teenagers do not go there unless it's to carry messages to their fathers. We need a place where we can get together after school to talk about school and other subjects that interest us.

At our own teahouse, we could also have meetings. These would be like club meetings. We could have a debating society, a poetry reading group, or a political club. We could have our meetings once or twice a week after school.

We need a place where we could just relax away from our families. Our home life is very hectic. There are a lot of younger children making a lot of noise in the evenings. We need a quiet place to study, read, or just sit.

If our town had a teahouse reserved for teenagers, it would be good for our parents. They would always know where we were. They would know that we were at the teahouse socializing, having a meeting, or just relaxing with our friends.

▼

| 53 | AD | Do you agree or disagree with the following statement? The most important aspect of a job is the money a person earns. Use specific reasons and examples to support your answer. |

I certainly agree that the most important aspect of a job is the money a person earns. When I get a job, I want to earn a lot of money. If I earn a lot of money, people will know I am successful, smart, and a good candidate for marriage.

Money equals success. If I earn a lot of money, I can wear nice clothes, get a big car, buy my parents a nice apartment, and spend a lot of money on my friends. Everyone will know I am rich and very successful.

Earning a lot of money will show people how smart I am. Everyone knows you can't be stupid and earn a lot of money. Who will trust someone stupid to do a job?

When I earn a lot of money, my mother will be able to find me a good wife. She will be able to tell everyone what an important job I have. It will make it easy for her to find someone for me since all girls want to marry a rich man.

I don't care what kind of work I do as long as I earn a lot of money. That is the most important thing for me. Having a well-paying job will show everyone that I am successful, smart, and a good catch.

▼

| 54 | AD | Do you agree or disagree with the following statement? One should never judge a person by external appearances. Use specific reasons and details to support your answer. |

In most cases, you shouldn't judge a person by external appearances. It is better to reserve judgment until you have had a chance to get to know the person. Judgments based on external appearances prevent you from really getting to know a person, reinforce stereotypes, and can lead you to conclusions that aren't true.

When you judge people by their external appearance, you lose the chance to get to know them. In high school I stayed away from students who were called "bad students" because they dressed a certain way. I wanted nothing to do with them. Later, I had a chance to meet a "bad student" because his mother was a friend of my mother. Then I realized that we actually had a lot in common. My impression of him was very different once I got to know him.

Judging people based on external appearances just reinforces stereotypes. You might think that a person with a tattoo, for example, is not a nice person. It's easy to start thinking that all people with tattoos are not nice people. Then you will never make friends with people who have tattoos or want to work with them or like to live near them. You will feel uncomfortable around them because all you will see about them is their tattoos.

Judgments based on external appearances can often lead you to conclusions that aren't true. Maybe you know someone who dresses in old, unfashionable clothes. If all you see are the clothes, it is easy to think that the person has bad taste or bad habits. But maybe the truth is different. Maybe that person comes from a less fortunate family than you and doesn't have money. Maybe the person is working hard to save money for school. You will never know if all you do is look at external appearance.

You should always take time to get to know new people before making judgments about them. External appearance often does not tell us anything about a person. Judging someone by their appearance is misleading, reinforces stereotypes, and doesn't lead to the truth. It can prevent you from making a true friend.

▼

| 55 | AD | Do you agree or disagree with the following statement? A person should never make an important decision alone. Use specific reasons and examples to support your answer. |

You should never make an important decision alone. You should think out your important decisions carefully, and you need other people to help you do this. People close to you can give you good advice, give you a different perspective, and share their own experiences. It is hard to make big decisions without this kind of help.

It is very important to have advice when making decisions. When I had to decide which courses to take in high school, I talked to the school counselor. He had the knowledge and expertise to help me determine which classes were best for my goals. Without his advice, I might have chosen unsuitable courses.

Getting a friend's perspective on a situation is also usually helpful. I have always loved drama, but I thought I wasn't good enough to act in the school play. When a friend of mine found this out, she was shocked. She was able to provide me with another perspective on myself and my talents. I changed my mind and decided to audition for the school play. Imagine my surprise when I got an important part.

When other people share their experiences with you, that can help you in making your decisions. When I was trying to decide if I should study overseas, I talked with a friend. She had studied overseas the year before. She really helped me because I was very unsure about my decision. After hearing about her experiences, I decided it would be a good experience for me too. I went and it was amazing.

Whenever I am faced with an important decision, I seek advice from others so that I am well-informed and have the benefit of their experience and perspective.

▼

| 56 | MA | A company is going to give some money either to support the arts or to protect the environment. Which do you think the company should choose? Use specific reasons and examples to support your answer. |

Deciding between supporting the arts and protecting the environment is a difficult choice to make, but I think I would choose protecting the environment. We need a healthy environment in order to survive, so we must protect it. We need to protect the environment now to help prevent health problems, to maintain the ecosystem, and to preserve the Earth for our children.

Pollution from factories and cars can cause damage to the environment. It makes the air dirty. Breathing this dirty air causes health problems, particularly for children and the elderly. We need to control the amount of pollution we produce in order to prevent health problems.

We also need to pay attention to the ecosystem. Plant life, animal life, and people all depend on each other. An unhealthy environment disturbs this ecosystem. For example, changes in the environment might cause a certain kind of plant to die. If that plant is food for a certain kind of animal, the animal will die too. If people use that animal as a food source, there could be big problems.

If we do not protect our environment now, it will continue to get worse and our children will suffer the consequences. The air and water will get dirtier, and more plants and animals will die. Our children won't have as much natural beauty to admire. Even worse, their well-being will be threatened.

Without clean air to breathe, a healthy ecosystem, and a future for our children, the human race will not survive. That's why protecting our environment is important. If we have a healthy environment, we have healthy children who can participate in and appreciate the arts.

▼

| 57 | PR | Some movies are serious, designed to make the audience think. Other movies are designed primarily to amuse and entertain. Which type of movie do you prefer? Use specific reasons and examples to support your answer. |

Movies have the power to make you laugh, cry, or think about an issue that you might not otherwise think about. Although I sometimes watch movies that are serious, I prefer movies that amuse and entertain. When I see an amusing movie, it makes me relax, laugh, and keeps me in good spirits.

After a long day at school and work, I need a break and something to take my mind off the troubles of the day. I can do that with an entertaining movie. When I watch an amusing movie, I don't have to think. I just sit back and relax. After a movie, I feel ready to get back to work and study.

Amusing movies make me laugh. Laughing is important for the soul. Laughing not only makes me feel good, it connects me with other people. When I laugh with other people, we become friends.

When I watch an entertaining movie, I feel good. When I feel good, I can focus more on important things like my studies and work. Being in good spirits makes me feel better about myself and gives me a positive outlook on life.

While I can appreciate serious movies that make you think, I prefer to be amused and entertained after a long day of work. Such movies allow me to take a break from the rigors of daily life by helping me relax, making me laugh, and putting me in a good mood.

▼

| 58 | AD | Do you agree or disagree with the following statement? Businesses should do anything they can to make a profit. Use specific reasons and examples to support your position. |

After I get my degree, I plan to start a business. My goal is to make money, a lot of money. However, I can't forget that there are more important things in life than earning a profit. I must consider the people I work with, the customers I serve, and the community I live in.

My colleagues are a very important part of my business. Without them, I would not have a business. I depend on them to carry out the day-to-day operations. I depend on them for their advice on what to sell and how to sell it. I must compensate them for their work. I can't take a large profit without sharing with the people who made it possible.

Similarly, I would not have a business without my customers. I can never forget that they could take their business elsewhere. I must give them good value for their money. I can't overcharge them. I want my customers to trust me and keep coming back.

My employees and I are a part of the social life of our community. We must play an active part in it. I feel it is important that some of the profits my business earns from *the community be returned to the community. We need to support community programs like summer jobs for high school students, campaigns to clean up parks, and efforts to make the shopping area more attractive.*

A business must make profits, but we all—workers, customers, community—must profit from a successful business.

▼

59	PR	Some people are always in a hurry to go places and get things done. Other people prefer to take their time and live life at a slower pace. Which do you prefer? Use specific reasons and examples to support your answer.

Life is short. Haste makes waste. What's your hurry? These three sayings character-ize the way I manage my day-to-day chores. I don't want to rush through things; I prefer to take my time.

Life is short. You never know what may happen tomorrow, so it is important to enjoy today. By doing just a few things slowly and doing them well, you can savor the experience. You can truly enjoy what you are doing.

Haste makes waste. We are not machines. We can't just rush through our chores. If we do, we might forget something. We might take shortcuts and do a poor job. Then we'll have to do the job all over again. That certainly doesn't save us any time. By going more slowly, we can do a chore carefully, completely, and correctly.

What's your hurry? Where's the fire? I don't see any need to rush to the next experience. There's still a lot to see and learn from the chores around you. Taking care of your baby brother, for instance, can be very rewarding. If you are in a hurry to get many things done, you can just keep the baby near you while you work on other chores. Or, you could devote your whole attention to him and observe his reactions to the environment. You can't observe carefully if you are rushing to do other things at the same time.

To twist a common saying, "Don't just do something, sit there!" Take life easy and savor each minute. Life is shorter than you think.

▼

60	AD	Do you agree or disagree with the following statement? Games are as important for children as they are for adults. Use specific reasons and examples to support your answers.

Everyone likes to play games. Games are important at any age to keep your mind sharp, learn new things, and maintain social skills.

When you play games, you exercise your mind. This becomes more important as you grow older. By concentrating on the tactics of a game, memorizing moves, and following your opponent's strategies, you can keep your brain functioning and growing.

Playing games can teach you a lot. Games that ask questions, for example, show you what you don't know. You can learn about things like geography and history when you play certain games. It's a fun way to learn, and adults enjoy this as much as children do.

Games require the use of social skills. When you play games, you interact with other people. You have to be considerate of them and you have to play fairly. Playing games allows you to maintain personal contacts. This is important for people of all ages.

Regardless of your age, playing games can help you keep your mind alert, learn new things, and build friendships.

▼

| 61 | AD | Do you agree or disagree with the following statement? Parents or other adult relatives should make important decisions for their older (15–18 year old) teenaged children. Use specific reasons and examples to support your opinion. |

No one knows me as well as my parents, and no one cares about me like they do. It is natural that I should allow my parents to make important decisions for me. I think all older teenagers should take their parents advice on decisions that concern their education, their social life, and their future careers.

My parents are the ones who can make the best decisions about my education. They have always chosen the best schools for me to attend. They have hired tutors to make sure I understood my classes well. They have sent me to special prep classes to help me prepare for exams. When it is time to choose a college, I know they will choose the right college for me.

My parents make good decisions about my social life. When I was young, they invited children over to play with me. I became very close to these children and we are still friends. Even though I am older now, my parents still guide me in my social life. I know they don't want me to hang out with the wrong crowd. I know they want me to marry a good person who is right for me. They have more experience than I have and they can help me make decisions about my social life.

I need my parents to help me make decisions about my future career. Both my parents have successful careers of their own. My father runs a business and my mother is a well-known politician. I want to be as successful as they are, so of course I will listen to their advice about my career.

If all children follow their parents' wishes, they will be happier. They will be more successful in school, in work, and in their social life. After all, parents want only the best for their children.

▼

| 62 | MA | What do you want **most** in a friend—someone who is intelligent, or someone who has a sense of humor, or someone who is reliable? Which **one** of these characteristics is most important to you? Use reasons and specific examples to explain your choice. |

I like people who are intelligent and I always enjoy someone with a good sense of humor. What I look for first, however, is a friend who is reliable. I need to be able to rely on my friends to provide me with companionship, to support me, and to encourage me.

I depend on my friends for companionship. If I want to see a movie or go to a concert, of course I ask some friends to accompany me. If I feel sad or lonely, I can count on my friends to spend some time with me. If I feel happy, I can invite all my friends to a party. I know they will come over to have a good time with me.

When I am having troubles, I turn to my friends for support. If I fail an exam, or have a fight with someone, I call up a friend. I rely on my friends to be willing to talk to me and help me solve my problems. I expect my friends to be there when I need them, and I do the same for them.

I need my friends to encourage me. If I am afraid to do something such as enroll in a difficult course or apply for a job to earn some extra money, my friends help me. They talk to me and give me the confidence I need to try new and difficult things. I know I can count on them to give me encouragement when I need it.

We all like to spend time with smart and entertaining people. I think the people who make the best friends, though, are people who are reliable. If someone is reliable, you know he or she will always be ready to give you companionship, support, and encouragement when you need it. That's what friends are for, isn't it?

▼

| 63 | AD | Do you agree or disagree with the following statement? Most experiences in our lives that seemed difficult at the time become valuable lessons for the future. Use reasons and specific examples to support your answer. |

People say that experience is the best teacher, and I believe this is true. Difficult experiences, especially, can teach us valuable lessons. They can help us overcome fears, they can teach us better ways to do things, and they can show us that we have friends who are ready to help us.

Difficult experiences can help us overcome fears. I remember the first time I had to give a presentation to my classmates. I was very shy and afraid to speak in front of the whole class. I spent a long time preparing for my presentation. I was nervous and didn't sleep well the night before. I was surprised when I gave my presentation and everyone listened. No one laughed at me. They asked questions and I could answer them. Now I know I can talk in front of the class and do a good job.

Difficult experiences can teach us better ways to do things. I had a very embarrassing experience when I took the test to get my driver's license. I didn't practice for the test because I thought I was such a good driver. But I failed. I didn't really know what to expect so I got nervous and made mistakes. I was embarrassed about my failure and my parents were disappointed. Now I know that it is always better to prepare myself for something, no matter how ready I think I am.

Difficult experiences can show us that we have friends. Once I was very sick and I missed several months of school. I thought I would have to repeat the year. I didn't have to because there were a lot of people who helped me. My teachers gave me extra time to do my work. My classmates explained the homework to me. People who I didn't even know well helped me make up the work I lost. I learned that I had friends where I hadn't expected any.

Nobody looks for difficult experiences, but we all have to go through them from time to time. They help us overcome fears, learn better ways of doing things, and show us who our friends are. These are all valuable lessons for our future.

| 64 | PR | Some people prefer to work for themselves or own a business. Others prefer to work for an employer. Would you rather be self-employed, work for someone else, or own a business? Use specific reasons to explain your choice. |

Many people have dreams of becoming self-employed or starting their own business, but I don't understand this. I think it is much better to work for someone else. When I work for someone else, I don't have to take risks or make difficult decisions alone. I have someone to tell me what to do, someone to evaluate my work, and most important of all, someone to give me a regular paycheck.

As an employee, I don't have to decide what to do every day. My employer gives me work to do and she gives me deadlines for it. I don't have to worry about what needs to be done next on a project. That's my employer's job. Without this worry, I can just focus on getting the job done right.

When I have an employer, I never have to wonder if my work is good or bad. My employer tells me if I did a good job, or if I need to do something over again. I don't have to worry if a client will like my work or if a product is good enough to sell. That is my employer's concern. My employer lets me know how my work is and if necessary, I will do it again or do it better the next time.

I know I will get a paycheck every two weeks when I work for someone else. I don't have to worry if the clients have paid or if we have sold enough merchandise. If I go to work every day, I get my paycheck on a regular basis. I work so I can get paid and I want to be able to be sure of receiving my money.

Many people want to feel independent and that is why they want their own business. For me, however, it is more important to feel secure. I feel secure knowing that I have an employer to give me directions, evaluate my work, and pay me regularly. That is why I prefer to work for someone else.

| 65 | MA | Should a city try to preserve its old, historic buildings or destroy them and replace them with modern buildings? Use specific reasons and examples to support your opinion. |

Of course a city should preserve its old, historic buildings. New buildings can always be built, but old ones can never be replaced. They are usually more beautiful than modern buildings, they represent the city's history, and they can even help the city by attracting tourists. Historic buildings should always be preserved.

Old buildings are usually very beautiful. Depending on when they were built, they show different periods of architecture. They have a lot of character. They were made by hand, the old-fashioned way. You can feel the personalities of the people who built them and of the people who have lived and worked in them. Modern buildings, on the other hand, are usually not so beautiful. They seem like impersonal giants that have no character.

Old buildings represent a city's history. Important things may have taken place in an old building. Maybe a peace treaty was signed there or an important meeting took place. A famous person may have lived there. Maybe it was a former president or a famous writer. When we have historic buildings around us, we learn more about our history and we appreciate it.

Old buildings attract tourists to a city. People want to see old buildings because they are beautiful or because important things happened in them. If a city has a lot of old, interesting buildings, many tourists will visit the city. That is good for the city's economy. People usually don't visit a city in order to see its modern buildings.

A city's old, historic buildings are among its greatest treasures. They are a source of beauty and a representation of history. It would be a crime to try to replace them.

▼

66	AD	Do you agree or disagree with the following statement. Classmates are a more important influence than parents on a child's success in school. Use specific reasons and examples to support your answer.

I believe that parents have more influence on a child's school success than classmates do. Classmates have an important social influence on each other, especially as they get older, but the influence of parents is stronger than this. Parents are the most important model a child has, parents love their children, and they have expectations of them. All of these things are important influences on a child's success in school.

Parents are important role models for their children. Young children like to copy other children, but they like to copy adults more. When children see their parents read, they read too. When children hear their parents talk about books or news or politics, they will think these are interesting subjects, too. Children may learn other things from their classmates, but the examples they get from their parents are stronger.

Parents are the most important people who love and care for a child. Children know how important this is, and they love their parents, too. They may have close friends in school, but their feelings for their parents are more important. If they feel loved and cared for at home, they will have the necessary confidence to do well in school.

Parents have expectations for their children. They expect them to behave well and be good people and be successful in school. Children want to please their parents so they try to fulfill their parents' expectations. They want to be nice to their classmates and get along with them, but this is not the same as fulfilling their parents' expectations.

Many people have influence on children while they are growing up, but parents are the ones who have the strongest influence. They are the most important role models their children have, they love them the most, and they have the greatest expectations of them. Nobody can influence a child more than a parent can.

▼

67	PR	If you were an employer, which kind of worker would you prefer to hire: an inexperienced worker at a lower salary or an experienced worker at a higher salary? Use specific reasons and details to support your answer.

If I were an employer, I would prefer to hire an inexperienced worker at a lower salary. Of course it would save me money, at least at first. I could also train an inexperienced person exactly as I want, and he or she might be willing to work longer hours, as well.

As an employer, my first concern is money. I have to make sure the business brings in more money than it spends. When I save on salaries, I save a lot of money. I don't want to pay my employees less than the salary they expect, but I want to save on salaries when I can. Hiring inexperienced workers is one way to do this.

I like to train my employees to work according to my company's methods. Experienced people are used to doing things a certain way. If they get their experience at another company first, it is hard to change their methods when they come to my company. It is much easier to train inexperienced workers to follow my company's methods.

I don't like to ask my employees to work overtime, but sometimes I have to. Sometimes we have a lot of work to do in a short period of time. Inexperienced workers want to gain experience, so they more often volunteer to work extra hours.

People may think it is not good for a company to hire inexperienced workers, but I disagree. I think everyone benefits this way. The workers get training and experience and the company saves money. I think it is the best plan.

▼

68	MA	Many teachers assign homework to students everyday. Do you think that daily homework is necessary for students? Use specific reasons and details to support your answer.

I believe that daily homework is not necessary. Students already spend most of the day in school. They need their time outside of school to do other things. They need time to spend with their families, to work, and to just relax. They can learn their lessons with homework two or three times a week, but every day isn't necessary.

All students need to spend time with their families. They are still young and they need the guidance and support their parents can give them. They need the companionship of their brothers and sisters. In addition, many families rely on their older children to help out at home. They take care of the younger children and help with the cooking and cleaning. If students have too much homework, they won't have time for their families.

Many high school students have jobs. They go to their jobs after school and on weekends. Some work in order to help their families. Others work to save money for college. Students' jobs are important to them. If they have too much homework, they won't have time and energy to go to work.

Students need time to relax. They study hard in school all day and many work at jobs after school. But they are still young. They need to spend time with their friends and have fun. When students relax with friends, they then have more energy for school and work. They have a chance to develop social skills or to pursue their own interests. Having free time is important for a child's development. If students have too much homework, they won't have time for relaxation.

Homework is important for students, but other things are important, too. Some homework is good, but daily homework can take time away from a student's family, job, and relaxation. There needs to be a balance.

▼

69	MA	If you could study a subject that you have never had the opportunity to study, what would you choose? Explain your choice, using specific reasons and details.

I have always been interested in art and literature, so people will think my choice is strange. If I could study something I have never had the opportunity to study, I would choose calculus. If I could actually learn something as difficult as that, it would give me a lot of confidence. Besides that, I think I would like it and it could help me learn some useful skills.

The only mathematics I have studied are the required courses in high school. I finished those requirements early and since then I have chosen to study other subjects. I never liked my math classes and I didn't do well in them. I have always thought that I couldn't learn math. But now I would like to try it. I think if I made the effort, I could learn calculus. If I learned calculus, I would feel very smart.

I like art and literature because I like beauty and creativity. I never liked math because I didn't think it was beautiful and creative. I like solving problems, however. And I might actually discover something beautiful and creative about math. I think if I tried studying calculus, I would actually like it.

There are some new skills I would like to develop. There are some electrical problems in my house and I would like to learn how to fix them myself. I would like to learn how to do repair work on my CD player or even on my computer. If I learned calculus, it would help me develop the skills I need to do these things.

I think it would be really interesting to try learning something completely new. For me, calculus would be a big challenge. If I learned it, I would feel smart, I would enjoy myself, and I could develop new skills. It would be a big accomplishment for me.

▼

70	MA	Some people think that the automobile has improved modern life. Others think that the automobile has caused serious problems. What is your opinion? Use specific reasons and examples to support your answer.

There is no question that the automobile has improved modern life. It has opened up job opportunities to people, it has allowed families to stay connected, and it has given people the chance to travel to new places. The automobile is one of the best modern inventions.

With an automobile, a person has more choices of places to work. He can work near his home or farther away. He can even take a job in another city without having to go there to live. Without an automobile, a person can work only near his home or near a bus stop. His choices are much more limited.

With an automobile, it is much easier for a person to visit his family. Families these days often become separated. When children grow up, they find jobs in other cities. If they have cars, it is easy for them to visit their parents and other relatives whenever they want to. Without an automobile, they have to spend time and money taking a bus or train. It is not easy to visit their relatives as often.

With an automobile, a person can explore new places. He can just get in the car and drive wherever he wants to go, whenever he wants to. He has the opportunity to see new places and new people. He learns more about the world. Without an automobile, a person can go only where the bus, train, or plane takes him. It is not very convenient.

The automobile has greatly improved modern life. It has opened up new worlds and new opportunities to people. It has made many things possible. Where would we be without it?

▼

| 71 | MA | Which would you choose—a high-paying job with long hours that would give you little time with family and friends **or** a lower-paying job with shorter hours that would give you more time with family and friends? Explain your choice, using specific reasons and details. |

At this time in my life I would definitely choose a higher-paying job even if I had to work long hours. If I want a good future, first I have to gain experience, move up in my company, and save a lot of money. I will have plenty of time for friends and family later, after I get a good start on my career.

When I finish school, I will have a lot of knowledge. I won't have any experience, however. I can get experience only by working. I want a lot of experience so that I can be among the best in my career. The only way to get experience is to work a lot of hours.

I want to have a high position in my company. I don't want to be just an employee, I want to be a supervisor, and someday, director or president. I can't do this if I work only forty hours a week. The only way to move up is to work long hours.

Living a comfortable life is important to me. I want to have a nice house, fashionable clothes, and a couple of cars. When I get married, I want my family to have nice things too. This takes money. The best time to save money is now, before I have a family. The only way to save a lot of money is to work hard and earn a high salary.

A high-paying job with long hours will give me the experience, opportunities, and money that I want. After I reach a high position in my company and have a big bank account, I can take all the free time I want to relax with friends and family.

▼

72	AD	Do you agree or diagree with the following statement? Grades (marks) encourage students to learn. Use specific reasons and examples to support your opinion.

Grades are very important for students. Without grades, students don't know how well they are doing in class. They don't have a goal to study for. They don't have anything to show their parents. Students need grades to help them be motivated to learn.

Grades show students their progress in class. A student might work very hard to write a report. Without a grade, how does the student know if the report is good or bad? Without a grade, how can a student know if she is improving?

Grades give students a goal. A good grade is like a reward. If a student receives 100% on a test, he feels like all his hard work was worthwhile. If a student gets a bad grade, he will study harder next time so he can improve his grade.

Grades give students something to show their parents. Students want to please their parents. They want to work hard so they can show them good grades. When parents see good grades, they know their children are studying and learning. If the grades aren't good, the parents know they have to give their children extra help and support.

Grades are an important part of education. All students want to get good grades, so they will study hard to get them. Grades show students their progress, present them with a goal, and give them something to show their parents. Grades motivate students to learn.

▼

73	MA	Some people say that computers have made life easier and more convenient. Other people say that computers have made life more complex and stressful. What is your opinion? Use specific reasons and examples to support your answer.

Almost everything these days is done with the help of a computer. Computers make communication much more convenient. They make many tasks of daily life easier. They help many people do their jobs better. Overall, computers have made life easier and more convenient for everybody.

Through the Internet, computers make communication much more convenient. E-mail makes it possible to communicate with people instantly at any time of day. This is important for both our work and our personal lives. The Internet makes it possible to find out the latest news right away—even if it is news that happens someplace far away. The Internet makes it possible to get almost any kind of information from anyplace quickly, right in your own home or office.

Although we may not realize it, computers make many daily tasks easier. Checkout lines at stores move faster because a computer scans the prices. The bank manages your account more easily because of computers. The weatherman reports the weather more accurately with the help of computers. A computer is involved in almost everything we do, or that is done for us.

Most people these days do their jobs with the help of a computer. Architects use computer programs to help them design buildings. Teachers use computers to write their lessons and get information for their classes. Pilots use computers to help them fly planes. With the help of computers, people can do complicated jobs more easily.

We are living in the computer age. We can now do more things and do them more easily than we could before. Our personal and professional lives have improved because of computers.

▼

| 74 | AD | Do you agree or disagree with the following statement? The best way to travel is in a group led by a tour guide. Use specific reasons and examples to support your answer. |

When I travel, I always prefer to go with a group led by a tour guide. The tour guide makes all the necessary arrangements for the trip. The tour guide knows the best places to visit. The tour guide is familiar with the local language and customs. When I travel with a tour guide, the only thing I have to do is relax and enjoy myself.

If I travel in a group with a tour guide, I don't have to worry about arranging the trip. I just look for a group that is going to a place I like, and I let the tour guide take care of the rest. The tour guide makes the hotel reservations and chooses the restaurants and plans the activities for each day. I don't have to worry about anything because the guide does everything for me.

If I travel in a group with a tour guide, I don't have to figure out which places to visit. The tour guide knows which are the best museums. The tour guide knows where the good beaches are and which stores have the best prices. If I had to figure this out myself, I might make the wrong choices. With a tour guide, I am sure of having the best possible experience on my trip.

If I travel in a group with a tour guide, I don't have to know the local language and customs. The tour guide knows the language and can speak for the group when necessary. The tour guide knows when the local holidays are, or how to dress appropriately for each situation. I don't have to worry about confusions with the language or customs because the tour guide can help me.

When I go on vacation, I want to relax. I don't want to worry about making hotel reservations, or learning the museum schedules, or speaking the local language. A tour guide can take care of all these things for me, and I can have a good time.

▼

| 75 | MA | Some universities require students to take classes in many subjects. Other universities require students to specialize in one subject. Which is better? Use specific reasons and examples to support your answer. |

Universities offer opportunities to study many different subjects and university students should take advantage of this. Studying many subjects can help students better prepare for their careers. It can also help them become responsible members of society and can add to their personal enjoyment, as well.

Studying many subjects can help students be better prepared for their careers. A doctor doesn't need to know only about medicine, for example. She also needs to know how to respond to patients' emotional needs. She might need to know about accounting and legal contracts so she can run her own office. Each profession requires certain specialized skills, but all professionals also need other, more general skills in order to do their jobs well.

Studying many subjects can help students become more responsible members of society. They need to understand the economic and social issues of their communities so that they can vote responsibly. They might want to do volunteer work at a community organization. They will need to be able to educate their children, no matter what their children's abilities and interests are. They will need to know about more than just their profession in order to do these things.

Studying many subjects can add a great deal of enjoyment to a student's life. If students understand art and music, they will get a lot of enjoyment from museums and concerts. If they study literature, they will continue to read good books. Life is about more than just career. If students know about a lot of subjects, they will get a lot out of life.

Some university students think only about their careers. If the choice is left to them, they might only study courses for their future profession. They will have a much better future, however, if they study subjects in addition to their career. Therefore, universities should require students to take classes in many subjects.

▼

| 76 | AD | Do you agree or disagree with the following statement? Children should begin studying a foreign language as soon as they start school. |

Children should begin studying a foreign language as soon as they start school. Childhood is the best time to learn a foreign language. It is easier at that time, it contributes to a child's development, and it helps children expand their knowledge.

Everybody knows that it is much easier to learn foreign languages when you are young. Children's minds are ready to learn many new things. When children learn foreign languages, they learn them as well as their native language. If they wait until they are older to study a language, it is much harder to become fluent.

Many studies have shown that learning a language helps the child's mind develop. Children who learn foreign languages also do better in their other subjects. It helps their intellect develop more. This isn't so true for older students.

Learning foreign languages can help children expand their knowledge of the world. If they learn a foreign language, they will be interested in the people who speak that language. They will want to know about their country and customs. They will want to understand them instead of becoming afraid of them because they are different.

Learning a foreign language has many advantages for everybody. It contributes to our intellectual development and our understanding of the world. The younger a language student is, the more advantages he or she gets from learning the language. So, the best time for a child to start studying a foreign language is when he or she starts school.

▼

| 77 | AD | Do you agree or disagree with the following statement? Boys and girls should attend separate schools. Use specific reasons and examples to support your answer. |

I don't think it is a good idea for boys and girls to attend separate schools. They will not be separated when they finish school and start their careers, so why should they be separated in school? When boys and girls study together, they are assured of getting equal quality of education, they learn how to work together, and they learn how to become friends. It is a much better preparation for life than studying in separate schools.

When boys and girls attend the same school, they get equal education. They are in the same classrooms with the same teachers studying from the same books. If they attend separate schools, the schools might be different. One school might be better than the other. By studying together, girls get the same education as boys. This helps them work toward having equality in society.

By attending the same schools, boys and girls learn how to work together. Some people say they should study separately because they have different learning styles. I think it's better to study together, however. It gives them the chance to learn to work together despite their differences. This will help them in the future when they have to work together professionally.

When boys and girls see each other in school every day, they have the chance to become friends. They see each other as normal people, not as strangers. If they attend separate schools, they don't know each other. It's easy to misunderstand, or even fear, each other. When boys and girls have the chance to become friends, their lives are much richer. They will have better relationships in the future.

By studying together, boys and girls get equal education, they learn to work together, and they become friends. This prepares them for adult life where men and women live and work together everyday.

▼

| 78 | MA | Is it more important to be able to work with a group of people on a team or to work independently? Use reasons and specific examples to support your answer. |

The ability to work on a team is one of the most important job skills to have. It is usually necessary because most jobs involve teamwork. It is usually the best way to work because a team can get more work done than an individual. In addition, a worker on a team has a lot of support from his coworkers.

Most work is done in groups or teams. Professionals work with their professional colleagues, and they also usually have assistants and support staff. Construction workers work with other construction workers, auto mechanics work with other auto mechanics; they all have assistants, and almost nobody works alone. It is necessary for all coworkers to get along and work well together.

More work can be done by a team than by individuals working alone. On a team, each member is responsible for one part of the job. Each member has to concentrate only on her part and do it as well as possible. Then all the parts are put together and the job is done. An individual working alone has to worry about every aspect of the job. He might not do such a good job because he has to think about everything at once.

A worker on a team has the advantage of support from his coworkers. If a worker can't finish a job on time or doesn't understand a task or needs help planning, he has a group of people to help him. The team supports him and he can get the job done. An individual working alone has to solve all her problems herself. She has to stop work while she finds a solution, or do a poor job.

Most jobs involve teamwork. Teams can usually do a better job than an individual working alone. A person who cannot work well on a team will have a hard time in today's workplace.

▼

79	EX	Your city has decided to build a statue or monument to honor a famous person in your country. Who would you choose? Use reasons and specific examples to support your choice.

The person I would choose to honor is not one specific famous person, but a famous type of person. I come from a small rural town. Most people here are farmers, so I would choose a farmer as the subject for a statue. The farmers of my town deserve the honor. They work hard so the rest of the country can eat, but they are not rich. They deserve to be appreciated.

The farmers in my town make an important contribution to our country. They grow the food that the rest of the country eats. Our major products are corn and milk. These things are a basic part of everyone's diet. Without our farmers, it would be harder and more expensive for people to have these things to eat.

The farmers in my town are not rich even though they work hard. A farmer's job begins at sunrise and doesn't stop until dark. A farmer rarely has a chance to take a vacation because there are always things to do on a farm. Farming is not a profitable business. If the weather is bad one year, there might be no profits at all. Still, farmers do their work because people need to eat.

The farmers in my town work hard, but they are not appreciated. People in other parts of the country don't pay much attention to my town. Nobody comes to visit because there are no tourist attractions. Nobody wants to work here because there aren't many professional jobs. Nobody thinks about the contributions our farmers make. They just buy our products in the stores without thinking about the work it takes to put them there.

Nobody thinks about the farmers in my town, but they deserve to be honored. They work hard to grow food for everyone in the country. I think we should put a big, shiny statue of a farmer in the middle of our town park. It would make everyone in town feel proud.

▼

| 80 | EX | Describe a custom from your country that you would like people in other countries to adopt. Explain your choice using specific reasons and examples. |

In my country, many people in the towns still follow an old custom that people in the cities no longer practice. This is the custom of taking a big break at noon. In the towns, all stores and businesses close from noon until 2:00 P.M. This not only gives people a needed rest in the middle of the day, it also allows them time with their families and contributes to a slower pace of life.

In the towns, all workers get a good rest in the middle of the day. They go home, enjoy a nice meal, take a nap, and then they return to work for the rest of the afternoon. They have energy and enthusiasm for the rest of the day's work. Their afternoons can be as productive as their mornings. Without this rest, they might be tired all afternoon and not get much work done.

In the towns, most families eat their noon meal together. They have time to enjoy their food, talk about their morning activities with each other, and just be together. It is good for families to have this time together. Parents hear about their children's activities. Husbands and wives learn about each other's daily concerns. Without this opportunity, families might not be together until evening. They are usually tired then and just want to rest.

In the towns, there is a slower pace of life. Nobody can do any business at lunchtime. They have to wait until the afternoon. Because of this, people don't expect things to be done in a hurry. They have more patience. If something doesn't get done today, it doesn't matter. This is a much healthier way to live.

A big rest at noon contributes to a better quality of life. In the towns, people don't worry about getting a lot of work done fast. They are more interested in spending time with their families and enjoying their lives. I think that in the long run this actually improves work. In any case, it is a better way to live. I think everyone everywhere should follow the custom of taking a big break at noon.

▼

| 81 | AD | Do you agree or disagree with the following statement? Technology has made the world a better place to live. Use specific reasons and examples to support your statement. |

Technology has made our lives better in many ways, but it has also made them more complicated. Technology is often expensive to buy and run, it can be difficult to use, and it often isn't easy to repair.

Technology isn't cheap. The more technology we depend on in our daily lives, the more money we have to spend. Everybody wants a modern TV, a digital camera, a DVD player, etc. Even though these things might be considered luxuries, people want them. In addition, some technology is more than a luxury. For example, teachers nowadays expect their students to have computers at home for their schoolwork. Parents have to buy the latest computers so their children can keep up with their classmates. This can be a real hardship for some families.

Technology isn't always easy to use. In fact, it is getting more and more complicated. The computers of today do many more things than the computers of even just five or ten years ago. That means a lot more things that computer users have to learn how to do. Even a simple thing like using a VCR to record a movie takes some practice and learning.

Technology isn't easy to repair. If the average person has a problem with his computer or DVD player, he probably doesn't know how to fix it himself. He'll have to spend time and money taking it to a place to get fixed. In the past, a lot of people enjoyed doing routine maintenance work on their cars. Modern technology has made today's cars more complicated. It is harder to learn how to repair and maintain them.

People think modern technology has made our lives easier. In a way this is true, but in other ways it has made our lives much less convenient. Modern technology costs us money and time and can add complications to our lives.

▼

| 82 | AD | Do you agree or disagree with the following statement? Advertising can tell you a lot about a country. Use specific reasons and examples to support your answer. |

Advertising is like a window onto the life of a country. It tells a lot about the people there. Advertisements show what kinds of things the people in a country like to buy. It shows what kinds of situations are attractive to them. It even shows whether or not the people tend to be affluent. You can learn a lot by looking at advertisements.

By looking at advertisements, you can see what kinds of things people like to buy. Are there more advertisements for soda or for juice? For movies or for music? For vacations or for furniture? You can see what kinds of food people prefer, how they like to spend their free time, or what they save their money for. You can learn just about anything about the average lifestyle in a country.

By looking at advertisements, you can see what kinds of situations are attractive to people. If an ad shows someone driving a car freely down an open highway in beautiful scenery, you can see that people value feeling free. If an ad shows a professional-looking person in an expensive car in front of an elegant house or office building, you will know that people value success.

By looking at advertisements, you can know whether or not a country is affluent. If ads are usually about food, clothes, and other necessities of life, the people in the country may not have a lot of money. If more ads are for luxury items and expensive, high-quality products, then you know that more people in that country have money.

Advertisements can tell you a lot about a country. They show how the people there live. They show what the people want to buy and can buy. Ads give a picture of a country's daily life.

▼

83	AD	Do you agree or disagree with the following statement? Modern technology is creating a single world culture. Use specific reasons and examples to support your answer.

Modern technology is creating a single world culture. This is because it is now much easier to communicate with people who are far away. Satellite TV, modern transportation, and the Internet have all brought people closer together. People the world over share the same sources of information and this leads to the creation of a single world culture.

Because TV is broadcast by satellite, TV programs can be received anywhere in the world. Now people in every part of the world can have access to all the same TV programs. Everybody knows that TV is one of the biggest cultural influences there is. When people everywhere see the same news, educational, and entertainment programs, they move toward the development of a single world culture.

Because modern methods of transportation are fast, a trip to a faraway place becomes easy. People from all different places are together more now than they ever were before. They can see how people in other countries dress, eat, and spend their time. People have more exposure to customs from other countries and might start to adopt some of those customs. This also contributes to the development of a single world culture.

Because of the Internet, people have access to information and news from all over the world. They can communicate easily with people far away and share sources of information. This can do a lot toward international understanding but it can also have another result. When people share sources of information on the Internet, they come more and more under the same cultural influence. They move toward the creation of a single world culture.

Modern communications technology has brought people from all around the world closer together. People these days have more and more opportunities to share ideas and information. In this way they are coming more and more under the same cultural influence. A single world culture is being created.

▼

84	MA	Some people think the Internet provides people with a lot of valuable information. Others think access to so much information creates problems. Which view do you agree with? Use specific reasons and examples to support your opinion.

The Internet provides us with a lot of valuable information. This is important because it keeps us informed about the world today, contributes to children's education, and even helps us shop better. It helps improve our lives in many ways.

When we want to know the latest news, we can just go to the Internet and get it right away. We don't have to wait for a news program on TV or the radio. We also don't have to listen to just one source of news. On the Internet we can get news from different newspapers and different countries. We can get information from different points of view. This greatly contributes to our understanding of current events.

When children need information for their schoolwork, they can find it on the Internet. Most schoolchildren these days do their research on-line. They have access to more information than they could probably find in their school libraries, and they can get the information more easily. In addition, any time a child wants to know something or needs the answer to a question, he can probably find it on-line.

When we want to buy something, we can usually get the information we need for our purchase on-line. Of course you can order almost anything you want on the Internet, but this isn't the most important part. On the Internet it is easy to find information about the quality of different products and to compare prices. This really matters if you plan to buy something expensive.

The ability to get information from the Internet has improved our lives in many ways. We can learn more about the news, improve our children's education, and become more informed shoppers. The Internet is one of the most important tools we have in modern society.

▼

| 85 | MA | A foreign visitor has only one day to spend in your country. Where should this visitor go on that day? Why? Use specific reasons and details to support your choice. |

A foreign visitor with only one day to spend in my country should definitely spend that day in the capital. Spending time in the capital is the easiest way to see many aspects of our country in one place. In this city, the visitor can learn about our history, see examples of our culture, and buy our best products.

Our country's history is represented in several ways throughout the city. In the Government Palace, a visitor can learn about the history of our independence. In our National Museum, a visitor can see exhibits that show all the different stages of our history, from ancient times to the present. In parks all around the city, a visitor can see monuments to famous historical people and events.

It is also possible to see different representations of our culture throughout the city. Our art museums and galleries show paintings and sculptures by our artists. Plays written by national playwrights are performed in the theaters. Folk ballet performances show examples of our traditional dances. Many restaurants in the capital serve our native dishes.

The best products of our country are sold in the capital city. The large department stores sell clothes, furniture, and household items manufactured in our country. The Central Market sells fruit and vegetables from the surrounding agricultural region. Tourist and craft shops sell native handicrafts made in the countryside.

The capital city is the best place to learn a lot about our country in one place. Of course, it is difficult to see all of the city's attractions in one day. With some planning, though, it is possible to see at least a few examples of our country's history, culture, and products in one day.

▼

| 86 | MA | If you could go back to some time and place in the past, when and where would you go? Why? Use specific reasons and details to support your choice. |

If I could go back to a time and place in the past, I would go back to ancient Egypt. I would like to find out how they built the pyramids. People today cannot understand how the ancient Egyptians cut the stones so precisely, how they moved them to the building site, and how they lifted such heavy stones to build the pyramid walls. I would like to solve this mystery.

The stones that were used to build the pyramids were cut very precisely. All the stones fit together exactly without any space between them. How were the ancient Egyptians able to cut the stone blocks so well? Nobody knows.

The stones that were used to build the pyramids are very heavy. They weigh several tons each. The ancient Egyptians didn't have any kind of motorized machinery to move them around. Yet, they got the stones from one place and moved them to another place to build the pyramids. How were they able to do this? Nobody today can figure it out.

The pyramids are very tall. They were built by placing stone blocks on top of each other. The ancient Egyptians didn't have any cranes or other type of modern lifting equipment. Yet they built huge pyramids out of heavy stone blocks. How did they do this? We still aren't able to understand.

One of the great mysteries of the ancient world is the Egyptian pyramids. Nobody knows how the Egyptians cut, transported, and lifted heavy stones to build the pyramids. If I could go back to ancient Egypt, I could find this out. Then I would return to the modern world and tell everyone the answer.

▼

| 87 | MA | What discovery in the last 100 years has been most beneficial for people in your country? Use specific reasons and examples to support your choice. |

A discovery that has been beneficial to people in my country and everywhere is the use of electricity. Electricity has made the development of modern technology possible. Without electricity we wouldn't have modern communications technology, we wouldn't have computers, we wouldn't even have electric light. Almost everything about modern life depends on electricity.

Electricity has made modern communications technology possible. Telephones, television, and radio all depend on electricity. Because we have these things, we can communicate with friends and business associates instantly. We can hear the latest news almost as soon as it happens. We can follow the newest developments in music. Both our personal and professional lives are completely different now from what they were 100 years ago.

If we didn't have electricity, we wouldn't have computers. We use computers in almost every aspect of our lives. We use them to get information in school. We use them to make our jobs easier. Computers help people fly airplanes and design buildings. We couldn't do many of the things we do today without computers. And we couldn't use computers without electricity.

Because of electricity, it is easier to light up buildings and streets at night. This seems so simple that sometimes we forget it. Before electricity, people used candles. It was hard to read at night, to go anywhere, or to do any work. Now we can live our lives as fully at night as we do during the day. We can work or play at any hour we choose. It really is an amazing thing.

Electricity has made many things possible in modern life. We wouldn't have any modern technology without it. It is the most important discovery of the modern world.

▼

88	AD	Do you agree or disagree with the following statement? Telephone and e-mail have made communications between people less personal. Use specific reasons and examples to support your opinion.

Some people think that telephone and e-mail have made communication between people less personal, but I disagree. If anything, they have made communication more personal. This is because these types of communication are easy, informal, and inexpensive.

It is easy to communicate with someone by phone or e-mail. You just pick up the phone or turn on the computer, and that's it. E-mail is especially easy because you can send your message at any time. If the receiver isn't available when you send the message, it doesn't matter. The message will be there when she's ready to answer. Because this sort of communication is so easy, people communicate more frequently. This brings them closer together, so it becomes a more personal form of communication.

Communication by phone or by e-mail is informal. On the phone you converse with someone as informally as you do in person. When you write e-mail messages, you usually use less formal styles of writing. Traditional letters, on the other hand, have formal conventions that the writer must follow. Even friendly letters have certain rules to follow. Communication that is informal is more personal than formal communication.

Telephones and e-mail are inexpensive to use. Nowadays even long distance phone calls are cheap, and local ones are free. E-mail costs nothing if you already own a computer. Letters are cheap, but seeing someone in person isn't always. Even if the person lives nearby, it still costs something for the bus or gasoline to go meet them somewhere, and it takes time, too. Since e-mail and telephone are cheap, people communicate more frequently and, therefore, more personally.

Some people think you have to meet face to face in order to have personal communication, but this isn't so. Telephones and e-mail make frequent communication convenient. They help maintain personal relationships.

▼

| 89 | MA | If you could travel back in time to meet a famous person from history, what person would you like to meet? Use specific reasons and examples to support your choice. |

If I could meet a famous person from history, I would like to meet Leonardo da Vinci. There has probably been no other person like him in all of history. He was a talented artist and an imaginative inventor. He was a unique person and I would like to know what that felt like.

Da Vinci's artistic talents are well known. The Mona Lisa is, of course, his most famous painting. It is beautiful, and he painted and drew many other beautiful works of art as well. I like to draw and paint, too. Of course my talent will never approach da Vinci's, but it would be inspiring to meet him.

Da Vinci invented many things. For example, he made drawings of a flying machine. This was centuries before the first airplane was ever built. Perhaps his inventions never became reality in his life, but he still was able to imagine them. He created things in his mind that were well ahead of his time. I think this is amazing and inspiring.

Da Vinci was a smart and talented person. His ideas were well ahead of his time. There was no one else like him around. I wonder what that felt like. It must have been difficult at least some of the time. If I could meet him, I could ask him about this.

To tell the truth, I haven't read much about da Vinci. I would like to learn more about him, however, because of his unique talents and ideas. It would be an inspiring experience to meet him.

▼

| 90 | MA | If you could meet a famous entertainer or athlete, who would that be, and why? Use specific reasons and examples to support your choice. |

If I could meet a famous entertainer, I would like to meet Madonna. She used to be an ordinary person, and now she has achieved fame, power, and money. I think that is amazing. I have never met anybody like her.

Madonna was a normal college student and now she is famous all over the world. She worked hard to make her name known. There are better actors and singers than she is, but few people are as famous. Her goal was to become famous, and she made it happen. I think that is admirable.

Madonna is one of the most powerful people in the entertainment industry. People pay attention to what she says. Everybody listens to her music. She can set fashions. Teenagers everywhere like to dress like her. She can do whatever she wants in both her business and personal life. I have never met such a person.

Madonna has a lot of money. She owns several houses. She can travel anywhere she wants to go. She pays a lot of people to work for her. It would be interesting to meet a person with so much money.

Madonna was an ordinary person who became famous, powerful, and rich. I am an ordinary person too. I would like to meet Madonna to learn how she made these achievements.

▼

| 91 | EX | If you could ask a famous person **one** question, what would you ask? Why? Use specific reasons and details to support your answer. |

If I could ask a famous person one question, I would ask Neil Armstrong what it felt like to walk on the moon. Sometimes I think it would be scary; sometimes I think it would be fun. On the other hand, maybe Neil Armstrong was too busy to feel scared or have fun while he was walking on the moon.

I think it could be very scary to go to walk on the moon. Neil Armstrong was the first person to do it. He was well prepared for the event, but he still couldn't be sure what he would find. Also, maybe he worried that something might happen. What if he had a problem with his oxygen or couldn't get back to the spaceship on time? I wonder if he thought about these things, or if he just did his job.

On the other hand, maybe Neil Armstrong had fun walking on the moon. The gravity is different so just taking steps would feel different. I think that would be fun. If I went to the moon, I would want to run and jump and shout, "Hurray! I am on the moon!" I wonder if Armstrong felt that way.

Maybe Armstrong didn't have time to feel scared or happy or anything else. He had a very important job to do. The whole world was watching him. He had to be serious and focus on his work. His time was short. He probably didn't have time for anything except to get his job done.

It can be a scary thing or a fun adventure to do something for the first time. Being the first person to walk on the moon is one of the most incredible adventures of all time. I would like to meet Neil Armstrong so I could ask him how it felt.

▼

| 92 | PR | Some people prefer to live in places that have the same weather or climate all year long. Others like to live in areas where the weather changes several times a year. Which do you prefer? Use specific reasons and examples to support your choice. |

I would prefer to live in a place that has warm weather all year. My life would be easier and more comfortable this way. I would be healthier, I would have more fun, and I would save money if I lived in a warm climate.

I would always be healthy if I lived in a warm climate. Where I live now, I get sick every winter. I wouldn't have this problem in a warm climate. Also, I could be outside all year long. I would play sports and get more exercise. That would make me healthier, too.

I would have more fun if I lived in a warm climate. I like outdoor activities. I like going to the beach, playing soccer, and riding my bicycle. I can't do these things in cold weather. In a warm climate, I could do my favorite activities all year long.

I would save money if I lived in a warm climate. It costs money to heat a house in the winter. This can get very expensive. I wouldn't have this expense in a warm climate. It costs money to buy new clothes every time the season changes. In a warm climate, I could wear the same clothes all year.

My life would be better in a warm climate. My health, my free time activities, and my bank account would all improve. In fact, I plan to move to a warm climate as soon as I finish school.

▼

| 93 | MA | Many students have to live with a roommate while going to school or university. What are some of the important qualities of a good roommate? Use specific reasons and examples to explain why these qualities are important. |

It is important to have a good roommate. A good roommate can become your best friend, but a bad roommate can be your worst enemy. A good roommate is considerate, flexible, and fun.

A good roommate is considerate of your needs. He doesn't make noise when you want to sleep or study. He doesn't plan a party or use your things without asking. A good roommate doesn't think only about himself; he thinks about you, too.

A good roommate is flexible. He can adjust to your habits. If you are neat and your roommate is messy, for example, you each try to change a little bit. Your roommate tries to be a little neater and you try to live with a little mess.

Finally, a good roommate is fun. If he knows about a party or a concert, he invites you to go with him. He introduces you to his friends. You plan some free time activities together. A good roommate may be serious about his studies, but he knows that it is important to have fun, too.

It is great to have a roommate who can be your friend, too. If your roommate is considerate, flexible, and fun, you are sure to get along well together.

▼

| 94 | AD | Do you agree or disagree with the following statement? Dancing plays an important role in a culture. Use specific reaons and examples to support your answer. |

I agree that dancing plays an important role in a culture. It keeps us connected with our traditions, it brings people together, and it helps people release energy.

Folk dances keep us connected with our traditions. Folk dances were developed hundreds of years ago. People used to dance together to celebrate important events, such as harvests or weddings. When we dance folk dances now, we are connected to our ancestors. We do the same dances they did and remember the things that were important to them.

Dancing brings people together. When we dance at an event such as a birthday or graduation party, we celebrate a happy occasion together. We might go out dancing with our friends on weekends. Then we celebrate being together and enjoying life. Dancing is a way of enjoying good times together.

When we dance, we release energy. We work hard all week at school or at our jobs. At the end of the week, we feel stress. We need a change of activity and a way to relax. Dancing is a good way to do this. When we dance, we can release all our extra energy, and any frustrations or anger we might feel. We relax and have fun. Then we can feel ready start a new week of work and school

Dancing keeps us connected to our traditions and to each other. It helps us release energy so we can perform our responsibilities at work and school. These are important roles that dancing plays in our culture.

▼

95	AD	Some people think governments should spend as much money as possible exploring outer space (for example, traveling to the moon and other planets). Other people disagree and think governments should spend this money for our basic needs on Earth. Which of these two opinions do you agree with? Use specific reasons and details to support your answer.

I believe that we should spend whatever money is required to explore outer space. It is true that we have many needs here on Earth, and many problems to solve. Exploring outer space, however, has invaluable benefits for people on Earth. It helps medical research, it leads to useful inventions, and it can help solve our overpopulation problem. I think space exploration is worth the cost.

Research carried out in space contributes a great deal to medical science. There is some research that can be conducted only in space. The research on the effects of gravity on bone marrow is one example. Research such as this will continue to contribute to advances in medicine. It benefits everybody on Earth.

Many useful inventions have happened because of space exploration. Different kinds of plastics that were developed for space travel are also now used on Earth. Things we use in our daily lives are made from "space age" materials. This is another aspect of space exploration that benefits everyone.

The search for other planets can help solve our overpopulation problem. People are living longer and healthier lives these days. That's a good thing, but it means more people on Earth. The Earth will not get bigger. Through space exploration, we may be able to find other planets where people can live. This is one more thing that will have a benefit for all people.

Space exploration results in benefits for people everywhere on Earth. It contributes to medical science, to inventions, and to a solution to overpopulation. It is expensive, but the benefits are worth the price. Space exploration is one of the best ways governments can spend our money.

▼

96	MA	People have different ways of escaping the stress of modern life. Some read, some exercise, others work in their gardens. What do you think are the best ways of reducing stress? Use specific details and examples in your answer.

Stress is one of our biggest enemies. It affects all aspects of our lives. In order to get rid of stress, I first have to identify the cause. My solutions to stress depend on the cause. The most common causes of stress in my life are work, friends, and myself.

Work-related stress is the easiest to combat. I simply stop working for a while. Sometimes I get up from my desk and go down the hall to talk to my colleagues. Of course, I don't talk about work-related topics. Other times, I take a short walk around the block. Work-related stress can be cured just by getting away from work.

Stress caused by my friends is more difficult to cure. A friend might be angry with me or vice versa. A friend might be anxious about something, and that makes me anxious, too. The best cure for this kind of stress is talking about the problem and spending time with my friends. Unlike work, you can't walk away from your friends.

Stress I cause myself is not very easy to get rid of. If I feel bothered by an exam or anxious about the future, there is very little for me to do. I just have to tell myself that I can only do my best and leave the rest up to fate.

It is important to try to lead a stress-free life. If you can avoid stress by walking away from it (as at work), talking about it (as with friends), or facing it head on (as with yourself), you will benefit in all aspects of your life.

▼

| 97 | AD | Do you agree or disagree with the following statement? Teachers should be paid according to how much their students learn. Give specific reasons and examples to support your opinion. |

It is a bad idea to pay teachers according to how much their students learn. It just encourages teachers to teach only the material on a test. It discourages them from paying attention to slow students. It is unfair because teachers can't decide which students will be in their class. Instead of improving teaching, it keeps teachers from doing the best job they can.

If a teacher is paid according to how well his students do on a test, then he will teach only what is on the test. He will spend time teaching his students to memorize facts. He won't be able to teach them other things. The students will miss the opportunity to gain a wider variety of knowledge. They won't have the chance to develop skills besides memorization. They will learn less, not more, in this way.

Another problem is that teachers may ignore the slower students. Some students learn more quickly and easily than others. The teacher won't want to spend time with the few slowest students. She will prefer to focus on the average and fast students to make sure they get high scores on tests. She can't waste time with the students who can get only mediocre scores. These students, who need the most help in school, will get very little help at all.

Finally, a teacher has no control over which students are placed in his class. One teacher may get all the best students in a school. Another may get several of the worst. If the teacher has some average students, a few below average, and no students who are above average, then of course the class will get lower test scores on their tests. People will think those students didn't learn much. It is not fair to base a teacher's salary on something over which he has no control.

Most teachers, like other professionals, want to do the best job possible. They want to teach their students useful skills and knowledge and they want to help the students who need help. Teachers need encouragement and support, but basing their salary on their students' performance is not a good way to provide this.

| 98 | MA | If you were asked to send one thing representing your country to an international exhibition, what would you choose? Why? Use specific reasons and details to explain your choice. |

If I were asked to send one thing representing my country to an international exhibition, I'd send something unexpected: one week's worth of television programming. These programs best represent my country. They show how we live, what we value, and what we teach our children.

Television programs show how people in my country live. They show how different people earn a living. They show the different kinds of houses people live in. They show routines of day-to-day living. They show the different kinds of relationships people have. They give a broad representation of daily life in my country.

Television programs show what the people in my country value. Comedies indicate what we think is funny. Documentaries show what issues we're concerned about and how we want to resolve them. Sports programs show what we think about winning and losing. In general, the range of programs shown on television demonstrates what we think is important and interesting.

Children's programs show what we teach our children. Some programs teach school skills such as reading and math. Others tell stories from literature or folk traditions. Many focus on teaching children right from wrong. And some, like cartoons, are just meant to entertain.

You can learn a lot about a country by watching its television programs. You can learn about daily life, values, and education. That is why I would send a week's worth of television programs to an international exhibition.

| 99 | PR | You have been told that dormitory rooms at your university must be shared by two students. Would you rather have the university assign a student to share a room with you, or would you rather choose your own roommate? Use specific reasons and details to explain your answer. |

I'd rather have the university assign a roommate to share a room with me. I don't know many people at the university I plan to attend. I'm sure the university will choose a roommate who is compatible with me and this will give me the chance to make new friends.

None of my close friends will attend the university with me. We all plan to attend different schools. I have a few acquaintances at my university, but I don't know them well. I don't think they are people I would choose to live with. At this time, I really can't choose my own roommate. I am glad the university can do it for me.

The university has a very good system for assigning roommates. All the students have to fill out information sheets. We write about our majors, our interests, our study habits, and our goals. The university uses this information to match roommates. They can match people who have similar habits and interests. I think it is a good system.

When the university assigns me a roommate, I have a chance to make new friends. For one, my roommate will be a new friend. We already know that we will have similar habits and interests, so we will probably enjoy spending time together. In addition, my roommate's friends could become my friends, too. My roommate can introduce me to new people, and I can do the same for him.

I think it's a good idea for a university to choose roommates for the students. They can match people who are compatible and give everyone a chance to make new friends. Meeting new people is an important part of a university education, and this is one way to make that happen.

▼

100	PR	Some people think that governments should spend as much money as possible on developing or buying computer technology. Other people disagree and think that this money should be spent on more basic needs. Which one of these opinions do you agree with? Use specific reasons and details to support your answer.

Developing computer technology is important for the development of the country as a whole. However, we have some basic needs and issues in our country that are even more important than technology. Our children need to get a good education. Our transportation system needs to be improved. We need to develop new sources of energy. We need to work on these issues before we put a lot of money into computers.

Our children need to get a good education. We need to make sure that every child in the country has the opportunity to learn to read and write. In addition, they all need to learn skills for the modern world. They need to learn how to use computers. It costs money to buy computers for schools and train teachers to use them. If children don't learn basic computer skills in school, who will be able to use modern computer technology?

We need to improve our transportation system. In big cities, the roads are very crowded and it is hard to get around. It takes a long time for people just to get to work every day. We need to spend money developing a good public transportation system. We need to get cars off the road and have more buses and trains. Computer technology helps people at work. If it is difficult for people just to get to work, computer technology won't help them much.

We need to develop new sources of energy. Our current methods of generating energy cause a lot of pollution. We need to develop the use of solar energy and other nonpolluting energy technology. Energy research and development costs a lot of money, but it is necessary. If we don't have clean, cheap sources of energy, what will we use to run our computers?

Computer technology is important. However, we can't take advantage of it if we don't solve some problems first. We need well-educated children, good public transportation, and clean sources of energy before we can spend money on computers.

▼

| 101 | PR | Some people like doing work by hand. Others prefer using machines. Which do you prefer? Use specific reasons and examples to support your answer. |

I prefer using machines to doing work by hand. Machines can work faster and more neatly than I can, and they never get tired.

Machines are fast. If I want to write a letter, it takes me a certain amount of time. If I write ten letters by hand, it takes ten times as long. If I use a computer, on the other hand, I just write the letter once, then tell the printer to make ten copies. Or I can use a photocopy machine. Either way, it's much faster than doing all the work by hand.

Machines are neat. They don't make mistakes and cut the wrong way. They don't get distracted and spill coffee on the paper. They do a job over and over again, each time as neatly as the time before. I could never be as neat as a machine.

Machines never get tired. You can set a photocopy machine to make 25 copies or 250 copies. It makes no difference to the machine how many copies it has to make. An answering machine answers calls in the middle of the night as well as it does in the morning. If I work a lot, I get tired, and I can't work at all in the middle of the night.

I can depend on machines, but I can't always depend on myself to be fast, neat, and tireless.

▼

| 102 | AD | Schools should ask students to evaluate their teachers. Do you agree or disagree? Use specific reasons and examples to support your answer. |

I think it is a good idea for schools to ask students to evaluate their teachers. It is good for the teachers, good for the school administrators, and good for the students themselves.

Teachers can get a lot of useful information from student evaluations. They can find out what the students like about the class and what they don't like. They can learn what the students think is easy or difficult. They can discover which kinds of activities the students prefer. Generally, they can find out the ways they reach the students and the ways they don't. All of these things can help teachers improve their classes.

Student evaluations are also helpful for school administrators. Student evaluations help administrators learn which teachers are most effective. They give an idea of how students are satisfied or dissatisfied with their school program. With this kind of information, administrators can work better with the teachers. They can work together to improve the school program where necessary.

Evaluating teachers is a good exercise for students. They have to organize their thoughts about their teacher. They have to think about how they themselves learn best and what kind of help they need. This can help them do better in class. Evaluations also give students a chance to develop honesty and responsibility. Evaluations with real and useful information are valuable to the school. Evaluations that are used as a way of being mean or getting favors aren't worthwhile.

Student evaluations can provide a lot of useful information to a school. They help the teachers, the school administrators, and the students. I think they are a very good idea.

▼

| 103 | MA | In your opinion, what is the most important characteristic (for example, honesty, intelligence, a sense of humor) that a person can have to be successful in life? Use specific reasons and examples from your experience to explain your answer. When you write your answer, you are not limited to the examples listed in the question. |

Although honesty, intelligence, and a sense of humor are all worthwhile characteristics, I feel the most important one to have is sensitivity. A sensitive person is aware of the way his or her actions affect others. A sensitive person knows the place of honesty, intelligence, and a sense of humor.

Honesty is not always the best policy. There is such a thing as a white lie. You don't want to tell someone that her expensive new dress doesn't look good on her. You wouldn't tell your friends that you don't like their house. Sensitive people know when it is necessary to tell the truth and when it is better to tell a white lie.

Intelligence is a wonderful thing to have, but not all intelligent people use their intelligence sensitively. It isn't good to show off your intelligence and make other people feel dumb. Sometimes you might have to say, "My answer might be wrong. We should check it." Sensitive people know when to use their intelligence and when to step back and let others answer.

A sense of humor is always valued. Different people, however, laugh at different things. A joke that is funny to you might be offensive to someone else. Some people can laugh at their mistakes but others are uncomfortable about them. A sensitive person knows when it's O.K. to laugh or tease, and when it's better to be sympathetic or just quiet.

A sensitive person can make everyone feel comfortable. A sensitive person knows that people are different and that honesty, intelligence, and humor need to be applied to each situation differently.

▼

| 104 | EX | It is generally agreed that society benefits from the work of its members. Compare the contributions of artists to society with the contributions of scientists to society. Which type of contribution do you think is more valued by your society? Give specific reasons to support your answer. |

Artists and scientists make very different types of contributions to our society, and the contributions of both are valuable. Although the contributions of both are important, however, our society seems to value the contributions of scientists more.

Artists lift our spirits and show us who we are. A painter or writer shows us in pictures and words what we're like as a people. Performing artists entertain us. Artists take our minds off our troubles and remind us of the beauty of life. Artists also help keep society mentally and emotionally healthy, because they provide us with a means of expression. Art of all types is necessary to the human spirit.

Scientists make contributions to our material lives. The cars we drive, the computers we use at school and work, the appliances we use to clean our houses, are all results of the hard work of scientists. We can grow more food, and cure more diseases, and live healthier lives thanks to scientific research. Scientists have helped improve our material lives in many ways.

Artists make valuable contributions to society, but society seems to value scientists more. Scientists are more often rewarded with money than artists are. They generally earn higher salaries, and it is easier for them to get government funding for their work. They have more social prestige and are generally considered to be smarter people than artists. There are always exceptions, of course. Some scientists struggle to earn money. Some artists are very rich and have a great deal of prestige, but they are few. Overall, scientists have a better position in society.

The contributions of both artists and scientists are valuable to our society. They each contribute to different aspects of our lives. Unfortunately, artists don't always get the recognition they deserve.

▼

| 105 | PR | Students at universities often have a choice of places to live. They may choose to live in university dormitories, or they may choose to live in apartments in the community. Compare the advantages of living in university housing with the advantages of living in an apartment in the community. Where would you prefer to live? Give reasons for your preference. |

I think it is better for university students to live in a dormitory. It makes their lives much easier, it gives them more opportunities to make friends, and it helps them become more involved in the university community.

Dormitory life is much easier than apartment life for a university student. If a student rents an apartment, that means she has to buy furniture and kitchen utensils. She has to shop and cook for herself every day. She has to spend time keeping the apartment clean. A dormitory room, on the other hand, already has furniture, and meals are served in the dormitory dining room. The student doesn't have to spend time taking care of household things and can just concentrate on her studies.

A student living in a dormitory has potential friends living all around her. First she'll make friends with her roommate, then with the other students living on her floor. She can make friends in the dormitory dining room and the lounge. If she feels lonely, if she needs help with her classwork, if she misses her family, there is always someone to turn to. If she lives in an apartment, she won't have all this support. She might have a roommate, but otherwise she will be alone. She'll have to put more effort into making friends in her classes.

By living in a dormitory a student is right in the middle of the university community. She is close to all the university activities and it is easy to participate in them. She can become involved in clubs, sports, or the student government. If she lives in an apartment, she is farther from all these activities. It takes more time to get to club meetings.

It is harder to find out what activities are going on. It's more difficult to be part of the community.

　　Living in an apartment has advantages for some people, but for me dormitory life is much better. It makes daily tasks, meeting new friends, and being involved in university activities much easier. It is a convenient and fun way to live.

▼

| 106 | EX | You need to travel from your home to a place 40 miles (64 kilometers) away. Compare the different kinds of transportation you could use. Tell which method of travel you would choose. Give specific reasons for your choice. |

　　When I choose a method of transportation to go 40 miles, I have three common choices: my bike, my parents' car, or public transportation. When I choose among them, I think about how much it will cost, how long it will take, and why I need to go from point A to point B.

　　My bike is a less expensive alternative. The only cost is my manual labor to pedal from my home to a place 40 miles away. This method, however, is extremely time-consuming. I imagine it would take me all day. Biking is excellent exercise. If my only goal is to burn calories and strengthen my muscles, I should go by bike.

　　Public transportation is another alternative that is inexpensive. The cost is minimal and shared by everyone on the bus or train. Where I live, you cannot depend on public transportation. It might take me all day to go 40 miles by public transportation if I include waiting time. However, using public transportation is good for the Earth. By sharing resources, we waste less.

　　Taking a private car is the most expensive, especially since I don't own a car and I must borrow one from my parents. They want me to pay for my own gas, which is a lot, and I must also pay for parking the car when I get to my destination. A car is the most dependable way to go if I need to get there fast. When convenience is your goal, you should pick a car.

　　When I consider these points, I must confess that I am spoiled. I prefer the convenience of the car over the exercise of a bike and the virtues of public transportation. I like to go and come when I want to without waiting, even if it costs me more.

▼

| 107 | MA | Some people believe that a college or university education should be available to all students. Others believe that higher education should be available to only good students. Discuss these views. Which view do you agree with? Explain why. |

　　Some people believe that only the best students should go to a college or university, but I don't. Academics are not the only purpose of a university education. Another important goal is to learn about yourself. When you are separated from your parents, you have to learn to be independent and make decisions about your future. I believe every student should have the opportunity to have this kind of experience.

I can understand why some people think that a college or university education should be available to only good students. Higher education is very expensive. It might seem like a waste of money to send a mediocre student to college. If a better student will learn more, why not send only the better student to college? Higher education is also a big investment of time. Maybe a mediocre student could spend his or her time in a better way, by getting a job or going to trade school.

I don't agree with this position. I think higher education should be available to all students. It is true that it is expensive and takes a lot of time, but I think every student deserves the opportunity to try it. People change. A student who didn't like school as a teenager may start to like it as a young adult. Also, having the opportunity to make independent decisions is part of a good education. A student may try college for a while and then decide that trade school is a better place for him or her. Or a student may decide, "I will work hard now because I want a good future." At a college or university students have the opportunity to make changes and decisions for themselves.

All students who want to should be given the chance to go to a college or university. In college they will have the opportunity to learn independence and to make adult decisions about their future. This is a basic part of education and an experience every student should have.

▼

| 108 | PR | Some people believe that the best way of learning about life is by listening to the advice of family and friends. Other people believe that the best way of learning about life is through personal experience. Compare the advantages of these two different ways of learning about life. Which do you think is preferable? Use specific examples to support your preference. |

Both learning through personal experience and learning through the advice of others can help you a lot in life. I think learning through personal experience comes first, however. No one can teach you how to get along with other people, how to judge your own abilities, or how to understand who you are. You can learn this only through experience.

When we are small children, adults tell us, "Play nicely with the other children. Don't fight. Don't hit." In this way, we learn that it is important to get along with others. Only through our own experience, however, can we learn how to do this. If another child hits us, we learn that hitting isn't a nice thing. If we fight with other children, we learn that fighting doesn't always get us what we want and maybe there are other solutions. Through our own experiences, we begin to learn about ourselves and we carry this learning into our adult lives.

Friends and relatives might say to us, "You are good at science. You should become a doctor." Or, "You are a talented artist. You should study painting." Our friends and relatives can observe our abilities and point them out to us. But they can't know everything about us. Maybe you get good grades in science but you think its boring. Maybe you are a talented artist, but you like sports better. Through our daily experiences we have the chance to learn about our abilities and our tastes. If we value these experiences, we pay attention to them and use them to make decisions for our future.

The people who know us might say, "You are so hardworking." Or, "You are too shy and quiet." They can point out our good qualities to us and that is good. We need our own experience, however, to tell us who we really are. Maybe you really are shy, or maybe it just looks that way to another person. Your own experience will tell you if this is true and if it is important to you or not. When we pay attention to our own experiences, we learn a lot about who we are and who we want to be.

The advice of other people can be very helpful. It isn't much good, however, if we don't have our own experiences to compare it to. I like to ask other people for advice, but I always pay attention to my own experience first.

▼

| 109 | PR | When people move to another country, some of them decide to follow the customs of the new country. Others prefer to keep their own customs. Compare these two choices. Which one do you prefer? Support your answer with specific details. |

When you move to another country, you have to change some of your customs of daily living. For example, you will have to make some changes in your language, your food, and your work habits. It is also important, however, to maintain some of your old customs because they are part of your identity.

The most important thing to do in a new country is learn the language. Daily life will be very difficult without it. You will need the language to find things in stores, to understand TV programs, to go to school, and for many other things. You don't have to stop speaking your own language, though. You can continue to speak it with family and friends. You need your language to maintain your connection with your own country and origins.

It is a good idea to learn to eat the food in a new country. It will make your life easier. You can't always find stores and restaurants that sell your country's food. Eating the new country's food also helps you get to know something about the country and the people. If you shop and eat only in places that sell your country's food, you will get to know only people from your country. You should also eat your country's food sometimes. You will probably prefer it on holidays, for example. It is also a good thing to share with new friends from your new country.

When you get a job, it is important to learn your new country's work habits. If the custom in the country is to arrive at work on time, you must do it. If the custom is to be friendly with clients, invite them to restaurants, and so on, then you must do that. You will not be successful in your job if you don't adapt to the work habits. You might also have some useful customs from your own culture. Maybe you have more efficient methods of organizing work. Share your ideas with your coworkers. They might appreciate it.

If you want to be successful in a new country, you have to adapt to its customs. You also need to maintain some of your own customs because they are part of who you are. The important thing is to find a good balance between the two.

| 110 | PR | Some people prefer to spend most of their time alone. Others like to be with friends most of the time. Do you prefer to spend your time alone or with friends? Use specific reasons to support your answer. |

I cannot understand people who like to be alone. I always choose to be with friends whenever possible. My friends keep me company, they are enjoyable to talk with, and they teach me new things. I always feel good when I spend time with friends.

My friends keep me from feeling lonely. If I want to do something, I invite a friend or friends and we do it together. It is fun to go to the movies, shopping, or even to the library to study with friends. It isn't fun to do anything alone.

I like talking with my friends. If I have a problem, I talk it over with my friends and they help me solve it. If something interesting happens to me, I share it with my friends. They share their problems and experiences with me, too.

I learn a lot from my friends. A friend might invite me to a movie that I haven't ever heard of. A friend might tell me about a trip she took or a book she read. A friend might have a different point of view about a political issue. I learn a lot of new and interesting things by sharing with my friends.

Friends make our lives richer. They keep us company, share their problems and experiences with us, and teach us many things. Life would be sad and lonely without friends.

| 111 | PR | Some people prefer to spend time with one or two close friends. Others choose to spend time with a large number of friends. Compare the advantages of each choice. Which of these two ways of spending time do you prefer? Use specific reasons to support your answer. |

We all need to have friends, and I think the more friends we have the better. When you have a lot of friends, you are never alone. You always have people who will entertain you, people you can trust, and people who teach you about life.

I want to have a lot of people I can have fun with. If I have a lot of friends, I always have people to laugh and joke with me. I have people to go to the movies or the mall with me. I have people to go to parties with me. If I have only a few friends, they might be busy when I want to do these things, or they might not enjoy some of the things I enjoy.

I need to have a lot people I can trust. If I have a problem, I want to share it with several friends. If I make a mistake or fail a test or have a fight with my parents, I need my friends to help me. I want to be able to pick up the phone and know I can easily find some friends to talk with. If I have only a few friends, they might not be available when I need them.

I like to have a lot of people who teach me about life. If I have a lot of friends, I have a lot of different people to learn from. Each person has different experiences and a different point of view. I can learn a lot of things from a lot of different people. If I have only a few friends, I will see only a few points of view.

I like to have a lot of friends around me. I like to have fun with them and to learn from them and to know that I can rely on them. My life is better because of all the friends I have.

▼

| 112 | AD | Some people think that children should begin their formal education at a very early age and should spend most of their time on their school studies. Others believe that young children should spend most of their time playing. Compare these two views. Which view do you agree with? Why? |

Should a child spend more time on school studies or more time on play? The answer to this question depends on the quality of the school and the quality of the play. Wherever children spend their time, they should be active participants, not passive observers.

Not all schools are the same. In some schools, children must sit quietly all day and memorize dates and facts. In other schools, children are encouraged to participate in different kinds of activities. They are encouraged to ask questions, to interact with other children, and to experience things.

Not all children play the same way. Some children prefer to watch TV or video games. Other children enjoy games that involve physical activity, using the imagination, or playing with other children.

Not all children are the same, but all children have the same requirements for learning. They learn when their minds and their bodies are active. They learn when they socialize with other children. They can do these things during school time or during play time. It doesn't matter when or where they do these things; it only matters that they do them.

Children can learn a lot from formal education and they can learn a lot from play. Parents need to make sure that the time their children spend in school is quality time. They need to make sure that the time their children spend at play is also quality time. Then they can feel assured that their children are getting the experiences they need to learn and grow.

▼

| 113 | MA | The government has announced that it plans to build a new university. Some people think that **your** community would be a good place to locate the university. Compare the advantages and disadvantages of establishing a new university in your community. Use specific details in your discussion. |

A university can contribute a lot of good things to a city, but it also brings some disadvantages. If we built a university here, it would bring jobs, culture, and interesting new people to our town. On the other hand, it would also destroy land, cause traffic problems, and be a burden on city services. There are two sides to every story.

A university would bring jobs, but it would also destroy land. During construction, the university would have to hire carpenters, electricians, plumbers, etc. After the building is finished, they would hire people to help run and maintain the campus. We need jobs in our community, so this is a big advantage. On the other hand, the university needs land to build on. Would they take over one of our city parks, or tear down some of our houses? Either way, they would destroy things that we use and enjoy now.

The university would bring culture to our community, but it would also bring crowds. The community could take advantage of events at the university such as concerts, lectures, and art exhibits. But a lot of people from all over would also attend these events. They would fill our streets with traffic and cause parking problems. Our community would no longer be a quiet place.

The university would bring interesting people, but it would also cause a burden on our city services. People such as professors, researchers, and visiting lecturers would work at the university. They are sure to contribute a lot to our community life. However, they are also sure to have families. They will need houses, schools, and transportation. How can our city suddenly provide services for a lot of new residents?

A university would bring many advantages to our city, but it would also have some big disadvantages. The fact is, we already have two universities here and I don't think we need any more.

▼

| 114 | PR | Some people think that family is the most important influence on young adults. Other people think that friends are the most important influence on young adults. Which view do you agree with? Use examples to support your opinion. |

Although friends make an impression on your life, they do not have the same influence that your family has. Nothing is as important to me as my family. From them, I learned everything that is important. I learned about trust, ambition, and love.

Your family is with you forever. They are not going to leave you because they find another daughter or son they like better. They are not going to leave you because they think you are too much trouble. Friends come and go, but a family is permanent. You can always trust your family.

Your parents are your role models. They will encourage you to do your best, to push yourself, and to improve yourself. Friends want you to stay the same; they don't want you to be different. Your family is ambitious for you. Friends are not.

A family's love is not judgmental. They love you for everything you are. Friends may love you because you have a new car or because you go out with them on Saturday evenings. Friends may only like you, but your family loves you.

Without my family, I wouldn't know what to do. I wouldn't feel as secure. I might not have the ambition to go to school. I probably would be afraid to love. My family is my greatest influence.

▼

> | 115 | PR | Some people prefer to plan activities for their free time very carefully. Others choose not to make any plans at all for their free time. Compare the benefits of planning free-time activities with the benefits of not making plans. Which do you prefer—planning or not planning for your leisure time? Use specific reasons and examples to explain your choice. |

My free time is very valuable. I don't have a lot of free time, so I want to be sure to spend every minute of it well. Therefore, I always try to make plans ahead of time. In this way I don't waste any of my free time, I have a chance to make any necessary preparations, and I can invite my friends to join me.

If I make a plan for the weekend ahead of time, I don't waste any of my free time trying to decide what to do. If I don't have a plan, I might spend all morning thinking about the different things I could do. Before I knew it, half the day would be gone. I would lose half my free time making decisions and it would be too late to start a lot of activities.

If I make a plan for the weekend ahead of time, I can also make my preparations ahead of time. Then I can spend the whole weekend just enjoying myself. For example, if I want to go on a picnic, I can have my food all prepared beforehand. If I want to go to a concert, I can get my tickets ahead of time. By making plans ahead of time, I am sure I will be ready to do just what I want to do.

If I make a plan for the weekend ahead of time, it's easier to invite friends to join me. If I wait until the last minute, my friends might already have plans to do something else. If I make plans ahead of time, I can invite any friends I want to. And even if those particular friends are already busy, I still have time to invite somebody else.

It's always best to plan anything ahead of time. I think it is especially important to plan free time, because my free time is my best time. I want to enjoy every minute of it.

▼

> | 116 | PR | People learn in different ways. Some people learn by doing things; other people learn by reading about things; others learn by listening to people talk about things. Which of these methods of learning is best for you? Use specific examples to support your choice. |

I have never been able to learn well from reading or from listening to someone talk. My mind wanders and I can't grasp the situation. The best way for me to learn is by doing things. It helps me understand and remember information better, and it is much more interesting for me than reading and listening.

Doing things helps me understand. Someone may explain to me how a musical instrument works, for example. I don't really understand this, however, until I try to play the instrument myself. Then I can hear and see and feel how the sound is made. I can feel how hard I have to push a key or pluck a string to make the sound I want. Or I could read a recipe in a cookbook. But I don't really understand how to prepare the food until I try to make it myself.

Doing things helps me remember. A teacher could explain some grammar rules to me, but it's hard for me to remember them. However, when I practice using the grammar rules by speaking the language, then I will remember them better. The more I speak the language, the better I remember the rules. I could also read about math formulas in a book. But I can't remember them unless I use them to try to solve some math problems.

Doing things holds my attention. When I listen to a lecture, my thoughts wander to other things and I don't hear the information at all. When I read something, it is hard for me to follow the ideas unless I concentrate really hard. When I do something, on the other hand, I am always interested in it. I have to pay attention because I am the one who is doing it.

We all have our own learning styles. For me, it is clear that I learn best by doing things. It is the only way I can really focus my attention on information, understand it, and remember it.

▼

| 117 | PR | Some people choose friends who are different from themselves. Others choose friends who are similar to themselves. Compare the advantages of having friends who are different from you with the advantages of having friends who are similar to you. Which kind of friend do you prefer for yourself? Why? |

There are a lot of advantages to having friends who are different from you. They can introduce you to new food, books, and music. They can present you with a different way of looking at the world. However, there are times when you need a friend who really understands you. That is why I enjoy having all kinds of friends—both those who are different from me and those who are similar.

Someone who is different from you can show different ways of looking at things. If you tend to be a spontaneous person, a scheduled person can help you be more organized. And you can help that person loosen up a bit at times, too. If you are impatient, a patient friend can help you calm down. If you are a little bit timid, an assertive friend can help you develop more self-confidence.

Someone who has different tastes from you can introduce you to new things. A friend might persuade you to read a book that you thought you wouldn't like. A friend might get you to try new kinds of food. You can share your different tastes and interests with your friend, too. Together you can dare to try new things.

There are times, however, when you really need a friend who is similar to you. Sometimes you get tired of compromising on what you want to do. You want to be with someone who has the same tastes as you. A friend who is similar to you probably has the same reactions to situations as you do. Therefore, if you feel unhappy, a friend who is similar to you can understand just why you feel that way.

Friends who are different from you have a lot to offer. Friends who are similar offer something else. That is why it is important to know all kinds of people.

▼

| 118 | PR | Some people enjoy change and they look forward to new experiences. Others like their lives to stay the same, and they do not change their usual habits. Compare these two approaches to life. Which approach do you prefer? Why? |

It is true that some people prefer things to stay the same while others prefer change. My preference is to establish a routine and follow it, although this has not always been true of me. My circumstances have changed since I was young.

When I was younger, I enjoyed change. During school vacations I was free from responsibility. I would travel, go away with friends at a moment's notice, and make decisions from day to day. In this way, I could have lots of new experiences, meet new and interesting people, and learn a lot about life.

These days, I enjoy following a routine. It makes my life easier because I am the mother of two small children. Their lives are happier if I don't upset their schedules too much. For example, we give the children a bath every night at 8:00, put them in their pajamas, read them stories, and put them to bed by 9:00. It is not always convenient to do this, but everyone in the family is happier when we follow our routine. In addition, our friends know when we are free, which makes visiting easier.

In conclusion, my preferences have changed with the circumstances of my life. Now, my family's needs force me to have a routine. The stability of a household routine is better for me now, even though I preferred the excitement and adventure of change when I was young. I think the people you spend your time with often dictate your lifestyle.

▼

| 119 | AD | Do you agree or disagree with the following statement? People behave differently when they wear different clothes. Do you agree that different clothes influence the way people behave? Use specific examples to support your answer. |

People behave differently depending on what they are wearing. The reason is not because they have changed, but because people's reactions to them have changed. Strangers react to your appearance because it is all they know about you. A friend may be influenced by your dress also, if it is inappropriate for a situation. In addition, appearance is almost always important at work.

Strangers can judge you only by the clothes you wear. Once I was wearing an old army coat. I went into a fancy candy shop to buy some chocolates. The woman saw my coat and was very suspicious of me. Because of the woman's negative reaction to me, I acted more politely than usual. The woman reacted to my clothes and that made me behave differently.

With friends clothes are less important because friends know more about you. However, friends can also react to you because of your clothes. Imagine you arrive at a friend's party. Everyone is wearing formal clothes and you are wearing casual clothes. You might have a good reason for this mistake, but your friend will still be disappointed. You will probably feel uncomfortable all evening because you disappointed your friend and because you are dressed differently from everyone else.

Certain clothes are appropriate for certain jobs. For example, business clothes are appropriate for some jobs; uniforms are appropriate for others. If you are not dressed appropriately for your job, clients and coworkers take you less seriously. You might begin to take yourself less seriously also, and your work could suffer. On the other hand, if you are wearing the right clothes, people will have confidence that you are the right person for the job, and you will feel this way, too.

Clothes don't change you into a different person, but they can make you behave differently. If you are dressed inappropriately for a situation, people will react to you in a different way. This reaction can, in turn, change your behavior. If you want good reactions from people, make sure to dress appropriately for every situation.

▼

| 120 | AD | Decisions can be made quickly, or they can be made after careful thought. Do you agree or disagree with the following statement? The decisions that people make quickly are always wrong. Use specific reasons and examples to support your opinion. |

I don't agree that quick decisions are always wrong. Sometimes they can be the best decisions we make. A quick decision made about a familiar situation is usually correct. Quick decisions based on a gut feeling, or instinct, can usually be relied on. It's the decisions made out of fear or desperation that we need to watch.

In familiar circumstances you can usually trust yourself to make a good decision quickly. For example, your boss might offer you the opportunity to do a certain job. She doesn't have time to explain the details right away but needs an immediate decision from you. It is probably safe for you to accept the assignment. You know your boss and your boss knows you. You can trust that if your boss thinks this is a good assignment for you, she is probably right.

We can also usually rely on our instinct. You might be looking for a new apartment, for example. You look and look, but none of the apartments you see are right. Then you walk into one and right away you know it is the place for you. You don't know anything about the neighborhood or the landlord and you aren't sure about the rent, but you immediately sign the lease. Some people might think this is crazy. I think you will probably be very happy in that apartment because you listened to your instinct. Your instinct doesn't need a lot of information to make good decisions.

On the other hand, we can get into trouble when we make decisions out of desperation. Let's say you are on a lonely road late at night and your car breaks down. Another driver arrives and offers you a ride. There is something strange about this person. You accept the ride, however, because you are tired and cold. This is not a good decision; in fact, it is a very dangerous decision. It would be better to wait in your own car, all night if necessary, for the police to arrive. You would realize this if you made the decision more carefully.

Not all decisions need to be made carefully. We can usually rely on familiar situations and instinct to guide us in making quick decisions. We need to stop and think more carefully, however, when we make decisions in more difficult circumstances.

▼

| 121 | MA | Some people trust their first impressions about a person's character because they believe these judgments are generally correct. Other people do not judge a person's character quickly because they believe first impressions are often wrong. Compare these two attitudes. Which attitude do you agree with? Support your choice with specific examples. |

Some people think it is unfair to judge others based on first impressions, but I dis-agree. People can show us who they really are in just a few minutes. Even if someone is having an unusually bad day, it is still easy to see their true character. If I don't like someone at first, I don't want to waste time being friendly just because he or she might change later. First impressions give us valuable information.

It doesn't take long for people to show their true character. Some people think you have to see how people act in different situations and talk to them a lot to get to know them. I don't believe this is true. When you meet someone, pay attention to how the person greets you. You can see right away if the person is friendly or shy, polite or rude. See how the person tries to make conversation and you will know what topics are inter-esting to him or her. All of this gives us a lot of information about a person.

Even on a bad day, you can see what a person is really like. Some people think that it isn't fair to judge people quickly because they might be having a bad day. I dis-agree. A bad day tells you a lot about people. You can see how they react to bad situa-tions. Do they get very angry or take it all in stride? Do they get depressed and cry or just try to forget the problem? These are important parts of a person's character.

I feel I can learn a lot about a person in a few minutes, so I don't want to waste my time if the first impression isn't good. If I don't like the way a person greets me, or if I am uncomfortable with the way a person responds to a bad situation, will my impres-sion change later on? Probably not. If I spend more time with the person, I'll probably just see more of the same. I would prefer to spend that time looking for people who I like.

First impressions can tell us a lot about a person, no matter what the circum-stances. We can learn enough to decide whether or not we want to spend more time with that person. I always rely on first impressions.

▼

| 122 | AD | Do you agree or disagree with the following statement? People are never satisfied with what they have; they always want something more or something different. Use specific reasons to support your answer. |

II believe that it is part of human nature to never be completely satisfied with what we have. This is true throughout our entire lives, from the time we are small children, through adolescence, and on into adulthood. We are always trying to have something more or better or different than what we already have.

The desire for something different begins in early childhood. Give a small child a toy to play with, and she's happy—until she sees another toy. Then she wants to play with the other toy. Give her a cookie and give another cookie to her brother.

She'll probably think that her brother's cookie is bigger than hers, or somehow different, and cry for it.

The dissatisfaction with what we already have continues into adolescence. A teenager may buy some new clothes. Then he sees his friend has shoes in a different style or pants of a different color. All of a sudden his new clothes are no good; he wants what his friend has. Being like their friends is very important to teens and they constantly change their desires in order to match their friends.

Even in adulthood, we are not free from dissatisfaction. A young adult may be excited to get her first job, but right away she starts thinking about moving up and getting a better job. A young couple is finally able to buy a new house after saving for several years. But soon they start thinking about buying another, bigger house. A man may finally reach a high position in his company after years of hard work. Not long after that, he starts thinking about retirement. We are never satisfied.

It is part of the cycle of life to never be entirely satisfied with what we have. This is actually a good human quality because it pushes us on to each new stage of life. Without dissatisfactions, we would probably always stay in the same place.

▼

123	AD	Do you agree or disagree with the following statement? People should read only those books that are about real events, real people, and established facts. Use specific reasons and details to support your opinion.

It is just as important to read fiction as nonfiction. Fiction can actually teach us about real things. It also helps develops our creativity and express our emotions. These things are just as important as learning about facts.

Fiction can teach us about real things and give us a deeper understanding of them. Nonfiction tells us only facts. Novels, on the other hand, can tell us some facts and also about what those facts mean, or meant, to real people. Reading novels by Charles Dickens, for example, helps us really understand the consequences of poverty in Victorian England.

Fiction helps us develop our creativity. When we read stories, we try to imagine what the places and characters look like. We try to imagine what it feels like to live a character's life. Developing creativity is just as important as knowing a lot of facts.

Fiction helps us understand and express our emotions. When we read romances or tragedies or comedies, we read about feelings that we ourselves have. Reading helps us explore these feelings more. It gives us a mirror for our emotional lives.

It is important to learn facts, but it is also important to develop creativity and explore feelings. Reading fiction as well as nonfiction helps us do this. We should all read a wide range of things to deepen our understanding of ourselves and of the world around us.

▼

| 124 | AD | Do you agree or disagree with the following statement? It is more important for students to study history and literature than it is for them to study science and mathematics. Use specific reasons and examples to support your opinion. |

In my opinion, it is much more important for students to study science and mathematics than it is for them to study history and literature. Science and mathematics are much more practical. It is easier to get a job with science and math skills. Scientists and mathematicians have more social prestige, and they can earn higher salaries.

People who study science and mathematics get jobs more easily than people who study history and literature. There are always jobs in fields such as medicine, computer science, engineering, and other professions that require a science or math background. People who study history or literature can only become writers or college professors. It is difficult to get well-paying jobs in those fields.

Scientists and mathematicians have a lot of social prestige. Let's face it—our society values science and math. If you go to a party and say, "I am a rocket scientist," people will be interested in you. They will want to talk to you and be your friend. If you say, "I am an historian," no one will pay any attention to you.

Scientists and mathematicians also earn more money than people in other fields because society values them more. A doctor, a chemist, a medical researcher,—a person in any one of these professions usually earns a far higher salary than a literature professor, for example, or a history expert.

Our society values science and math, so it is important to develop skills in these areas. If you have a science or math background, you are sure to get a good job, have lots of social prestige, and earn a good salary. Faced with this fact, who would want to study anything else?

▼

| 125 | AD | Do you agree or disagree with the following statement? All students should be required to study art and music in secondary school. Use specific reasons to support your answer. |

I agree that all students should be required to study art and music in high school. Art and music can teach us many things. They can teach us about ourselves, about our society, and about the world we live in.

By studying art and music, students can learn a great deal about themselves. Both are natural forms of self-expression. Just as our ancestors drew on the walls in caves and made music with drums, people today use art and music to explore their emotions. Students also explore their likes and dislikes when they choose the music they want to learn, or when they decide which subjects they want to draw. The process of making music or making art is a process of self-exploration.

Studying art and music means more than drawing or playing an instrument. Students go to museums and concerts, too. By studying pictures in museums or listening to the selections in a musical program, students learn about their own culture. They learn about what their society values. They also learn about the history of their society and how lifestyles and values have changed over time.

By studying art and music from other cultures, students learn about other people around the world. They learn about what is important in other societies. They learn about similarities and differences between cultures. They learn about the history and lifestyles of other places. New worlds are opened up to them.

By studying art and music in high school, students begin to understand themselves as well as their own culture and other cultures. What could have more value than that?

▼

126	AD	Do you agree or disagree with the following statement? There is nothing young people can teach older people. Use specific reasons and examples to support your position.

Many of us believe that young people have nothing valuable to teach older people. However, that is not always the case. Young people can teach older people about technology, popular culture, and current social issues.

Young people are usually better than older people at using new forms of technology. For example, children these days become familiar with computers at an early age. Older people can learn to use computers from young people. Many older people have difficulty learning to use a videocassette recorder, while for young people this is usually easy. I taught my grandparents how to use a VCR when I was thirteen, and now they use it regularly.

Older people are usually not familiar with popular culture, and younger people can help here too. For example, most older people don't know much about popular music. When young people teach them about it, however, they may come to enjoy it. I introduced my grandmother to some of my favorite music, and now she and I listen to it together often. I plan to teach her about a popular sport—rollerblading—very soon!

There are also more serious things that younger people can teach older people about. Today's children have grown up knowing about AIDS and school violence. These are serious social issues, but older people don't always understand them. Talking about them with younger people can help the older people learn more.

I know there are people who say, "You can't teach an old dog new tricks." However, it is plain to me that the young have plenty to teach the old if they take the time to try. When they do, I think both gain a new appreciation for each other.

▼

127	AD	Do you agree or disagree with the following statement? Reading fiction (such as novels and short stories) is more enjoyable than watching movies. Use specific reasons and examples to explain your position.

Reading fiction is definitely more enjoyable than watching movies. Written stories have more depth than movies. Readers are more actively involved in the stories, and they can read their stories at any time and place they choose.

Most novels and stories have more depth than movies. Of course there are bad books and excellent movies, but usually books contain more than movies. They explain more about the characters and show more details about the action. Part of the reason for this is that most movies have to be close to two hours long. Books, on the other hand, can be as long as the author wants.

Readers are more actively involved in a story than movie watchers are. A movie watcher just has to sit and watch. A reader, on the other hand, has to think and imagine. The reader can't see the scenes like a movie watcher can. He has to picture them in his mind and understand what they are about.

The most enjoyable thing about books is that you can read them at any time and place. You don't have to go to the movie theater or rent a video or wait for a movie to appear on TV. If you want to enjoy a story for a few minutes before dinner or while riding the bus, you can. If you want to relax for a while before going to sleep, there is always a book ready for your enjoyment. Books are the most convenient form of entertainment there is.

Movies are fun, but books are better. Books keep the reader involved and entertained. Books can be read at any time or place. I never go anywhere without a book.

▼

| 128 | MA | Some people say that physical exercise should be a required part of every school day. Other people believe that students should spend the whole school day on academic studies. Which opinion do you agree with? Give specific reasons and details to support your answer. |

While physical exercise is important, I do not believe that it is a school's responsibility to provide physical training for its students. If physical exercise is part of the school program, that means that students have to receive grades for it and that the school has to pay for the necessary space and equipment. This seems a waste of effort and resources when students can usually get enough physical exercise on their own.

If a school offers physical education classes, then students will have to be graded in them. It is not always easy to do this fairly. Some schools, especially smaller ones, may not be able to offer activities that interest everyone. Then some students might get poor grades simply because the school couldn't offer an activity they enjoy or do well in. In addition, research suggests that participation, not excellence, in physical activities is what benefits the body.

Another issue is economic. Physical education costs money and many schools do not have the money to provide gym facilities, playing fields, and athletic equipment for their students. Other schools are located in cities where that kind of space just isn't available. A few schools would rather keep money for academic purposes.

Many students get plenty of physical exercise as part of their daily life or recreation. Some students walk or ride their bicycles to schools. Some participate in soccer teams or tennis leagues outside of schools. Young people are usually active and have plenty of chances to get exercise outside of school, whether in organized activities or not.

It is important to get plenty of physical exercise, and young people usually do this. They don't need the school to focus effort and money on their physical education. It is much better to direct the school's resources toward academic achievement.

▼

| 129 | MA | A university plans to develop a new research center in your country. Some people want a center for business research. Other people want a center for research in agriculture (farming). Which of these two kinds of research centers do you recommend for your country? Use specific reasons in your recommendation. |

Business research and education is already well developed in my country, so I recommend an agricultural research center. Farmers in my country still follow old-fashioned methods. We need to do research to learn how to grow more crops, grow disease-resistant crops, and educate farmers in modern methods so they can raise their standard of living.

We need to increase agricultural production for several reasons. One is that the population of my country is growing so we need to produce more food. In addition, if we could export more crops, it would be good for our economy. An agricultural research center could develop methods for growing more crops.

We also need to develop disease-resistant crops. Farmers spend a lot of time trying to protect their crops from disease. Often, they lose their crops anyway, so a lot of money and effort are lost. Some farmers end up losing their entire farms because disease kills their crops. An agricultural research center could develop methods to save crops from disease.

Farmers need to learn modern farming methods. They need to learn how to grow more and better crops and they need to learn more efficient work methods. This would benefit the country as a whole and it would also make things better for farmers. Their work would be easier and they would earn more money. An agricultural research center could develop better farming methods and teach them to farmers.

An agricultural research center would benefit everybody. We would all have more food to eat, agricultural exports would help our economy, and the farmers' standard of living would improve.

▼

| 130 | MA | Some young children spend a great amount of their time practicing sports. Discuss the advantages and disadvantages of this. Use specific reasons and examples to support your answer. |

Participating in sports is good for children. It helps them stay in good physical shape, it helps them learn teamwork, and helps them learn to develop excellence. However, too much of a good thing is never good, and children need to balance sports with other types of activities.

It is important to stay in shape, and participating in sports is a good way to do this. In sports, children get a chance to run and jump, to develop their muscles and lungs. This is especially important after spending most of the day sitting at a desk doing school-work. However, if children focus too much on sports, they might neglect their homework. They might also be too tired to pay attention in school.

Participating in sports helps children learn to work on a team. They have to pay attention and cooperate and do what is best for the team. This is an important skill that will help them throughout their lives. If children always play on a team, however, they don't have the chance to learn to do things alone. They don't learn to enjoy solitary activities such as reading or drawing, and they don't learn how to play with just one or two other children and no adult supervision. These activities also help develop important skills.

Learning to play sports helps children learn to develop excellence. They want to be really good in the sports they choose. Each one wants to be the best ball player or gymnast possible. While it is good to learn to work toward goals, it is also good to participate in other types of activities. Children need activities that are just for relaxation and enjoyment. They need activities that don't involve competition. If they focus too much on sports, they might not get a chance to do these other activities.

Playing sports is an important part of a child's development. Other activities, however, are equally important. Adults should encourage children to find a balance between different types of activities in their lives.

▼

| 131 | AD | Do you agree or disagree with the following statement? **Only** people who earn a lot of money are successful. Use specific reasons and examples to support your answer. |

Many people believe that a large income equals success. I believe, however, that success is more than how much money you make. Some of those measures of success include fame, respect, and knowledge.

Most people assume that famous people are rich people, but that isn't always true. For example, some day I would like to be a famous researcher. Few scientists are rich by today's standards. Still, I will feel myself successful if I am well known. Additionally, there are many famous humanitarians who are not rich. Mother Theresa was one. Certainly no one would say she was not successful.

I also believe that being respected by coworkers indicates success. Without that respect, money means very little. For example, I once did some work for a top attorney in a law firm. He made a very good salary, but he wasn't a nice man. No one ever did work for him willingly. He ordered everyone around, and we didn't respect him. In contrast, however, I had a wonderful band director in high school. He had to take extra jobs just to make enough money to support his family. However, his students had great respect for him and always listened to what he said. As a result, we were a very good band. In my opinion, my band director was more successful than the attorney was.

Finally, I think one of the most important indicators of success is knowledge. Wealthy people don't know all the answers. For example, in the movie Good Will Hunting, *the only person who could solve complex problems was the janitor. He knew a lot and decided what he wanted to do with that knowledge rather than just think about money. In my opinion, he was extremely successful.*

When we think of history, there are few people we remember simply because they were rich. Overall, we remember people who did something with their lives—they were influential in politics, or contributed to science or art or religion. If history is the ultimate judge of success, then money surely isn't everything.

| 132 | EX | If you could invent something **new,** what product would you develop? Use specific details to explain why this invention is needed. |

If I could invent something new, I'd invent a device or pill that could put people to sleep immediately and would have no side effects. The proper amount of sleep is important for our concentration, mental health, and physical health.

When we don't get enough sleep, our concentration is strongly affected. We're easily distracted, we can't remember things, and we don't notice what's happening around us. For example, a lot of car accidents are caused by tired drivers. When we get enough sleep, our powers of concentration are sharper. We're more focused on what we're doing. We perform better.

Mental health is also affected by lack of sleep. When we don't get enough sleep we're irritable. We lose our tempers easily and overreact to situations. In fact, experiments have shown that lack of sleep over a long period of time can cause a complete mental breakdown. When we get our proper rest, we're more alert and responsive. Our outlook is positive, and we're much easier to get along with.

Sleeplessness also affects our physical health. We have less energy, and everything seems like a major effort. Over a long period of time, we become slow and unresponsive. The wear and tear on the body from lack of sleep can be a very serious health problem. Every doctor will tell you that getting enough sleep is important for your health.

Wouldn't it be great to go to bed every night knowing you'd have no problem getting to sleep? Getting enough sleep is always going to be an important part of how you respond to your situation. I think this device would be very helpful to all of us.

| 133 | AD | Do you agree or disagree with the following statement? A person's childhood years (the time from birth to twelve years of age) are the most important years of a person's life. Use specific reasons and examples to support your answer. |

I think I'd have to agree that a person's childhood years are the most important. These are the years that form us. During these years we learn about relationships, begin our formal education, and develop our moral sense of right and wrong.

No doubt, the early years are the time when we learn about relationships, first with our family, then with the rest of the world. We learn how to respond to others based on the way others treat us. If we're loved, then we learn how to love. If we're treated harshly, then we learn to treat others in the same way. We also form our ideas about self-worth based on the way others treat us during these years. They can teach us that we're worthless, or they can show us that we deserve love and respect.

These are the years when we begin our formal education. In school we learn the basic skills of reading, writing, and working with numbers. These are skills that we will use throughout our lives. We also learn how to analyze and use information. This is perhaps the most important thing we learn during these years. Presumably, these are skills that will always be useful.

Most important, from my point of view, we develop our moral sense of right and wrong during these years. At first others teach us about good and bad. As we grow, we begin to decide for ourselves. During this time we also begin to develop self-discipline to live according to our morals.

I believe a person grows and changes throughout the many stages of life. However, the foundation is laid, by and large, in those first few years of life.

▼

134	AD	Do you agree or disagree with the following statement? Children should be required to help with household tasks as soon as they are able to do so. Use specific reasons and examples to support your answer.

I believe that children should be required to help with household tasks. It helps them learn skills and responsibility, and it helps the family. Sharing in household tasks benefits children of all ages.

First of all, household tasks build skills. Very young children learn motor skills and classification skills when they pick up their toys and put them away. Older children learn skills they'll need as adults. They learn cooking and cleaning, which may seem dull, but that are undoubtedly useful skills they'll need when they leave home.

Children learn responsibility when they help with household tasks. They learn to organize their time so they can fulfill their responsibilities. They learn that chores have to be completed before they can play. Children who understand that effort pays off will be more successful later in life.

When children help with household tasks, everyone in the family is happier. When parents come home from their jobs, they're faced with all the housework. If children share in the housework, everything is easier. The work gets done more quickly, and then the family can relax together. The children are helpers and the parents don't have to feel like servants to them.

Kids should not work all the time. A happy life needs balance. But if they can successfully handle tasks at home, they will handle life better, too. They will know the satisfaction of doing a good job, be involved in family life, and become more confident and responsible adults.

▼

135	MA	Some high schools require all students to wear school uniforms. Other high schools permit students to decide what to wear to school. Which of these two school policies do you think is better? Use specific reasons and examples to support your opinion.

Many high schools require students to wear uniforms. I think this is an excellent policy because uniforms can make things more equal for all students. When all the students dress alike, no one will be treated differently because of economic level, personal looks, or who his or her friends are.

Uniforms make students equal on an economic level. With uniforms, students from poor families dress the same as students from rich families. This can prevent envy and jealousy about stylish clothes. It can also encourage students to form friendships based on personality, not clothes.

Uniforms can reduce unequal treatment by teachers. Research suggests that teachers often have higher expectations for more attractive students, and this includes students with nicer clothes. Uniforms help teachers make judgments based on ability, not appearance.

Uniforms encourage the individual students of a school to feel like part of a bigger group. Their feelings of being together, working together, and having something in common are all helped by uniforms. Students are less likely to be left out because they belong to the "wrong crowd."

It is my opinion that all schools should have a policy requiring uniforms. Uniforms give every student an equal chance.

▼

| 136 | AD | Do you agree or disagree with the following statement? Playing a game is fun only when you win. Use specific reasons and examples to support your answer. |

I agree with the old saying, "It's not whether you win or lose, it's how you play the game." I have fun playing all games because they give me time to be with my friends, learn new things, and work as a team.

Tennis is one game that I enjoy. It's a great opportunity to socialize. First, I have to talk to my partner in order to arrange a time to play a game. We also talk about other things at the same time. We have another opportunity to talk while we are waiting for the tennis court to be free. After the game, we almost always go out for coffee and talk some more. We often don't even talk about tennis. The game is just an excuse for us to get together.

The board game Scrabble provides a good opportunity to build my language skills. It's a challenge to try to form words from the letters that are in front of me. I always learn new words from my opponents, too. Often we don't even keep score when we play the game. We just enjoy being together and improving our English.

The game of soccer gives me the chance to be on a team. I like traveling with the group when we go to other schools to play games. I like learning how to play as a team. Our coach tells us that the most important thing is to play well together. It's also important to have fun. Winning is secondary.

I play games because they are fun. Playing games gives me the opportunity to do things that I enjoy and be with people that I like. You can't win every time, but you can always have fun.

▼

| 137 | AD | Do you agree or disagree with the following statement? High schools should allow students to study the courses that students want to study. Use specific reasons and examples to support your opinion. |

I think the basic subjects, such as mathematics, literature, and science, should be required for all students. However, I also believe it is important to allow high school students to choose some of the subjects they study. In this way, they get to explore subjects they might want to study in college. They also get a chance to learn responsibility and to take some subjects just because they like them.

Students can start exploring possible career interests when they are allowed to choose some of their own subjects. If they have the chance to take a journalism class, for example, they may discover that field as a possible career. Or, students who like science may have the chance to learn about different branches of science. Then they can make better choices about a course of study when they go to college.

When students choose some of their own subjects, they have the chance to learn responsibility. They have to decide which courses are most compatible with their goals and interests. They have to think about what is the best way to spend their time in school. They will have to make decisions and choices for themselves throughout life. They should begin to get some experience with this in high school.

Students should also have a chance to enjoy themselves in school. If they can choose some of their own subjects, they can choose subjects they are interested in. A class such as international cooking may not be the start of a brilliant professional career, but it can be an enjoyable learning experience. Students should be able to spend some of their time exploring their interests and doing things they enjoy.

When students are allowed to choose some of their subjects, they get a chance to explore their interests and goals and take responsibility for themselves. This is an important part of education.

▼

| 138 | AD | Do you agree or disagree with the following statement? It is better to be a member of a group than the leader of a group. Use specific reasons and examples to support your answer. |

It is always better to be a leader than a follower. It is a much more interesting role to have. Leaders have skills and a chance to use them, they are constantly challenged to do the best job possible, and they are responsible for their actions. Followers, on the other hand, only have to follow and do what they are told.

It takes skills to be a good leader. Not everyone can do it. Leaders have to assess situations and decide how to approach them. A job supervisor, for example, has to decide the best way to get a project done, organize the work, and assign tasks to each worker. The workers only have to do their assignments. In fact any one worker may have to do the same job over and over again on each new project, while the leader's job is different every time.

Being a leader is a challenging position to be in. Any time there is a problem, the leader has to decide how to solve it. If a job supervisor assigns tasks to the workers, then one or two workers get sick, the supervisor has to reorganize the work. If some workers aren't getting along with each other or need support or if supplies start to run out, it is the supervisor's job to figure out how to get the job done and keep everyone happy. The leader must do his or her job as well as possible so that everyone's work gets done well.

Leaders have responsibility. Each follower is responsible for his or her part, but the leader is responsible for the whole. If a project succeeds or fails, the leader is the one who gets the credit or the blame. This motivates the leader to do the best job possible. A follower with less responsibility is not as motivated.

It is better to be a leader because a leader has a more interesting and challenging role than a follower. A leader will always strive to do his or her best, while a follower may not be motivated to do this. I like to be challenged and I want to do my best, so I prefer being a leader.

▼

139	EX	What do you consider to be the most important room in a house? Why is this room more important to you than any other room? Use specific reasons and examples to support your opinion.

My favorite room in a house is the kitchen. I love kitchens because they are the place where the family gathers and where food is prepared, and I have many happy memories of kitchens.

In my family, we have always had the custom of gathering in the kitchen. When my brother and I come home from school, we go straight to the kitchen for a snack. We usually do our homework at the kitchen table. Often, we are still there when my parents come home from work. Then we might help them prepare dinner. A lot of our time together is spent in the kitchen. When relatives come to visit, they also spend time in the kitchen. We usually all end up there, drinking tea while we talk.

I like eating, and I enjoy cooking too, so of course I like the kitchen. I especially love holidays when I spend all day in the kitchen with my cousins preparing special holiday food. The cooking is fun and sharing the work is even more fun. Sometimes our meals turn out well and other times not so well, but the fun of preparation is the most important part.

I have many happy memories of kitchens. I remember visiting my grandmother when I was small. Following family custom, those visits usually took place in the kitchen. I watched my grandmother cook and listened to her and my mother talk. I learned a lot about cooking and a lot about life. Now my grandmother is dead, but I always feel her near me when I am in the kitchen.

For me, many happy things happen and have happened in kitchens. When I have my own house, I will be sure that the kitchen is the biggest and most beautiful room in it.

| 140 | PR | Some items (such as clothes or furniture) can be made by hand or by machine. Which do you prefer—items made by hand or items made by machine? Use reasons and specific examples to explain your choice. |

Some people prefer to buy handmade items because of their beauty. I don't think this is important, however. I prefer machine-made items. Machine-made items are cheaper, more available, and easier to dispose of.

It is much cheaper to buy machine-made items than handmade items. A lot of time and effort goes into making things by hand, while a machine can turn out hundreds of copies of an item in just minutes. They're easier to make, so cheaper to buy. I can afford to have twenty or thirty machine-made dresses. If I bought only handmade clothes, on the other hand, I could buy only very few.

It is much easier to find machine-made items than handmade items. Go to any store in your neighborhood. How many sell handmade items? Very few, if any. Usually only specialty shops sell handmade items. If I wanted to buy a handmade chair, for example, I might spend days or weeks looking for a store that sold one I liked. If I buy machine-made chairs, I have lots of choices right in my own neighborhood.

It is much easier to dispose of machine-made items than handmade items. If I break a handmade plate, I feel I must make the effort to repair it, and repair it nicely. This is not only because of the cost of buying a new one, but also because of its beauty. People don't like to throw away handmade things because they feel that they are throwing away beauty. However, if I break a machine-made plate, I can just throw it in the trash without a second thought. Then I can go to the store and buy a dozen new ones if I wish.

Handmade items look nice, but they aren't at all practical. Machine-made items are easier to buy and to dispose of when you are finished with them. I always choose machine-made items.

| 141 | MA | If you could make one important change in a school that you attended, what change would you make? Use reasons and specific examples to support your answer. |

A big problem at my high school is the foreign language program. This program is neglected in favor of the math and science program, but I think it is just as important. The school can improve it by offering more classes, hiring well-trained instructors, and introducing the use of modern technology.

The first thing we need is third- and fourth-year language classes. Right now we don't have any classes above the second year level. It's hard to learn much about a language in only two years. This is especially frustrating for those of us who want to continue language study in college because we won't be well prepared.

Next, we need well-trained instructors. The current teachers in the program don't speak the languages well enough. They frequently make errors that the students repeat. If the teachers were well trained, they would be good models for the students. We would learn languages better.

Finally, we need to use modern technology in our language classes. Even though our school has a computer laboratory, we never use it in our language classes. We need to have and use computer software that is made for learning languages. We also need to be able to use the Internet to search for current, real-life materials in the languages we study.

Understanding people from other countries depends on being able to communicate with them. Poor language instruction makes this impossible. Improving the foreign language program would really make a difference to the students of the school.

▼

| 142 | MA | A gift (such as a camera, soccer ball, or an animal) can contribute to a child's development. What gift would you give to help a child develop? Why? Use reasons and specific examples to support your choice. |

I remember the bicycle my sister gave me when I was ten years old. That bike meant a lot to me. It meant physical activity, transportation, and independence. If I wanted to give a gift to a child now, I would give a bicycle.

Bikes are a wonderful form of physical activity. They encourage outdoor play and exercise. Television and video games, which are the most popular children's activities nowadays, involve mostly sitting and watching. Riding a bike makes exercise fun.

Bikes are also a convenient form of transportation. A child with a bicycle can easily ride to school or to visit friends. She doesn't have to wait for an adult to take her somewhere. She can go whenever she wants.

Bikes give children independence. Not only can they go where they want, they can also do what they want on the way. A child on a bike can stop at the store or choose a more interesting road or explore new neighborhoods. He can stop to look at or do whatever seems interesting. The bicycle gives him plenty of opportunities to explore the world on his own.

My bicycle gave me fun exercise, easy transportation, and freedom. For all these reasons, I think that a bicycle is a good gift that can help a child develop.

▼

| 143 | MA | Some people believe that students should be given one long vacation each year. Others believe that students should have several short vacations throughout the year. Which viewpoint do you agree with? Use specific reasons and examples to support your choice. |

I think several short vacations throughout the year are better than one long vacation. Students can concentrate on their studies better if they have more frequent breaks. Frequent breaks also make it easier to get a fresh start when necessary. Finally, I think students can make better use of their vacation time if it is shorter.

More frequent vacations make it easier for students to concentrate on their work. Students often get tired near the end of a long school year. Time seems to drag on during the last two months of school and nobody gets much work done. If the school sessions were shorter, they would be over before students had a chance to get tired. Then students could have a break, get rested, and return for the next school session with plenty of energy to start studying again.

With more frequent vacations, students can more easily get a fresh start when they need one. Sometimes a school year just starts out badly for some students, and no matter what they do, it's hard to change. They have to wait for a new school year to begin so they can start again. If the school year is long, a lot of time is wasted. With more frequent breaks, a student who is having a bad time doesn't need to wait a whole year to be able to start anew. That opportunity will come more quickly.

If students have more frequent, shorter vacations, they can actually make better use of that vacation time. A student may start a long vacation with plans, but those plans are soon used up. He becomes bored and just sits around doing nothing. With shorter vacations, a student can plan an interesting trip or project or take a job. Before he has time to get bored with those activities, it's time for school to start again. Then he has time to make fresh, new plans before the next break comes up.

I think shorter, more frequent vacations help students make better use of both their school time and their vacation time. It is a plan that every school should adopt.

▼

144	PR	Would you prefer to live in a traditional house or in a more modern apartment building? Use specific reasons and details to support your choice.

A modern apartment building is the best kind of place to live. Everything in it is new, everything works, and it is much easier to maintain than a traditional house.

In a modern apartment building everything is new and in good condition. There aren't holes in the walls or in the roof. The floors are clean and the paint is fresh. The kitchen appliances are modern and convenient. The lighting fixtures are modern so they give good light, and the electrical outlets are all in the right place. It is a comfortable way to live.

Since everything in a modern apartment is new, you can be sure it all works. You can rely on the heating system to keep you warm in the winter. You know the air conditioning will work all summer, even on the hottest days. You don't have to frantically call a repair company because your dishwasher breaks down on the day you plan a big party. You can count on all the modern systems and appliances to work whenever you need them.

A modern apartment is much easier to maintain than a traditional house. A house has grass that needs to be cut and a basement that needs to be cleaned and a furnace that needs to be maintained. In an apartment, you have none of these worries. You just have to do your housecleaning. Even that is easier, because an apartment is usually smaller than a house.

It is much easier and more comfortable to live in a modern apartment. I don't know why anybody would want to live in a traditional house.

▼

| 145 | MA | Some people say that advertising encourages us to buy things that we really do not need. Others say that advertisements tell us about new products that may improve our lives. Which viewpoint do you agree with? Use specific reasons and examples to support your answer. |

The purpose of advertising is to let people know what products are on the market. We need it so that we can make good decisions when we go shopping. Advertising tells us when new and improved products become available and lets us know which ones have the best price.

Through advertising we learn about new products. For example, many grocery stores now sell prepackaged lunches. These are very convenient for busy parents. They can give these lunches to their children to take to school. Busy parents don't have time to look at every item on the store shelf, so without advertising they might not know about such a convenient new product.

Even products we are familiar with may be improved, and advertising lets us know about this. Most people use cell phones, but new types of cell phone service become available all the time. There are different plans that give you more hours to talk on the phone, you can send text messages and photos, and next week probably some even-newer type of service will be available. By watching advertisements on TV it is easy to find out about new improvements to all kinds of products.

Advertisements keep us informed about prices. Prices change all the time, but any-one can look at the ads in the newspaper and see what the latest prices are. Advertise-ments also inform us about sales. In fact, some people buy the newspaper only in order to check the prices and plan their weekly shopping.

Advertisements improve our lives by keeping us informed about the latest product developments and the best prices. Advertisements serve a useful purpose.

▼

| 146 | PR | Some people prefer to spend their free time outdoors. Other people prefer to spend their leisure time indoors. Would you prefer to be outside or would you prefer to be inside for your leisure activities? Use specific reasons and examples to support your choice. |

I prefer to spend my leisure time outdoors whenever possible. It is more interesting and relaxing than staying indoors. Being outdoors gives me the opportunity to see new sights, try new things, and meet new people.

When I am outdoors, I have the opportunity to see new sights. I might go to a new park. I could go swimming at a beach I have never visited before or take a hike in a new place. The scenery is always different, too. Indoors I always look at the same four walls. Outdoors the scene is constantly changing. The flowers change with the seasons, the birds come and go, plants grow, trees fall down, nothing ever stays the same. It is fascinating to watch nature change.

When I am outdoors, I have the opportunity to try new things. I can learn how to sail a boat or climb rocks or swim farther and faster than before. I can also study nature and learn about the different kinds of plants and animals. There is always something new to learn, and some of these things are very challenging.

When I am outdoors, I have the opportunity to meet new people. I might meet someone casually while I am taking a walk or sitting on the beach. I can also meet people in a sailing class or a hiking club. Most of the people I meet during outdoor activities are interesting people. They enjoy the same activities that I enjoy. I think becoming involved in outdoor activities is actually one of the best ways to make new friends.

I am usually bored indoors, but I always enjoy the things I do and the people I meet when I am outdoors. Doing things outdoors is the most interesting way for me to spend my time.

▼

| 147 | MA | Your school has received a gift of money. What do you think is the best way for your school to spend this money? Use specific reasons and details to support your choice. |

Our school has many needs, but I think the best way to spend a gift of money is on new classroom equipment. Our school is old. We don't have enough desks and chairs for all the students and our classroom furniture is out of repair. If we buy new equipment, the students will feel better and want to work hard. The community will take pride in our school. New equipment will last a long time, so we will feel the benefit of the gift for many years.

It is hard for students to study when there aren't enough chairs in the classroom. It is hard for them to use old, broken blackboards. It is hard when there aren't good bookshelves and cabinets to organize the classroom supplies. With new equipment, students will feel like school is a nice place to be. They will feel like the teachers care about them. They will be motivated to study harder and do the best job they can.

It is hard for the community to feel proud of a school that looks old and broken. If members of the community visit the school and see new classroom equipment, they might feel better about the school. They might say, "This school has improved, and we can improve it more." They might be motivated to contribute money and volunteer time to further improve the school. Every school is better when community members become involved. New equipment can help motivate them.

We could spend the gift money on educational trips for the students. We could spend it on supplies such as paper and pencils or on books. All these things are important for education, but they don't last. Students this year will benefit, but students five years from now won't. Classroom equipment, on the other hand, lasts many years. If we spend the money on equipment, students will benefit for many years to come.

New classroom equipment will motivate both students and community members to improve their participation in school. Everyone will benefit from new equipment now and in the future as well. Therefore, I think this is one of the best ways we can spend a gift of money to our school.

▼

| 148 | AD | Do you agree or disagree with the following statement? Playing games teaches us about life. Use specific reasons and examples to support your answer. |

Almost everyone loves games. Playing games is both fun and useful because they teach us the skills we need in life. They teach us about cause-and-effect, about how to deal with people, and about following rules.

First of all, games teach us about cause-and-effect relationships. If we hit a ball, it will land somewhere or someone will catch it. If we make certain combinations with cards, we win points. We learn to pay attention to the results of our actions.

Playing games teaches us how to deal with other people. We learn about team-work, if the game has teams. We learn how to assign tasks according to each person's skills. We learn how to cooperate with team members. If the game doesn't have teams, we still learn about interacting with other people. We learn how to negotiate rules and get along with others.

Game playing teaches us how to follow rules to achieve something. We find out that if we want to reach a goal, we need to know the rules. We learn how to go step by step toward a desired end. We learn how to make a plan for reaching our goal. We learn strategy.

Most people understand that "all work and no play" is bad for you. Learning all these things would be much slower if we didn't play games. Life would be much duller, too.

▼

| 149 | MA | Imagine that you have received some land to use as you wish. How would you use this land? Use specific details to explain your answer. |

I would like to use my land for something that everyone can enjoy. Therefore, I would build a campground on it. Right now we don't have any good places for outdoor recreation in my town. A campground would be an inexpensive place for outdoor recreation and would provide activities that everybody would enjoy.

There aren't many opportunities for outdoor recreation in my town. We have only one small park and a playing field behind the high school. That really isn't enough space for our needs. In addition, the park is not well maintained so people don't like to use it. A well maintained campground would give our town a nice place to enjoy out-door activities.

We have many opportunities for indoor recreation, but they are all expensive. We have a brand new movie theater, but the ticket prices go up every day. It is especially hard to pay for tickets if you have several children. We have a museum of local history, but that, too, is expensive. Young people like to go to the mall, but of course that just encourages more spending. A campground, on the other hand, is an inexpensive place to spend time, even for large families.

At a campground, everybody can find activities that they enjoy. People can play different kinds of games outdoors, they can go hiking or study nature, or just sit and relax. At night they can enjoy talking around a campfire. It is a nice place for families to enjoy some free time together.

A campground would provide an inexpensive and enjoyable place for families and friends to spend time together. It would be a great asset to our town. I think it would be a very good way to use land.

▼

| 150 | AD | Do you agree or disagree with the following statement? Watching television is bad for children. Use specific details and examples to support your answer. |

I think television is very bad for children. It is bad for their health, it is bad for their minds, and it is bad for their values. They should rarely be allowed to watch it.

When children watch a lot of television, they don't get a lot of physical exercise. They just sit and watch all day. Often, they eat snacks while they watch TV. The snacks are probably cookies and potato chips and other food that is bad for their health. Children need to get a lot of exercise. They need to play active games. They also need to eat healthful food. Television watching does not encourage any of this.

When children watch a lot of television, they are exposed to a lot of information and ideas. Some of this is educational, but a lot of it is not. Children don't always know the difference. There is a lot of violence, sex, and other things on TV that children shouldn't see. If children learn about adult topics from TV, they will have a distorted view of the world.

When children watch a lot of television, they are encouraged to be materialistic. Advertising teaches children that having a lot of things is important. It teaches children that they must always have the newest, biggest, or most expensive thing. In addition, the characters on TV shows drive new cars, have fashionable clothes, and live in big houses. This also encourages children to want things.

Television can educate and entertain, but it also gives a distorted view of the world. It generally does not encourage healthful, intelligent, or moral living. It should not be a big part of any child's life.

▼

| 151 | MA | What is the most important animal in your country? Why is this animal important? Use reasons and specific details to explain your answer. |

The most important animal in my country is the dog. Almost everybody in my country has, or has had, a dog in his or her life. Dogs provide us with companionship, assistance, and protection. Most people like having dogs around.

The biggest reason people have dogs is for companionship. Dogs are companions for people who live alone. They are also good company for people who like to walk or go hunting. They are playmates for children. Dogs make good companions because they like being with people.

Dogs also provide some very important assistance. Seeing-eye dogs help blind people live independent lives. Sheep dogs and other types of herding dogs help farmers guard their animals. Police dogs are trained to find illegal drugs. Dogs' intelligence and desire to please people make them ideal for all kinds of work.

Dogs protect people from danger. Dogs have been able to find lost children. Dogs have alerted people to fires and other dangers. And we cannot forget guard dogs, which protect people and their property from burglars.

Dogs provide companionship to many people. They also assist and protect people. Most people in my country love dogs and appreciate the ways in which they can help us. This is why I think the dog is the most important animal in my country.

▼

| 152 | MA | Many parts of the world are losing important natural resources, such as forests, animals, or clean water. Choose one resource that is disappearing and explain why it needs to be saved. Use specific reasons and examples to support your opinion. |

An important resource that is disappearing is our trees. Thousands of acres of trees are lost every year all around the world. They are cut down for fuel or to make room for new houses and shopping centers. We need to save trees because they help us breathe, they provide us with medicine, and they protect our soil.

Trees are essential to our survival because they help us breathe. They are a major part of the process of photosynthesis. They take carbon dioxide from the air to produce oxygen. Oxygen is something we all need. The fewer trees there are, the more this affects our ability to breathe.

Trees are also important in the development of many medicines. Medical researchers are learning more and more about natural medicines from plants. Many drugs are made from plants, including trees. So, trees are important for our health.

Trees are important to soil conservation. This is why farmers usually have trees lining their fields. They know that tree roots help keep the soil in place and are also a factor in underground water distribution. Without trees, soil would be washed away and it would be difficult to grow things.

Trees are important to our lives in many ways. Without trees, we wouldn't be able to breathe, we wouldn't have certain medicines, and we wouldn't be able to grow food. You could say that our survival depends on them.

▼

| 153 | AD | Do you agree or disagree with the following statement? A zoo has no useful purpose. Use specific reasons and examples to explain your answer. |

Many people believe that zoos are unnecessary, harmful, and even cruel. If properly managed, however, I feel that zoos have a lot of value. They are educational, contribute to scientific research, and generate interest in environmental concerns.

Zoos can be wonderfully educational places. They provide opportunities to see animals up close. Zoo visitors can learn how animals eat, how they bathe, how they play and fight. They can learn about the different kinds of environments animals live in. They can discover new kinds of animals that they hadn't heard of before. A zoo is the best place to learn about animal life.

Zoos provide scientists with many opportunities for research. Research is safer and easier to conduct at a zoo than in the wild. Researchers have better access to animals and can set up controlled experiments. They are also in a safer situation.

Zoos can get people interested in environmental concerns. When people have the opportunity to see animals up close at a zoo, they become more interested in them. When they learn about how animals live, they can understand how animals become endangered. They are more likely to be concerned about protecting animals and their environments.

Zoos should provide animals with safe, clean, and comfortable homes. It is expensive to run a zoo properly, but it is worth it for the educational and research opportunities they provide.

▼

154	MA	In some countries people are no longer allowed to smoke in many public places and office buildings. Do you think this is a good rule or a bad rule? Use specific reasons and details to support your opinion.

It is not fair to ban smoking in public places. It is not fair to take away smokers' rights or ability to relax. Since it is possible to have special smoking (or nonsmoking) areas to protect nonsmokers, there is no reason to ban smoking in public.

Smokers have rights just like everybody else. Some people don't like smoke, but that doesn't mean that smoking should be banned. Some people don't like motorcycles, some people don't like dogs, some people don't like funny hats, but there is no law against having these things in public. People who don't like smoking have to learn to tolerate it, just as they tolerate anything else.

People smoke to relax. They don't smoke to harm other people. If they have to leave a restaurant or a park to go home and smoke, then it isn't relaxing. Other relaxing activities are allowed in public, so smoking should be allowed, too.

It is possible to have smoking areas in public places. Smokers can sit in a special section of a restaurant, airport, or any other public place. Nonsmokers can sit in another section. Then they won't be bothered by the smoke. In this way both smokers and nonsmokers can enjoy their use of public space equally.

It is true that smoking is bothersome to many people, and some people are even allergic to it. It isn't fair, however, to take away smokers' rights just because some people don't like it. It is possible for smokers and nonsmokers to share public space. It is the only fair thing to do.

▼

| 155 | MA | Plants can provide food, shelter, clothing, or medicine. What is one kind of plant that is important to you or the people in your country? Use specific reasons and details to support your choice. |

The coconut tree is a very important plant in my country. Coconut tree plantations are important sources of revenue, food, and shelter.

Our country earns a lot of money from the export of coconut tree products such as copra, coconuts, coconut oil, and coconut milk. This has been the main source of our foreign exchange for over a century. In fact, many of the coconut plantations were planted by various colonial powers and now, since independence, are run by our own citizens.

We not only export the food products of the coconut tree; we eat them ourselves too. The coconut is the basis of much of our national cuisine. We are famous for our curries made rich by coconut milk. We also use the oil to fry our food as well as to add shine to our skin and hair.

We use the fronds of the coconut tree to provide ourselves with shelter. The walls and roofs of many houses are covered with coconut fronds. The breezes pass through the fronds and cool the interior, but the heavy rains, which fall daily, do not enter.

The coconut tree is a very versatile and useful plant. It is a tree that has served our country well.

▼

| 156 | EX | You have the opportunity to visit a foreign country for two weeks. Which country would you like to visit? Use specific reasons and details to explain your choice. |

If I could visit any foreign country, I would go to Iceland. I imagine it is unlike any place I have seen before. In the middle of the summer the sun never sets. I would like to see that and the interesting scenery and learn more about Iceland's history.

I would like to experience some days when the sun doesn't set. Of course, I would have to go to Iceland in June in order to have this experience. It's hard to imagine going to bed while the sun is still in the sky. It would feel strange, but I would like to try it.

I would like to see some of Iceland's beautiful scenery. I have seen it in photos, and I am sure it is much better in real life. I would like to look at volcanoes and walk on glaciers. I want to see the places where steam rises from the ground and go swimming in the natural hot springs.

I would like to learn more about the history of Iceland. I know that Vikings went there from Norway over 1,000 years ago. Why did they want to live in that strange, cold place? How did they begin their lives there? How were they able to grow food and survive? I am sure Iceland has museums that explain these things. I would like to visit them and learn everything I can.

Iceland is a unique place. It would be wonderful to have the opportunity to visit there, to see the wonderful sights, and learn about the history. Maybe some day I really will be able to go.

▼

157	**PR**	In the future, students may have the choice of studying at home by using technology such as computers or television or of studying at traditional schools. Which would you prefer? Use reasons and specific details to explain your choice.

I believe that it is better to study at school than at home. I can learn a lot if I study alone at home, but I can learn more if I study at school with other people. I can gain a lot of information from other people. I also learn a lot by interacting with them. I am motivated to study more if I don't work alone. Therefore, I believe I can learn a lot more at school.

Information comes from technology, but it also comes from people. If I study at home, I can get a lot of information from my computer, DVD player, and television. If I study at school, I can get all this information, and I can also get information from my teachers and classmates. So, I learn more.

Interaction with other people increases my knowledge. At home I have nobody to talk to. Nobody can hear my ideas. At school I have the opportunity to interact with other people. We can explain our ideas to each other. We can agree and disagree. Together we can develop our ideas and learn to understand new things.

Competition motivates me. When I am at home, nobody can see my work. Nobody can tell me that I did a good job or a bad job. When I am at school, my teacher and my classmates see my work, and I can see my classmates' work. I want to do a good job like my classmates, or even a better job. So, I want to study harder.

Some people can study very well when they are alone at home, but I can't. I need to have other people near me. When I am with other people, I have the possibility to learn more information. I have the opportunity to develop my ideas more completely. I have the motivation to do a better job. Therefore, school is the best place for me.

▼

158	**MA**	When famous people such as actors, athletes, and rock stars give their opinions, many people listen. Do you think we should pay attention to these opinions? Use specific reasons and examples to support your answer.

Many people pay attention to the opinions of actors, athletes, and rock stars just because they are famous. Clearly this isn't a good idea. The opinions of famous people are not any better than those of ordinary people, and are certainly not as important as an expert's opinion. In addition, if we pay too much attention to fame, we might not hear what someone is really saying.

For some reason, people tend to think that famous people's opinions are better, but this isn't true. A rock star may know a lot about music, but why should she understand politics better than you do? An athlete may understand a lot or a little about a social issue, but you might, too, and so might your neighbors. It is better to discuss issues with people you really know than to listen to the opinions of someone you will never meet.

If we are going to listen to other people's opinions, we should listen to the experts. A political scientist will have an opinion on politics that is worth listening to. You might not agree with this opinion, but at least you know it is based on knowledge and experience. You don't know where a celebrity's opinion comes from.

Sometimes all we see is a person's fame, but we don't really hear what they say. You might admire a certain actor, for example. When that actor supports a certain political candidate, you might vote for that person just because you like the actor. You don't bother to learn something about the candidate and form your own opinion. You don't take the time to make sure that this candidate represents your beliefs. This is a dangerous thing to do.

We admire famous people for their achievements in their fields. This doesn't mean, however, that we should listen to their opinions about everything. We have the opinions of experts, of our friends and relatives, and of ourselves to examine, also. Often, these are the more important opinions to pay attention to.

▼

| 159 | MA | The twentieth century saw great change. In your opinion, what is one change that should be remembered about the twentieth century? Use specific reasons and details to explain your choice. |

There were many important changes, both technological and cultural, during the twentieth century. In my opinion, the most important of these is the advances that were made in medical science. The development of vaccines and antibiotics, increased access to health care, and improvements in surgical techniques are all things that improved, and saved, the lives of people all around the world.

Vaccines and antibiotics have saved the lives of many people. Fifty years ago, many people became crippled or died from polio. Now the polio vaccine is available everywhere. In the past, people could die from even simple infections. Now penicillin and other antibiotics make it easy to cure infections.

Increased access to health care has also improved the lives of millions of people. In the past, many people lived far from hospitals or clinics. Now hospitals, clinics, and health centers have been built in many parts of the world. More people have the opportunity to visit a doctor or nurse before they become very sick. They can be treated more easily. They are sick less and this leads to a better quality of life.

Improved surgical techniques make it easier to treat many medical problems. Microscopic and laser surgery techniques are more efficient than older methods. It is easier for the doctor to perform them, and easier for the patient to recover. Surgery patients can return to their normal life more quickly now than they could in the past.

Everybody needs good health in order to have a good quality of life. Advances in medical science have improved the lives of people all around the world. They are improvements that are important to everyone.

▼

| 160 | PR | When people need to complain about a product or poor service, some prefer to complain in writing and others prefer to complain in person. Which do you prefer? Use specific reasons and examples to support your answer. |

When I make a complaint about a defective product or poor service, I prefer to make my complaint in writing. It is easier to organize my thoughts this way and it is easier to control my emotions. Most important, it gives me written proof, just in case I need it.

When I write, I have a chance to organize my thoughts. I can take all the time I need, and I can write two or three or more versions, if necessary. In this way, I am sure of expressing my thoughts clearly. If I speak to someone in person, on the other hand, I might become confused and nervous. I can't take time to organize my thoughts. I can't erase my words and express my idea again in a different way.

When I write, I also have the chance to control my emotions. If I am making a complaint, I am probably angry. I can express this anger in writing in any way I want. Then I can throw out the letter and rewrite it in a more courteous way. I can express my anger without offending anyone because no one will see the first letter.

When I write a letter, I have written proof of my complaint. This might be important if we can't come to a friendly agreement. If we have to go to a lawyer, I will need to show documentation. A letter of complaint is one document the lawyer will need to prove my case.

Writing a letter gives me a chance to organize my thoughts and control my emotions. It also provides me with documentation. This is why I prefer to make complaints in writing.

▼

| 161 | EX | People remember special gifts or presents they have received. Why? Use specific reasons and examples to support your answer. |

I think we remember special gifts we've received because these gifts often hold special memories for us. They may be memories of special people, of special events, or even of ourselves as we once were in the past.

Gifts can remind us of special people in our lives. When we look at gifts, we remember the good times we have enjoyed with the giver. We think of the good feelings we have about that person. The giver may be someone we see frequently or infrequently. Either way, the gift is a special reminder of him or her.

Gifts may also bring back memories of special events in our lives. Some gifts mark special turning points in our lives such as school graduations. Some gifts may hold memories of special birthdays or anniversaries. They help us remember the special times in our lives.

Gifts can also be a symbol of our past. A gift received in childhood may remind us of games we enjoyed then. A gift received in high school makes us think of the music or clothes we loved when we were young.

Gifts are important to us because they remind us of the special people, events, and interests of our lives. They are a way of surrounding ourselves with our past.

▼

162	MA	Some famous athletes and entertainers earn millions of dollars every year. Do you think these people deserve such high salaries? Use specific reasons and examples to support your opinion.

Famous athletes and entertainers earn a lot of money and they deserve it. They work hard to achieve fame, they provide us with good entertainment, and they give up their privacy in order to do this. I think they deserve every cent they get.

Fame doesn't just appear overnight; people have to work hard to achieve it. If someone has a lot of fame now, it means he has spent years working hard to develop his talent. He has spent a lot of time at low-paying jobs in order to get experience and recognition. He continues to work hard now in order to maintain his talent and fame. Just like anybody else, famous people deserve to be rewarded for their hard work.

Athletes, actors, and musicians provide us with entertainment. On weekends, most of us attend at least one sporting event or movie or concert. After watching a famous person perform, we might even be inspired to learn to play a sport or a musical instrument ourselves. Famous athletes and entertainers help us make good use of our free time. They deserve to be paid for this.

Famous people suffer a loss of privacy. Since we admire them, we want to feel as if we know them. We want to know how they live and what happens in their daily lives. Therefore, journalists follow them all the time in order to find out the details of their private lives. These details, true or not, are published in magazines all around the world. This is a big disadvantage to being famous. Earning a lot of money can, in part, compensate for this.

Famous people work hard to entertain us, and then they lose their privacy. They contribute a lot to our lives. They deserve to earn a lot of money.

▼

163	MA	Is the ability to read and write more important today than in the past? Why or why not? Use specific reasons and examples to support your answer.

Today more than at any time in the history of the world it is important to be able to read and write. This change has been brought about by the Internet, which we use to communicate with one another, to get our news, and to buy products.

Millions of people today communicate through e-mail using the Internet. In the past, people had face-to-face meetings or called one another on the phone. Today they use e-mail and chat rooms. Of course it is necessary to be able to read and write in order to use the Internet for communication.

Today, one can subscribe to news and information on the Internet. When you turn on your computer in the morning, you see the headlines, financial news, sports scores, or social events that you requested. In the past, people got news and information from television or radio, and many still do. More and more people, however, get news from the Internet because they can subscribe to just the type of news that interests them. Again, reading skills are required to do this.

These days it is becoming more and more common to buy products on the Internet. People like this because it is more convenient than going to the store, and because it is easier to find certain products. In the past, people bought everything in stores. At a store one can just pick items off the shelf and ask the store employees any questions about the products. On the Internet, however, reading and writing skills are required to select products and order them. Buying things on the Internet will become even more common in the future.

The Internet will force us all to be literate not only in reading and writing, but also with computers. Today, we must be skilled readers and writers to be successful in the high-tech world.

▼

164	EX	People do many different things to stay healthy. What do you do for good health? Use specific reasons and examples to support your answer.

Our health is the only thing we really have in the world. You can take away our money, our house, or our clothes, and we can survive. Take away our health and we will die. That is why I eat healthfully, exercise regularly, and keep up my social life.

Eating healthfully is important to maintain health. I try to avoid foods high in fat such as french fries or cookies. I also rarely eat meat. I eat a lot of fruits and vegetables because they are full of vitamins. I try to cook foods properly so that they don't lose their nutrients.

Exercise is another part of staying healthy. I either walk or ride my bike everyday. A few days a week I work out at the gym, and on weekends I usually play tennis with my friends. I enjoy exercise so it is fun and easy for me to do it. It helps keep me strong and it is good for my heart, too.

Friends are an important part of one's health. Friends help keep you happy and help you deal with stress. Studies have shown that emotional health is related to physical health. Spending time with my friends helps keep me emotionally healthy.

By eating healthfully, exercising regularly, and spending time with my friends, I can keep both my mind and body healthy. Fortunately, I like to do all these things so I am a very healthy person.

▼

165	EX	You have decided to give several hours of your time each month to improve the community where you live. What is one thing you will do to improve your community? Why? Use specific reasons and details to explain your choice.

Volunteering a few hours each week is an important way of investing in the future of our society. I choose to spend my time helping children learn to read. Developing good reading skills will help poor readers keep up with their classmates, open new worlds to them, and help them succeed in life.

Students who are not good readers fall behind their classmates. They don't understand the lessons and they come to school unprepared. By learning to read, these students can keep up with their classmates. They can learn their lessons and be active participants in class.

When students improve their reading skills, they can read books on all different subjects. New worlds are opened up to them. They can travel to different places and experience new ideas without ever leaving their classrooms. Students who can't read well will know only what they see around them.

Students who are poor readers are severely handicapped. Someone without good reading skills will have to work at the most menial jobs. Good readers, on the other hand, have the whole universe open to them. They will have the possibility to learn any job that interests them.

By volunteering to help children learn to read, I help them not only today, but for the rest of their lives. I help them keep up with their peers and explore the world and themselves through books.

▼

| 166 | MA | People recognize a difference between children and adults. What events (experiences or ceremonies) make a person an adult? Use specific reasons and examples to explain your answer. |

It is not only age but also experience that makes people adults. The world looks at people as adults when they have had certain experiences. These experiences include graduation from school, having a job, and getting married.

Graduating from college is like graduating into adulthood. When a person finishes school, she is no longer dependent on her parents economically. She is prepared to earn her own living. She is experienced enough to make decisions about what kind of job she wants. She is ready to be on her own.

Getting a job definitely makes a person into an adult. A person with a job supports himself. He has responsibilities at work that he must fulfill. Unlike a child, he can't cry or complain to his parents if he doesn't like something about his job. He has to work it out with his boss and coworkers, or learn to tolerate it. The world looks on a job holder as a responsible person.

When a person gets married, she has made the final step into adulthood. She is no longer responsible only to herself; she is also responsible to her spouse and children. She has to be mature enough to make sacrifices for them and to love them unconditionally. She is also now considered old enough to take care of her parents when they need it.

The world looks on people as adults when they have had certain experiences. These are experiences that give people the chance to be independent and responsible.

▼

| 167 | MA | Your school has enough money to purchase either computers for students or books for the library. Which should your school choose to buy—computers or books? Use specific reasons and examples to support your recommendation. |

Our school already has books in its library and it already has computers. However, I think buying more computers is more important than buying more books. Computers provide access to more information than books, and they provide it more quickly. Also, in this modern world, every student needs to learn how to use computers skillfully. We need computers more than we need books.

Computers, unlike books, provide access to up-to-date information. Right now, the reference books in our library are very outdated. If we buy new books today, they will become old very quickly. Computers, on the other hand, provide the ability to access the latest information on the Internet. They are the best tool available.

Computers also provide information more quickly. Just type in a keyword and many sources of information appear instantly on the screen. It takes much longer to look up information in a book, and often the book you want is not immediately available. You have to wait for somebody to return it or order it from another library.

Computers are an important tool in the modern world, so students have to learn how to use them. If students do all their schoolwork on computers, they will develop the computer skills that they will need in the future. Therefore, we need to have a computer for every student in the school.

If we buy more computers for our school, all the students will have access to the latest information. They will be able to do their work more quickly and they will learn important skills, too. For these reasons, I feel that purchasing computers will benefit us more than buying books.

▼

| 168 | EX | Many students choose to attend schools or universities outside their home countries. Why do some students study abroad? Use specific reasons and details to explain your answer. |

Although students can get a good education in most subjects in their home countries, it is important to study abroad for at least part of one's college education. By studying abroad, students have the chance to learn a new language, to become familiar with another culture, and to grow in different ways.

It is important to be bilingual or even multilingual in today's world. International communication is important for our global economy. In addition, the Internet and satellite TV give us the opportunity to receive information from all over the world. We need to be familiar with different languages in order to take advantage of this.

Familiarity with other cultures is also important today. It teaches us respect for other ways of life. It can encourage peaceful solutions to conflicts. This will make the world a safer place for ourselves and our children.

Finally, living in a new environment opens us up to experimenting with different ways of doing things. We can have new experiences and try out different things. We can make changes in our habits if we want to. This gives us a chance to explore ourselves and the world more than we could at home.

Study abroad can be enriching. Not only can we learn a new language and understand more about a different culture, but we can learn more about ourselves, too. At the same time, of course, we get an education in the formal sense. Study abroad is a complete educational experience.

▼

169	EX	People listen to music for different reasons and at different times. Why is music important to many people? Use specific reasons and examples to support your choice.

Music has been a part of people's lives since the time civilization began. I think music is important because it helps us express our emotions, it helps us feel connected to others, and also simply because it is a beautiful thing.

Music is an expression of emotion. Music can be sad or happy, calming or agitating, angry or contented. Music can represent any human emotion. When people play or listen to music, they feel their emotions. Often people listen to certain music because they want to feel a certain way. Music has a lot of emotional power.

Music helps people feel connected to each other. When people go to a concert, they are with other people who share their musical tastes. Together they feel the emotions that the music evokes. Also, music has always played an important part in ceremonies, from ancient times to the present. This is because of its ability to make people feel connected.

Finally, people enjoy music because of its beauty. Music is art, an expression of beauty. Whatever emotion it expresses, positive or negative, it is beautiful. Listening to good music can be like looking at a beautiful flower or a spectacular sunset. It can be as beautiful as anything nature gives us.

Music brings a lot to our lives in terms of emotions, connections, and beauty. No culture has ever been without it.

▼

170	EX	Groups or organizations are an important part of some people's lives. Why are groups or organizations important to people? Use specific reasons and examples to explain your answer.

Groups or organizations are an important part of our lives because we are social people. We like to be with people who are similar to us. The most important groups for us are families, religious organizations, and political organizations.

Our families are obviously our most important group. They give us physical and emotional support. They are part of us; we are tied to them by blood. They are always there for us.

Religious organizations connect us to a larger sort of family. This is a family of people who share our beliefs. Our beliefs are based on tradition. These beliefs have been tested over time. They comfort us in times of stress. They tell us how to respond and act.

Political organizations connect us to people who share our ideas. We may be liberal or conservative or something in between. Whatever our political philosophy, we can find a group that matches it. Political organizations help us to be part of the larger community.

Family groups, religious groups, and political groups all serve a similar function in our lives. They help us feel as if we belong.

▼

171	MA	Imagine you are preparing for a trip. You plan to be away from your home for a year. In addition to clothing and personal care items, you can take one additional thing. What would you take and why? Use specific reasons and details to support your choice.

If I leave my home for a year, there is one thing I will definitely take with me: my cell phone. With my cell phone, I can call my friends or family whenever I feel lonely, need advice, or just want to talk.

If I am away from home for a year, I will feel very lonely. If I can call my parents, I will hear familiar voices and I will not feel so lonely. Calling my friends will also help me feel better.

I have never been away from home by myself, so there are many things I don't know how to do. I don't know how to open a bank account, cook, or drive a car. With my cell phone, I can call my parents to ask for help with cooking dinner, for example. I can ask them for any advice I might need.

Sometimes, I may just want to speak my own language. I can call my friends on my cell phone and tell them about my new life. This will make them jealous of me. I can call them a lot and tell them about all the wonderful things I am doing.

For me a cell phone is a necessity. On my trip I will need it when I feel lonely, when I need advice, and when I want to talk with friends. Of course, the phone bill will be sent to my parents.

▼

172	EX	When students move to a new school, they sometimes face problems. How can schools help these students with their problems? Use specific reasons and examples to explain your answer.

When students go to a new school, they often have a problem fitting in. They don't know how the school operates and they don't have any friends. The school administrators, the school counselors, and the teachers can do a lot to help new students become part of the community.

School administrators can help orient new students to their school. They can take the new students on a tour of the school, showing them classrooms, the gym, the cafeteria, the computer labs, and other school facilities. They can explain the school program and tell the students about what is expected of them.

The school counselors can talk to new students about their goals and interests. They should explain the school schedule and help the students choose the appropriate classes. They should also talk about extracurricular activities such as the school newspaper, sports teams, band, and language clubs. They should encourage new students to participate in such activities because it is a good way to make friends.

Teachers can help new students the most. They explain their coursework to them, of course. They can also encourage old students to be friendly with the new students and help them learn the school system. They are with the students all day, so they are aware if a student is having difficulties. Then they can try to help the student themselves, or ask for assistance from the counselors or administrators.

School administrators, counselors, and teachers can do a lot to help students adjust to their new school. It isn't easy, but it pays off with happier, more successful students in the end.

▼

| 173 | AD | It is sometimes said that borrowing money from a friend can harm or damage the friendship. Do you agree? Why or why not? Use reasons and specific examples to explain your answer. |

It is not a good idea to borrow money from a friend. It is not fair to the friend. It is hard for a friend to say no, to admit that she doesn't have enough money, or to ask for her money back when she needs it.

If you ask a friend for money, it is hard for her to say no. She may do many favors for you easily, but she still might feel uncomfortable about lending money. However, she doesn't want to be rude to you. If you ask her for money, she feels like she has to lend it. This puts her in an unfair position.

Your friend may not be able to admit that she doesn't have enough money. She may be embarrassed to tell you this. Or maybe she just doesn't want to disappoint you. She lends you the money, then she doesn't have enough for herself.

Your friend may feel awkward about asking for her money back. If some time passes before you repay the loan, the friend may feel embarrassed to ask you for it. Maybe she needs it, or maybe she just wants to know what is going on. But she also doesn't want to put pressure on you or make you angry. It is a difficult position to be in.

People all have different ideas about money and it can cause a lot of problems. It is better to borrow money from people you don't know well, such as bankers. Then, if necessary, you can have problems with them, and maintain good relationships with your friends.

▼

| 174 | EX | Every generation of people is different in important ways. How is your generation different from your parents' generation? Use specific reasons and examples to explain your answer. |

The one thing that makes the difference between my parents' generation and my own is modern technology. When my parents were growing up, they had TV, radio, and cars, but they didn't have the amount of technology we have now. They didn't have personal computers, they didn't have satellite TV, and they didn't have cell phones.

My parents didn't grow up with computers, but I did. They have a computer now, but they don't use it as I do. I write all my schoolwork and keep all my files on the computer. My parents still like to use paper. I do all my research and get all my news off the Internet. My parents still use newspapers and TV. Because of computers, I am accustomed to having more access to information than my parents are. I am used to doing more work more efficiently. It is a completely different way of living.

My parents had only local TV when they were young, but I have satellite TV. I grew up seeing programs from all over the world. I am used to seeing foreign movies and cartoons. I have some ideas about things in foreign countries and a lot of interest in them. Satellite TV exposes me to things that have opened up my mind. My parents didn't have the same opportunity when they were young.

Cell phones are common now, but they didn't exist when my parents were young. They didn't even have answering machines or voice mail. They couldn't talk to people at any time or leave messages easily. I can do this. Right now it is a fun part of my social life. When I have a job it will be more important. I will be able to contact people easily and that will make my work more efficient. Cell phones have made a big difference in the way we work.

Modern technology has made a big difference in the way we work, in our understanding of the world, and in the expectations we have of friends and colleagues. It has completely changed the way we live. The world of my generation is a different place than it was for my parents' generation.

▼

175	PR	Some students like classes where teachers lecture (do all of the talking) in class. Other students prefer classes where the students do some of the talking. Which type of class do you prefer? Give specific reasons and details to support your choice.

In my country, the lecture system is the most common system. It is the one I prefer for three reasons: I am used to it, it is an efficient system, and I am too shy to talk in class.

My classes have always been lecture classes. I am used to listening to the teacher talk. We students sit quietly at our desks and take notes. We never ask questions because we don't want to seem stupid. At the end of the course, we take a test. If we can repeat on the test what the teacher said in class, we get a good grade.

The lecture system is an efficient one. The teacher is the one who knows the subject, not the students. It is a waste of time listening to a student's ideas. What good will that do me? Time is short. I want the teacher to give me as much information as possible during the class period.

Even if we could talk in class, I would never open my mouth. I am much too shy. I don't want other students to laugh at me and make fun of my ideas. I prefer to listen to the lecture and memorize the teacher's ideas.

I hope I can always study at a school where they use the lecture system. I like it because I am used to it. I also want to learn information in the most efficient manner possible, and I don't want to interrupt a teacher with my foolish questions.

▼

| 176 | EX | Holidays honor people or events. If you could create a new holiday, what person or event would it honor and how would you want people to celebrate it? Use specific reasons and details to support your answer. |

October 24 is United Nations Day. This day is noted on calendars, but it is not generally observed as a holiday around the world. I want the entire world to celebrate the birth of the United Nations because of its attempts to promote peace and provide basic needs to people everywhere. United Nations Day should be a day to learn about the UN and about our neighbors around the world.

The most important mission of the UN is to promote peace. The sooner we can stop war, the sooner we can all have better lives. We need to appreciate and support the UN's efforts to create a more peaceful world.

The UN has done a lot of work to provide basic needs to people around the world. It has health programs and education programs. It provides assistance to refugees. The UN has done a lot to improve the lives of people everywhere. This work should be honored.

On United Nations Day, people should spend time learning about the work of the UN. Schools, universities, and community organizations can have workshops and fairs that provide information about the UN. The celebration should also include celebrating different cultures around the world. There could be food, games, and music from different countries. Learning about other countries is a first step toward world peace.

The United Nations has done a lot of work to promote world peace and provide basic human needs. This work is important to all of us. It needs to be recognized, supported, and celebrated.

▼

| 177 | MA | A friend of yours has received some money and plans to use all of it either

• to go on vacation
• to buy a car

Your friend has asked you for advice. Compare your friend's two choices and explain which one you think your friend should choose. Use specific reasons and details to support your choice. |

I advise my friend to spend his money on a car. A car is a much better investment. It is useful, it lasts a long time, and, most of all, my friend can use it to take me places.

A car is a very useful thing. If my friend buys one, it will be easier for him to get to school and work. He could even get a different job farther from home. He can help his parents with his car by going shopping for them. A vacation, on the other hand, is nice but not practical. It is not something my friend can use in his daily life. It is just a luxury.

A car lasts a long time. If my friend gets a good model and takes care of it, he can drive it for years. A vacation, on the other hand, is short. It lasts only a few days or weeks. Then my friend will be left with nothing but memories.

If my friend gets a car, then I will benefit. My friend can take me places with him. We can go to movies or for drives in the countryside. My friend might even be nice enough to drive me around while I do my errands. He wouldn't be able to share his vacation with me, however. I don't think he has received enough money to invite me along.

My friend shouldn't waste his money on a vacation. It isn't practical, it doesn't last, and he can't share it with me. Buying a car is the best use for his money.

▼

| 178 | EX | The 21st century has begun. What changes do you think this new century will bring? Use examples and details in your answers. |

The 21st century will bring many changes. Some of these changes have already begun. Some of the biggest changes of the new century will be in the areas of access to information, international relations, and family structure.

We have already entered the Information Age. The Internet has made information available to everyone. As time goes on, more and more people will use the Internet regularly. It will become a common part of everyday life. We will not have to go to libraries to do research, travel to hear an expert speak, or go to a store to buy a book. All the information we want will be available to us at home on our computers.

The face of international relations is changing. Countries will have to change the way they relate to one another because of the global economy. They will have to cooperate more. Already we have the European Economic Union. In the new century, countries will continue to form new alliances because of the global economy.

Family structure will also change. The traditional mother/father/children family will no longer be the only type. There will be more single-parent families and more families with adopted children. There will also be more couples who have few children or none at all.

Whatever the changes may be, whether in the way we receive information, the way nations cooperate with one another, or the way families are defined, you can be sure that there will be more change. Change is a constant.

▼

| 179 | EX | What are some of the qualities of a good parent? Use specific details and examples to explain your answer. |

I am fortunate to have good parents, so it is easy for me to identify the qualities that make them good. These qualities are unconditional love, trust, and respect for me and my brothers and sisters.

All parents love their children, but not all love is unconditional. Some parents would not love their children if they married someone of a different religion or ethnic group. Some parents would not love their children if they had a different sexual orientation. My parents would. My parents love us no matter what choices we make for ourselves.

Part of unconditional love is trust. My parents trust us to do what is right. They know we would never do anything to harm them. They trust us so we trust them. We know they won't hurt or mistreat us.

Because our parents love us, they also respect us. They treat us as individuals. They accept our differences. They do not expect us to be like them. They want us to make our own way in the world, not follow in their footsteps.

Without my parents' love, I would not feel confident. Without their trust, I would not feel free to do what I want. Without their respect, I would not feel comfortable on my own. All children should have such wonderful parents.

▼

| 180 | EX | Movies are popular all over the world. Explain why movies are so popular. Use reasons and specific examples to support your answer. |

Movies are popular because people are great watchers. We like to watch other people's lives. By going to the movies we can bring excitement into our lives, express our emotions, and imagine ourselves as someone else.

Our lives are not adventurous or glamorous like the movies. We don't fight the bad guys all day and then go home to a luxury apartment. We just go to school, do our homework, eat, talk to our friends, and sleep. We need a little excitement in our lives and we find excitement at the movies.

Humans are very emotional. We all like to cry and laugh. Sad movies give us a chance to cry about our sadness. Funny ones give us a chance to laugh about our joy. Sometimes it is easier to express our emotions in a dark movie theater.

Now I am a student, but I know some day I want to be a scientist or a politician or a famous model. When I go to the movies, I can see my role models. I can see what they wear and how they talk. I can imagine myself as they are, and maybe some day I will really be like them.

Even though my life is quiet, I can go to the movies and watch someone else's life. I can share their emotions and their everyday life. I wonder if they would like to share mine.

▼

| 181 | MA | In your country, is there more need for land to be left in its natural condition or is there more need for land to be developed for housing and industry? Use specific reasons and examples to support your answer. |

In my country we need to use land for building. Our country is developing and our industrial sector is growing. People are moving to the cities. We need to build more factories, houses, and stores.

Our industrial sector has grown a lot over the past decade. We have built many factories and we will continue to build more. The growth of industry has helped our economy. There are more jobs now. If we build more factories, there will be even more jobs.

Building more factories means that we need more houses. Many people are moving to the cities to get jobs in the new factories. They need places to live. Right now, we don't have enough houses in the cities. It is a big problem. We need to build more houses near the new factories.

We also need to build more stores. When people move to live in a city, they need to go shopping somewhere. They need to buy food and clothes. Right now, our cities have a lot of stores in their downtowns. We need to build more stores, however, in the neighborhoods around the factories. Then it will be easier for people to do their shopping. They won't have to travel to a crowded downtown.

Our economy is growing so we need to build many things. We need to build new factories, houses, and stores. This is the most important use for land in my country today.

▼

| 182 | MA | Many people have a close relationship with their pets. These people treat their birds, cats, or other animals as members of their family. In your opinion, are such relationships good? Why or why not? Use specific reasons and examples to support your answer. |

Pets are important because they provide us with companionship and even with love. It is not good, however, to have too close a relationship with a pet, or to treat it like a human being. Devoting too much attention to pets can prevent you from focusing on other activities and on relationships with people. It can also be a waste of money.

Sometimes people who love their pets don't want to become involved in other activities. If you invite such a friend out for coffee, for example, the friend might say, "I don't have time. I have to walk the dog." Sometimes people don't want to take a weekend trip because they don't want to leave their pets alone. They put their pets' interests before their own. Then they live life for their pets and not for themselves.

Loving a pet too much can interfere with good relationships with people. Sometimes people neglect their spouses and children in favor of their pets. A person who lives alone might devote all his attention to his pet. He might lose interest in making friends and being with people. A relationship with a pet is less complicated than a relationship with a person. Sometimes it seems easier to choose pets over people.

People spend thousands of dollars on their pets, but this money could have other uses. It seems strange to buy special food for a pet or take it to the doctor, when some people don't have these things. Children all around the world grow up without enough food, or never get medical care. It would be better to give a pet simple things and send the extra money to charity.

Pets give us a lot and they deserve our care and attention. It is never a good idea to go to extremes, however. It is important to balance your pet's needs with your own.

▼

| 183 | EX | Films can tell us a lot about the country where they were made. What have you learned about a country from watching its movies? Use specific examples and details to support your response. |

When I watch movies from other countries, I realize that people everywhere really are similar. We may have different languages and cultures, but we all want to get an education, need to make a living, and like to have fun.

Once I saw a movie made in China. It showed parents helping their children with their homework. My parents helped me the same way. Another time I saw a movie from Argentina. It showed schoolchildren playing a game during recess. My friends and I used to play the same game at school. Seeing these films showed me that education is a common goal in every country. Children go to school and their parents help them with their work and want them to do the best they can. Education is something we all have in common.

By watching foreign movies, I see the different ways people earn a living. In some countries, people choose their careers according to their interests and talents. In other countries, their parents choose their careers for them. But in every country, finding a way to earn a living is a major concern, and working hard is respected. Earning a living is another common goal.

Movies often show how people have fun. People everywhere want to be entertained and want to spend time with family and friends. Different cultures may enjoy different types of activities, but all cultures enjoy some form of sports, music, and dancing. Everybody likes to have fun.

The movies I've seen make it clear to me that no matter what the cultural differences are between countries, people everywhere have the same basic needs and goals.

▼

| 184 | PR | Some students prefer to study alone. Others prefer to study with a group of students. Which do you prefer? Use specific reasons and examples to support your answer. |

I don't like to study alone. I almost always prefer to study with a group of students. This helps me learn the material better, it keeps me focused, and it's fun. too.

I learn more when I study with a group. In a group, we can help each other out. If I missed something in class, another student in the group can give me the missing information. If I don't understand something, the other students can explain it to me. When we discuss topics together, we develop our ideas and understand the topic better.

Studying in a group helps keep me focused. I am with friends who are studying, so I study, too. If I study alone at home, I might get distracted. I might put my books down and go watch TV or call a friend. In a group, we decide a time and a place to study, and then we do it. We keep each other focused on the task.

It's more fun to study in a group than alone. I feel happy when I am with my friends, even when we are working hard. After we finish studying, we usually go out for coffee or to the movies. This is something to look forward to. It is always nice to spend time with my friends.

I look forward to being with my friends, so I look forward to studying when I study with them. The group helps me study better and learn more. Studying with a group is the best way for me.

▼

| 185 | MA | You have enough money to purchase either a house or a business. Which would you choose to buy? Give specific reasons to explain your choice. |

If I had enough money, I would purchase a business, not a house. A house is only a place to live, but a business is much more. With a business, I could earn enough money to buy a house and do other things as well. I could travel, for example, and I could help my family, too.

I have always wanted to buy a house, and a business would make this possible. With a business I would earn enough money to buy a house. It might not happen right away, but after a few years in the business, I am sure I would have enough money. Then I would have both a business and a house.

After I buy my house, I could use my money to travel. I would like to visit other countries. With a business, I could earn enough money to do this. I might also travel for business. I might have to go to other countries to attend conferences or meet clients. One way or another, a business would give me the chance to travel.

One of my goals is to help my family. My parents don't own a house. With a business, I could help them buy one. I could also take care of them when they get older. I would also like to be able to send them on a trip. If I had a good business, I could help my parents in all these ways.

A house is just one thing, but a business is so much more. A good business would give me the opportunity to buy a house, travel, and help my parents. Buying a business is an investment for the future.

ANSWER KEY

CHAPTER 2
PLANNING THE ESSAY

Practice 1

1. A   It asks for your opinion to be stated and explained.
2. B   It asks for your choice of two sides.
3. A   It asks *Do you agree or disagree?*
4. B   It asks for your opinion to be stated and explained.
5. B   It asks *Do you agree or disagree?*
6. B   It asks for your opinion to be stated and explained.
7. A   It asks *Which do you prefer?*
8. A   It asks for a choice to be made and explained.
9. A   It asks *Do you agree or disagree?*
10. A   It asks *Do you prefer...?*

Practice 2

1. B and C   They both mention a specific decision.
2. A   It answers the question *Do you agree or disagree?*
3. B and C   They both mention reasons why people visit museums.
4. A and C   They both state a preference.
5. B   It states an opinion.

Practice 3

5.1 weeds
5.2 tables
5.3 safe

Practice 4

5.1 travel
5.2 have lots of new experiences
5.3 read stories
5.4 stability of household routine

Practice 5

5.1 convenient
5.2 walk
5.3 quiet
5.4 park
5.5 affordable

Practice 6

5.1 to prepare for a career
5.2 meet new people
5.3 of other subjects

Practice 7

5.1 waste of money
5.2 time
5.3 people change

Practice 8

5.1 Scrabble
5.2 talk before the game
5.3 teamwork
5.4 learn new words from opponents

CHAPTER 3
WRITING THE ESSAY

Practice 1

1.1. Playing games also teaches us how to deal with other people.
1.2. We learn about teamwork, if the game involves being on a team.
1.3. We learn how to divide and assign tasks according to each person's skills.
1.4. We learn how to get people to do what we want, and
1.5. we learn that sometimes we have to do what other people want.
2.1. Cooking takes a lot of time.
2.2. Shopping for the food takes time.
2.3. Cleaning and chopping the food takes time.
2.4. Cleaning up the kitchen after the food is cooked takes time.
3.1. Watching movies and television can help us understand the world more
3.2. For example, seeing movies can expose us to people of different races and cultures.
3.3. We can then overcome some prejudices more easily.
3.4. Recently there have been more handicapped people in films, and this also helps prevent prejudice.
4.1. Our planet gives us everything we need, but natural resources are not endless.
4.2. Strip mining destroys whole regions, leaving bare and useless ground.
4.3. Deforestation removes old trees that can't be replaced.
4.4. Too much fishing may harm fish populations to the point where they can't recover.
5.1. The most important lessons can't be taught; they have to be experienced.
5.2. No one can teach us how to get along with others or how to have self-respect.
5.3. As we pass from childhood into adolescence, no one can teach us the judgement we need to decide on how to deal with peer pressure.
5.4. As we leave adolescence behind and enter adult life, no one can teach us how to fall in love and get married or how to raise our children.

Practice 2

1. In my opinion, people's lives are (or are not) easier today.

2. It seems to me that most people prefer (or do not prefer) to spend their leisure time outdoors.

3. To my mind, an apartment building is (or is not) better than a house.

4. From my point of view it is (or is not) good that English is becoming the world language.

Practice 3

1. I believe that high schools should (or should not) allow students to study what they want.

2. I guess that it is better to be a leader (or member) of a group.

3. I agree that people should (or should not) do things they do not enjoy doing.

4. I suppose that I would rather have the university assign (or not assign) me a roommate.

Practice 4

1. I am sure that children should (or should not) spend a great amount of time practicing sports.

2. I am positive that a shopping center in my neighborhood will (or will not) be a benefit to our community.

Practice 5

1. No doubt a zoo has (or does not have) a useful purpose.

2. Perhaps growing up in the countryside is (or is not) better than growing up in the city.

3. Certainly, our generation is (or is not) different from that of our parents.

4. Conceivably, a sense of humor can sometimes be helpful (or detrimental) in a difficult situation.

Practice 6

1. All things considered, the family is (or is not) the most important influence on young adults.

2. In general, parents are (or are not) the best teachers.

3. By and large, people are never (or are sometimes) too old to attend college.

Practice 7

1. In a way, it is better to make a wrong decision than to make no decision.

   or

   In a way, it is better to make no decision than to make a wrong decision.

2. To some extent, watching movies is (or is not) more enjoyable than reading.

3. More or less, you can (or cannot) learn as much by losing as winning.

Practice 8

1. **Opinion:** I think the more friends we have the better.

   Paragraph focus: learn how to trust others

   Paragraph focus: learn what to expect from others

   Paragraph focus: helps us profit from experiences

2. **Opinion:** I believe that playing games is both fun and useful.

   Paragraph focus: teaches cause-effect relationship

   Paragraph focus: teaches us about teamwork

   Paragraph focus: teaches us to follow rules

3. **Opinion:** Nothing is as important to me as my family.

   Paragraph focus: learned about trust

   Paragraph focus: learned about ambition

   Paragraph focus: learned about love

4. **Opinion:** I'd rather be alone.

   Paragraph focus: need time to pursue solitary activities

   Paragraph focus: need time to get to know myself better

   Paragraph focus: need time to reenergize mind and spirit

5. **Opinion:** Traveling alone is the only way to travel.

   Paragraph focus: meet new people

   Paragraph focus: have new experiences

   Paragraph focus: learn more about yourself

Practice 9

1.1 big portions
1.2 control ingredients
1.3 control size
2.1 print
2.2 audio
2.3 past
3.1 present opposite views
3.2 give additional information
3.3 show documentary films

Practice 10

1. options
2. choice
3. count on
4. transit
5. driving
6. quickly
7. purpose
8. admit
9. favor

Practice 11

1. a number of
2. benefits
3. introduce to
4. are apt
5. impulsive
6. relax
7. restless
8. shy
9. confident
10. trade off
11. responses

Practice 12

1.1 first—It introduces a sequence in time.
1.2 next—It continues the sequence in time.
1.3 we—It refers to *our* and *we*

previously mentioned in the sentence.

1.4 such as—It introduces a list of examples.

1.5 in addition—It adds information to the information in the preceding sentence.

1.6 as a result of—The last sentence describes the result of all the actions described in the rest of the paragraph.

2.1 in addition to—It adds information to the information in the main clause of the sentences.

2.2 before—explains when there is traffic.

2.3 whenever—means *every time*.

2.4 such as—introduces a list of examples.

2.5 consequently—introduces the result of the situation explained in the paragraph.

2.6 our—is a possessive adjective that identifies *neighborhood*.

3.1 a major part—explains the degree.

3.2 while—tells when children use the language.

3.3 on the other hand—contrasts the adults' situation with the children's situation.

3.4 first—shows the degree of importance.

3.5 usually—explains the frequency of the situation.

3.6 if—makes a cause and effect relationship between the two parts of the sentence.

4.1 for example—introduces a list of examples.

4.2 in order to—shows the reason for the children's help.

4.3 later—explains when attitudes changed.

4.4 hardly—explains the degree that the children are expected to work.

4.5 even—introduces additional information.

4.6 they—is the pronoun that refers to *modern children*.

5.1 on the contrary—contrasts this paragraph with the preceding one.

5.2 even though—makes a contrast between the two clauses of the sentence.

5.3 as well as—adds another example.

5.4 if—makes a cause and effect relationship between the two clauses of the sentence.

5.5 much as—compares the situation of farmers with that of businessmen.

Practice 13

1. maintain—matches the base form *learn*
2. think—matches the base form *analyze*
3. advancing—matches the gerund *educating*
4. in—matches *in a small city*

5. improve—matches the present tense *improves*
6. interesting—matches the adjective *interesting*
7. You—matches the pronoun *you*
8. engineers—matches the nouns *teachers* and *doctors*
9. where my cousins still live—matches the phrase *where my grandmother grew up*
10. to—matches the infinitive of purpose *to travel abroad*

Practice 14

1.1 A—matches *its product*

1.2 C—follows the pattern *If it's selling … it uses …*

2.1 C—follows the pattern *They studied …*

2.2 A—matches *They didn't have to learn*

3.1 B—follows the pattern *The ____ we ____*

3.2 A—matches the word *contributions*

Practice 15

1.1 B
1.2 A and B
2.1 C
3.1 A and B

Practice 16

Paragraph 1
1. S
2. Cx
3. S
4. Cx
5. S

Paragraph 2
6. Cx
7. Cx
8. S

9. S
10. Cx
11. Cx
12. Cx

Paragraph 3
13. S
14. Cx
15. S
16. Cx

Paragraph 4
17. S
18. S
19. C
20. Cx

Paragraph 5
21. S
22. S
23. C-Cx

Practice 17

1.1 A
1.2 C
2.1 C
2.2 A
3.1 A
3.2 C

Practice 18

Paragraph 1
1.1 like **active**
1.2 bring **active**
2.1 are outweighed **passive**
3.1 cause **active**
3.2 bring **active**
4.1 destroy **active**
5.1 is **active**
5.2 oppose **active**

Paragraph 2
6.1 cause **active**
7.1 build **active**
7.2 breathe **active**
7.3 will become **active**
8.1 will be covered **passive**
9.1 pollute **active**
10.1 will be **active**
11.1 will be hurt **passive**

11.2 will be affected **passive**

Paragraph 3

12.1 will say **active**

12.2 will be created **passive**

13.1 can have **active**

14.1 will grow **active**

15.1 will be built **passive**

16.1 will be **active**

17.1 can cause **passive**

Paragraph 4

18.1 will change **active**

19.1 is **active**

20.1 is **active**

21.1 knows **active**

22.1 brings **active**

22.2 will change **active**

23.1 will be **active**

Paragraph 5

24.1 would be helpful **active**

24.2 outweigh **active**

25.1 would be changed **passive**

26.1 cannot support **passive**

Practice 19

1. A
2. C
3. A
4. B
5. C

Practice 20

1. E—gives advice (*look for another opportunity; don't give up*)
2. E—gives advice (*maybe you shouldn't make it at all*)
3. C—explains what could happen (*it would bring more variety . . ., give us the opportunity to amuse ourselves . . ., bring more jobs . . . .*)

4. D—ends with questions (*Isn't it important . . . ? Don't you want . . . ?*)
5. D—ends with questions (*. . . would I?, Could you call me . . . ?*)

Practice 21

Topic Sentences

Introduction I think that people, weather, and politics determine what happens, not the past.

Paragraph 2 People can change.

Paragraph 3 The weather can change.

Paragraph 4 Politics can change.

Conclusion The direction of this change, in my opinion, cannot be predicted by studying the past.

Introduction focus: people, weather, politics

Opinion words

1. I totally disagree
2. To me
3. I think that
4. I don't believe
5. No doubt
6. On the whole
7. As a rule
8. in my opinion

Practice 22

Topic Sentences

Introduction I think I'd have to agree that a person's childhood years are the most important.

Paragraph 2 No doubt, the early years are the time when we learn about relationships.

Paragraph 3 These are the years when we begin our formal education.

Paragraph 4 These are the years when we develop our moral sense of what's right and wrong.

Conclusion The foundation is laid, by and large, in those first few years of life.

Introduction focus: learn about relationships, begin our formal education, and develop our moral sense of right and wrong

Opinion words

1. I think
2. to agree
3. No doubt
4. Perhaps
5. Presumably
6. from my point of view
7. I believe
8. by and large

Practice 23

Topic Sentences

Introduction I believe that success is more than how much money you make.

Paragraph 2 Most people assume that famous people are rich people, but that isn't always true.

Paragraph 3 I also believe that being respected by coworkers indicates success.

Paragraph 4 I think that one of the most important indicators of success is knowledge.

Conclusion If history is the judge of success, then money surely isn't everything.

Introduction focus: fame, respect, knowledge

Opinion words

1. people believe
2. I believe
3. definitely

4. certainly
5. I believe
6. In my opinion
7. I think
8. In my opinion
9. overall

CHAPTER 4 REVISING THE ESSAY

Practice 1

1. I agree that all students should <u>study</u> art and music in high school.
2. Complete sentence
3. I <u>am</u> assuming that this is true of teenagers.
4. All high school students must take physical education because it <u>is</u> good for their physical health.
5. Complete sentence
6. Both art and music are interesting and <u>help</u> students to express themselves.
7. Students <u>who</u> have never drawn a picture will be surprised when they start to draw.
8. It is always satisfying to try something new, even if you find <u>you</u> don't like it.
9. Complete sentence
10. Complete sentence
11. <u>It</u> gives us an avenue for our emotions and fears.
12. The teacher <u>who</u> taught me how to play the piano was very inspiring.
13. Complete sentence

Practice 2
1. Sentence OK.
2. This taught me important professional skills this assured me a successful career.
3. I was in college, computer science was relatively new.
4. Sentence OK.
5. They were learning how to be teachers, journalists, and economists I was learning how to write computer programs.
6. I graduated I had eight very good job offers.
7. My choice of college major gave me a lucrative career it helped in my married life.
8. I married a Naval officer through the years we've moved six times.
9. Sentence OK.
10. Sentence OK.

Practice 3
1. Students wonder why teachers are critical.
2. A birdbath is a source of water for birds when the weather is hot.
3. I'd like to have a garden where I could grow vegetables.
4. We have all we need, even though we want more.
5. As our population ages, we will need more services for the elderly.

Practice 4
1. There would be more money for schools, libraries, and other community needs.
   And combines a list of things.
2. Once the buildings were completed, the jobs would be those on the campus itself and would include teachers, office workers, custodians, and librarians.
   And combines two sentences with the same subject. The subject can be dropped in the second clause.
3. Our community is a place where everyone knows everyone else.
   Place can be replaced with the subordinating conjunction *where*.
4. Although playing sports is a wonderful way to learn discipline, it should not be the focus of a university education.
   Although combines two contrasting ideas.
5. Immigrant children learn their new language while playing with other children and while going to school.
   And combines two similar ideas.

Practice 5
1. A child growing up has exciting places to visit in the city.
   A child is the one who is growing up.
2. Children who study art do better in all subjects.

Children are the ones who study art.
3. Reading such as novels and short stories fiction is more enjoyable than watching a movie.
   Novels and short stories are examples of fiction.
4. English, which is very idiomatic, is the language of diplomacy.
   English is the thing that is idiomatic.
5. Computer science attracts many young people looking for a rewarding career.
   Young people are looking for a career.

Practice 6
Check Essay Model 21 for the correct punctuation.

Practice 7
Note: The asterisked corrections are examples. There are other possible correct revisions.
1. B
2. C
3. C
4. C*, There are many ways to make a difference in a community.
5. C, I believe that the activity learning to read brings hope to the future.
6. C, It teaches them that there are [other] ways to view situations.
7. C, Reading feeds a child's creativity.
8. C, and other cultures.
9. A
10. B
11. B Does the child prefer fantasy stories, adventure stories, or non-fiction?
12. C
13. B. . . . what happens to them is their own fault.
14. B. It teaches them that there are other ways to view situations.

Practice 8
1. A
2. A
3. B
4. C, The entrance is difficult to see.
5. C, A landscaper could plant trees suitable to the area.
6. B, beautiful
7. C, more attractive
8. A
9. A
10. B
11. C
12. A, Right now, we don't have a community recreation area, but we have empty land that isn't used.
13. B and C
14. C, for
15. B, a lot

Practice 9
1. D
2. C
3. C
4. A*, Our school already has books in its library, and it already has computers.
5. B, Right now the reference books in our library are very old.

6. C, You have to wait for somebody to return it or you have to order it from another library.

7. B, They will be able to do their work more quickly and they will learn important skills, too.

8. C

9. A

10. A

11. C

12. A

13. C, too

14. C, Look up.

Practice 10

Content

1. Thesis statement*; Paragraph 1, sentence 5; Parents can be very important teachers in our lives; however, they are not always the best teachers.

Grammar

2. Sentence fragment; Paragraph 2, sentence 2; For example, they may limit a child's freedom in the name of safety.

3. Sentence fragment; Paragraph 3, sentence 1; Another problem is that parents may expect their children's interest to be similar to their own.

4. Misplaced modifier; Paragraph 4, sentence 4; Sometimes parents, especially older ones, can't keep up with rapid social or technological changes.

5. Parallel structure; Paragraph 5, sentence 3; Our parents teach us, our teachers teach us, and our peers teach us.

Punctuation

6. Question mark; Paragraph 3, sentence 3; But what if the child prefers art?

7. Period; Paragraph 5, sentence 5; All of them are valuable.

8. Capital letter; Paragraph 3, sentence 2; If they love science…

Spelling

9. Spelling; Paragraph 4, sentence 1; … on their values…

Practice 11

Content

1. Thesis statement*; Paragraph 1, sentence 3; Overall, I believe that team sports have more to offer in this area.

2. Supporting details*; Paragraph 4, sentence 2-4: Team players have to show up for practices and games on time. They have to give their best to every game. If every player doesn't do the best that he or she can do, the entire team suffers.

Grammar

3. Run-on; Paragraph 3, sentence 2 + 3; Players must learn to communicate with other players to succeed. That is not true for individual sports…

4. Misplaced modifier; Paragraph 5, sentence 1; All sports teach important skills.

5. Parallel structure; Paragraph 2, sentence 4; Cooperation is important when throwing and catching the ball.

Punctuation

6. Indent; Paragraph 1, sentence 1.

7. Indent; Paragraph 1, sentence 2.

8. Indent; Paragraph 1, sentence 3.

9. Indent; Paragraph 1, sentence 4.

10. Indent; Paragraph 1, sentence 5.

11. Period; Paragraph 2, sentence 1; Both individual and team sports emphasize competition, but team sports have an added benefit.

12. Capital letter; Paragraph 3, sentence 4; In individual sports, on the other hand, there are no teammates to interact with.

Spelling

13. Spelling; Paragraph 4, sentence 1; Finally, team sports help…

Practice 12

Content

1. Conclusion*; Paragraph 5, sentences 1-2; By studying art and music in high school, students begin to understand themselves as well as their own culture and other cultures. What could have more value than that?

Grammar

2. Fragment; Paragraph 2, sentence 2; Both are natural forms of self-expression.

3. Misplaced modifier; Paragraph 2, sentence 3; Just as our ancestors drew on the walls in caves and made music with drums, …

4. Parallel structure; Paragraph 3, sentence 1; Studying art and music means more than drawing a picture or playing an instrument.

5. Parallel structure; Paragraph 3, sentence 3; By studying pictures in museums, by listening to the selections in a musical program, …

6. Cohesion; Paragraph 3, sentence 4; They learn about what their society values.

Punctuation

7. Indent; Paragraph 4

8. Capital letter; Paragraph 4, sentence 2; They learn about what is important in other societies.

BARRON'S BOOKS AND CASSETTES TO HELP YOU SUCCEED IN ESL AND TOEFL EXAMS

Barron's ESL Guide to American Business English • Focused to fit the needs of ESL students. Paperback handbook describes a variety of business writings and sample correspondence. Review section covers the basics of English grammar. $16.95, Canada $24.50.

Write English Right • This workbook presents exercises, assignment worksheets, and drills for TOEFL and ESL students. $11.95, Canada $17.50.

American Accent Training • Concentrates on spoken English, American style, with exercises in American speech rhythms and inflections. Exercises prompt ESL students to listen and imitate, in order to be better understood by Americans, while also increasing listening comprehension. Package consists of book and five audio CDs in a durable case. $39.95, Canada $55.95.

WritingAmerican Style:

An ESL/EFL Handbook • Instructs advanced high school, college, and graduate students who have little experience in writing academic papers in English. Explains and illustrates documentation rules using Modern Language Association parenthetical style and using endnotes, outlines documentation techniques, gives helpful grammar tips, and much more. $12.95, Canada $17.95.

Minimum Essentials of English, 2nd • A concise 72-page summary of English grammar, rules, and language forms. Explains MLA, APA, and CMS documentation. An indispensable aid and style sheet to help with all written assignments. Pages are punched to fit a three-ring notebook binder. $6.95, Canada $9.50.

Please send me the following titles:

_____ Barron's ESL Guide to American Business English, (0-7641-0594-9), $16.95, Canada $24.50.

_____ Write English Right, (0-8120-1462-6), $11.95, Canada $17.50.

_____ American Accent Training, (0-7641-7369-3), $39.95, Canada $55.95.

_____ Writing American Style, (0-7641-0792-5), $12.95, Canada $17.95.

_____ Minimum Essentials of English, 2nd, (0-7641-0745-3), $6.95, Canada $9.50.

BARRON'S EDUCATIONAL SERIES, INC.
250 Wireless Blvd. • Hauppauge, NY 11788
In Canada: Georgetown Book Warehouse
34 Armstrong Ave. • Georgetown, Ontario
L7G 4R9

I am enclosing a check or money order for $_____ which includes an additional 18% for postage and shipping (minimum charge $5.95). New York, New Jersey, Michigan, and California residents add sales tax to total.

Charge To My: ☐ Mastercard ☐ Visa ☐ American Express

Account # _____ Exp. Date _____

Signature_____

Name _____

Address _____

City _____State_____ Zip_____

Phone _____

If not satisfied, please return books within 15 days of the date of purchase for full refund. Prices are subject to change without notice. All books are paperback editions, and may be purchased at local bookstores or direct from Barron's.

Visit our web site at: www.barronseduc.com

(#6a) R 10/05